ABOLITIONISTS ABROAD

Abolitionists Abroad

American Blacks and the Making of Modern West Africa

Lamin Sanneh

HARVARD UNIVERSITY PRESS

Cambridge, Massachusetts

London, England

First Harvard University Press paperback edition, 2001

Published with the assistance of the Frederick W. Hilles Publications
Fund of Yale University.

Library of Congress Cataloging-in-Publication Data

Sanneh, Lamin O.
    Abolitionists abroad : American Blacks and the making of modern
West Africa / Lamin Sanneh.
        p.   cm.
    Includes bibliographical references and index.
    ISBN 0-674-00060-9 (cloth)
    ISBN 0-674-00718-2 (pbk.)
        1. Africa, West—History—To 1884.   2. Freedman—Africa,
West—History—18th century.   3. Freedman—Africa, West—History—
19th century.   4. Afro-Americans—Africa, West—History—18th century.
5. Afro-Americans—Africa, West—History—19th century.   6. Antislavery
movements—Africa, West—History—18th century.   7. Antislavery
movements—Africa, West—History—19th century.   8. Evangelicalism—
Africa, West—History—18th century.   9. Evangelicalism—Africa,
West—History—19th century.   10. Antislavery movements—United
States—History.   11. Antislavery movements—Great Britain—History.
I. Title.

DT476 .S26   1999
966—dc21   99-044227

To Kelefa and Sia,
in proud tribute
for dreams fulfilled
and hopes yet unrealized

To accomplish this magnificent design [of the formation of a civilized society], in Africa, let us form agricultural colonies on its coast, which present a variety of situations, where we shall be little, or not at all, disturbed in our operations. Let us kindly mix with the inhabitants, and assist them in cultivating their fertile soil, with the view of inviting them to participate with us in it's [sic] inexhaustible stores, and in the concomitant blessings of improving reason with progressive civilization. Let us give them a manly and generous education, which will make them feel the nobility of their origin, and shew them of what great things they are capable—an education which will teach them no longer to suffer themselves to be dragged, or to conspire to drag others, from their simple, but improvable and beloved societies—which will teach them to avenge themselves on the blind and sordid men who purchase them, only by becoming more useful to them as freemen, than ever they have been, or can be, as slaves. Thus, on the wreck of tyranny, let us build altars to humanity, and prove to the negroes that the Europeans, become just from sound policy, and generous from a sense of their true interests, are at last disposed to make some atonement for the irreparable mischiefs their perverted system of commerce has occasioned in Africa.

C. B. Wadström, *An Essay on Colonization* (1794)

CONTENTS

ACKNOWLEDGMENTS

I first worked on a history of the antislavery movement as my senior history essay in college, and then promptly abandoned the subject until now. The responsibility for returning to it in the present form is my own, but the credit for it in part belongs to my publisher, in particular, to Peg Fulton, who over several years gently goaded me into attempting a book-length study of the topic and with forbearance endured my procrastination. I am deeply indebted to her.

My initiation into historical study occurred at the hands of Henry Ferguson, whose love and passion for the discipline carried me beyond the view of the past as a mere weary chronicle to the understanding of it as a living testament. His scrupulous sense of social justice, of seeing the world from the bottom up, gave no quarter to indifference or complacency and brooked no compromise with simple credulity, antiquarian curiosity, or idle contemplation. For Henry, history as such belonged with the problem of the human condition, with the struggle to be humane, with what made the human enterprise coherent, challenging, and instructive, with new and different possibilities for living and experience, in fact with the emergence of a liberal and cosmopolitan sensibility. This book is a tribute to his professional vision and courage, even if an inadequate exemplification of his own exacting standards.

I am grateful to the Templeton Foundation, to Sir John Templeton and to Kirkley Sands personally, for the opportunity to present an earlier version of this material as the Templeton Lectures in Nassau, Bahamas. I similarly acknowledge my indebtedness to the Virginia Theological Seminary and to Richard Jones, for the honor they extended to me of delivering the Sprigg Lectures. The material for those lectures later formed the basis of this book. I took advantage of the invitation to deliver the Sprunt Lectures at the Union Theological Seminary in Richmond, Virginia, to refocus the connection between the antislavery movement and the missionary movement, and I am grateful to President Louis B. Weeks and his colleagues for their warm and generous welcome. Dean Clarence G. Newsome and Dean Emeritus Lawrence N. Jones of Howard University Divinity School convened the weekend seminar "Research and Writing African American Religious History" to discuss parts of the book then in manuscript form. I am grateful to them for their exceptionally warm hospitality and also to my colleagues at the seminar for their interest and their comments on and criticisms of the manuscript. All of that made the task of revision and rewriting much simpler and more rewarding.

The preparation for this book was facilitated by the extraordinary help and courtesy of the staff of the Public Record Office, Kew Gardens. I cannot think of a better, a friendlier, a more solicitous, a more efficient, a more dedicated, and a more accessible group of research staff anywhere. It is to my chagrin, therefore, that I am unable here to thank each one of them by name, but I hope they will nonetheless accept my deep-felt gratitude. They were a magnificent team of welcome and help that left me wondering, "How do they do it?" In the same vein I would like to mention the staff of the British Library for their prompt service at very short notice. I was fortunate to have the professional expertise and excellent resources of the Day Missions Library at Yale Divinity School as well as the Sterling Memorial Library, whose labyrinthine maze, not to say personnel changes, can haunt and daunt the most seasoned of even homegrown researchers. It was for this reason a source of much encouragement to have the help of my students at Yale; I make special mention of Steve Gold in this connection.

I am grateful to the fellows weekly discussion group of the Whitney Humanities Center for a chance to present some of the main conclusions of the research on which the book is based, and to the Griswold Fund of the same center for support toward the research costs for the book. I make grateful mention, too, of Richard C. Levin, the president of Yale University, for his assistance over many years.

It has made life much less difficult for me that several scholars had preceded me in the field, or at least in a different part of the field. My approach, it goes without saying, is different from that of many other writers on the subject, but to the degree that there is overlap between the work on slavery and the slave trade, on the one hand, and, on the other, that on antislavery as set out here, I have gained much from the insights of colleagues and of earlier works. The references in this book give evidence of their influence, but I would like to emphasize it here. J. F. Ade Ajayi took time from his busy schedule while in residence at Yale Divinity School to read the manuscript and to make extensive suggestions and comments. I thank him most sincerely for his generosity with his time and comments, and for calling my attention to numerous details of fact and interpretation. I also mention the encouragement of Robin Winks and David Brion Davis of the Yale History Department, and Margot Fassler of the Yale Institute of Sacred Music. To the anonymous readers of the manuscript I pay special respect for their helpful suggestions and critical observations. Much appreciation goes to Kelefa Sanneh for his help with the title of the book. I am also much indebted to Elizabeth Hurwit for transfusing clarity into the book with her meticulous attention to detail. All these people have saved me from countless hazards of embarrassment over carelessness, sloppiness, inattention, and inconsistency, though I alone must take full responsibility for any remaining flaws and blemishes in the book. An earlier version of Chapter 2 appeared in the *Journal of Religion in Africa,* 27, no. 2 (February 1997). It remains for me to beg the reader's indulgence for the outstanding errors and inadequacies of which I am guilty. I shall consider myself more than rewarded by knowing that the book has contributed to a vital field of historical inquiry.

Feast of the First Martyrs at Rome   L. S.

ABOLITIONISTS ABROAD

Introduction

Slavery was a widespread practice dating back to antiquity. In Africa, the origins of slavery are hidden in the mists of time, before there were any written records. The records we do have tell the story of slavery as a practice already well established in African societies. Over twelve hundred years ago, for example, Arabic chronicles described how Arab traders from the north came to Africa south of the Sahara bringing salt to exchange for gold and slaves. These trans-Saharan routes carried caravans that returned laden with slaves from black Africa. Slaves were also obtained from military raids, such as those on the black populations of Nubia, in the Sudan, and on places as far south as Borno. The slaves were taken to Cairo and other Arab centers, there sold, and then dispersed throughout the Arab world. It was a community of such slaves, called the Zanj, who led a major revolt in the salt mines of Iraq in the ninth century of our era.[1]

The Arab writer Ibn Khaldún says in his "Prolegomena to World History," written in 1377 C.E., that God made Africa a natural source of slaves, for "the Negro nations are, as a rule, submissive to slavery, because [Negroes] have little [that is essentially] human and have attributes that are quite similar to those of dumb animals."[2] The ruler of Borno thought differently. In 1391–92 he wrote a letter to the sultan of Egypt, complaining about slave raids into his territory by Arabs from the north, this in spite of the fact that he and his people were free and Muslim. These Arab raiders, he lamented, "have devastated all our land, all the land of Bornu . . . They took free people among us captive, of our kin among Muslims . . . They have taken our people as merchandise." The

1

Borno ruler asked the sultan to search out these unfortunate blacks scattered among the various slave markets and restore them to freedom and Islam, a plea that went unheeded.[3]

Africa continued to supply slaves for the Arab world well into the twentieth century, when French and British colonial policy intervened to try to ban slavery, often with little practical result. Domestic slavery had by then become an entrenched social institution, as the Baba of Karo, a Hausa woman of northern Nigeria, describes in her memoirs.[4] It enabled indigenous communities to differentiate themselves between slave and free. In that differentiation slaves had no honor and were valued simply as chattel.

The Transatlantic Corridor

Transatlantic slavery, which began in earnest in the sixteenth century from West Africa, accelerated the process of slave exploitation that the trans-Saharan trade propagated in tropical Africa. The Portuguese had established a slave market at Arguin in northern Africa in 1448 shortly after they rounded the bulge of Cape Verde, and it is possible that Arguin supplied the first black slaves taken to Europe and America. In any case, on Cape Verde itself the Portuguese founded San Iago, a slave market, from where slaves were taken to Lisbon and Spain. Portugal also had a slave base in the Kongo kingdom under Afonso I, who converted to Christianity after becoming king in 1506.[5] Thus between 1513 and 1516 just under 3,000 slaves were transported to Lisbon and over 370 to Spanish ports.[6] The impact of the voyages of Columbus on the slave trade was considerable. On his third voyage of 1498 to the Caribbean, for example, Columbus spoke of the economic value of introducing African slaves to replace Indian labor, saying it could all be done in the name of Christianity. He affirmed: "From here in the name of the Holy Trinity one could send as many slaves as one could sell, and also from Brazil . . . It is the custom to employ many black slaves in Castile and Aragon, and I think that a great many of them come from Guinea [West Africa]; now one of these Indians is worth three blacks . . . From these two commodities it seems to me that one could gain 40 million, if there were enough ships to bring them here."[7]

With the incentive and justification thus provided, Europeans brought all the skills of credit, organization, and efficiency to bear on slave production in Africa, measuring the risks involved against the high volume needed to ensure a high return on investment. Thus disease and death would be offset by factors such as the relative youth of the slaves, the size of the haul, and the conditions of travel on the high seas. A high-density formula was devised on the basis of which captains of tightly packed slave ships would determine how much cruelty they should inflict to deter the mutinous spirit and the general insolence that congestion tended to provoke without risking loss of a valuable investment.

Nevertheless, considerations of profit were not enough to prevent abuse. First, to ensure low prices, slave traders would buy slaves in bulk and store them in stockaded factories on the African coast or on offshore islands to await shipment. As a result, the African coast became what Sir Richard Burton termed "a broken line of broker settlements," and allowed the traders to buy when the market was buoyant and prices were low, and to ship when they gauged conditions favorable for the seller and prices high. The slaves so shipped would consequently not represent a high risk to investment, while the fortified stockades could be replenished when supplies were high.[8] Captains were thus able to afford a certain level of cruelty as a check or reprisal for slave insurrection. Second, slaves needed breaking in. As Orlando Patterson has argued, slavery meant total domination,[9] using violence and dishonor, though writers like Ibn Khaldún preferred to believe that slavery was the natural condition of blacks. (It is beyond the scope of this book to determine the extent to which coastal slave factories affected economic and political relations in hinterland Africa by regulating the market for slaves, but the reader can imagine the close link with local political institutions and structures.)[10]

Antislavery

In the course of time, the vested slave interests of Europeans, Africans, and Arabs came under direct challenge from the organized efforts of those opposed to the slave trade and slavery. One potent antislavery force emerged when Africans who were enslaved and taken to Europe or America gained, or agitated for, their freedom and led efforts to abolish the trade in slaves. They looked to European and American philanthropists, the human rights activists of their era, who shared their abhorrence of slavery, and together they organized a campaign to win wider support in government and society at large. However, the antislavery campaign in Europe and America was only half the story. It dealt with demand, not with supply, for which the strategy would have to shift to Africa.

Freetown in Sierra Leone fits into this scheme. Leaders of the Western antislavery movement were convinced that as long as Africans were willing to sell fellow Africans, there would always be people equally willing to buy them, with supply and demand becoming with time a chicken-and-egg question. Therefore, it was necessary to attack the problem at its source and to establish a colony that would be a haven for ex-slaves and an example to the rest of Africa. People were not sure precisely how such a colony would work, who would govern it, how it would be defended, who would pay for it, and, most crucial of all, if the Africans living in it would set a good enough example to uphold antislavery. Such was the lucrative draw of the slave trade that a colony of Africans without a viable alternative means of livelihood would likely revert to the trade or else perish. Not only coastal but hinterland Africa as well was littered with slave settlements, called in the Fula language *rimá'ibé* (singular: *roundé*). In these settlements the normal rules of humanity were suspended, with whole populations held in absolute servitude. Slavery was taken as a normal state of affairs, and one that would last into the indefinite future. In time scale, scope, focus, and intensity, slavery, both domestic and transatlantic, belonged with the most obdurate of human rights abuses. What would it take for Africans themselves to resist slavery of such magnitude?

Without answers to all the important questions connected with the project of a free settlement, the antislavery leaders in Europe and America decided to go ahead with plans and to meet whatever problems might arise as a consequence. In 1787 Freetown was established under the authority of the Sierra Leone Company as a free colony, a reversal of the *roundé*.

Even before knowing what the outcome would be, the advocates of antislavery had to confront certain issues. One of the most perplexing was whether a viable settlement could be established on the so-called Dark Continent, "dark," that is, in the double entendre of the absence of the light of knowledge and physical impenetrability. People in Europe and America realized that ignorance of Africa's peoples and geography had to be overcome before antislavery could make any progress there.

A second issue was the likely disposition of neighboring chiefs and tribes toward a free colony. Would a settlement created to oppose slavery and the slave trade, and set to bring about the remission of the malignant *roundé*, earn the abiding enmity of chiefs and thus pose too great a security burden for officials? Perhaps gifts and tributes, offered with lavish official blandishments, would allow chiefs' hearts to be knit in the cause of antislavery. Perhaps, too, a modest show of force, coupled with conciliatory gestures—what Theodore Roosevelt called carrying the big stick and speaking softly, borrowing the idea itself from Africa—might be all it would take to avoid costly entanglements with chiefs and offer the fledgling settlement a chance. There was no knowing, except that walking makes the road.

This issue of chiefly and tribal hostility was a major one. It would not be enough merely to restrain these chiefs and their subjects. On the contrary, they would have to have positive inducement to comply with the terms of a settlement otherwise so opposed to their interests, to be shown in effect how they stood to gain more from antislavery than from slavery. Thus legitimate trade as a source of wealth might succeed and reconcile the chiefs.

Legitimate trade required open competition, however, and that in turn required abandoning the monopoly and protectionism that favored the chiefs. If pursued single-mindedly, legitimate trade would produce a new middle class whose members would see that they owed their status to their own efforts rather than to chiefs' patronage. Such a middle class would soon come to regard the chiefs as at best irrelevant to their prosperity and well-being. The question remained why chiefs should embrace antislavery when it was grafted to legitimate trade and threatened their interests so directly.

One answer to this obstacle was to do away altogether with chiefs in the new society to be fostered in a free colony, though such a course would still leave the colony vulnerable to chiefs' reprisals. It was a difficult historical choice. Local rulers were too wedded to slavery and the slave trade, they were too entrenched as "courtyard chiefs" of slavery, to become natural allies of abolition. Yet they were too important, too embedded in the social structure, to be ignored by a foreign cause like antislavery. It would be unthinkable to trust the chiefs, yet impossible, too, to avoid them entirely. Concessions might incite the less scrupulous chiefs to blackmail, while opposition might antagonize potential allies.

That impasse led to the conclusion that antislavery must cease simply to be a foreign movement and become instead an African and an African American cause, something that blacks themselves deeply desired and for which they were prepared to take risks. It was not enough to plant a free colony in Africa, provide it with European protection, and raise it on the uncertain income from legitimate trade. Such a free colony had to set an example of justice, of equality, of the dignity of labor, and of reward for personal enterprise, if it was to have any meaningful and lasting impact on local attitudes to the slave trade and slavery. Only then might chiefs accept that they and their own people's welfare was better served by productive enterprise, and that antislavery was in the interests of their societies. As beneficiaries of the slave trade, chiefs would likely not lead in this cause, but, having sniffed the wind, they might be willing to cooperate, especially when cooperation at that stage carried none of the stigma it was to acquire in the high imperial era.

Establishment Structures

Until the cause of antislavery prevailed, and often well after it, Africans were inclined to view one another as potential slaves. Consequently, the chiefs, who were reared on the philosophy that you should beat your own kind so others may respect you, were unwilling to sign on as supporters of antislavery. What was required, then, was to break this vicious circle with the establishment of a free colony in close proximity to the centers of the slave trade.

Thus, a new and revolutionary conception of society was involved in the establishment of the Sierra Leone Christian colony, begun haphazardly in 1787, continued more hopefully with the American impetus in 1792, and then pursued vigorously with the influx of recaptured Africans skimmed off the high seas following the abolition of the slave trade in 1807 and the creation in 1808 of Sierra Leone as a crown colony. A Vice Admiralty Court was set up in Freetown to enforce the provisions of abolition, with the British naval squadron patrolling the coast and confiscating slave cargoes. In 1835 the British Parliament passed a law allowing even cargo ships carrying goods intended for slavery to be seized and brought to Freetown, and the cargo sold off by auction, all in an attempt to use mainland pressure to close loopholes in the maritime trade. In this contest between antislavery and commerce we have a hint that European traders felt, as the chiefs did, that Christianity was an obstacle to their interests.

On the negative side, the creation of such a free colony involved the removal of hereditary chiefs from any controlling role in the community. Chiefs were too invested in the means of slave production, too rooted in the genealogy of power, too much at the beck and call of competing power groups, and too fettered by dynastic factors to be enlightened agents of freedom and progress. Chiefs would need long apprenticeships to accept the imperatives of a slave-free new world order. Yet apprenticeship seemed too subtle a response to their provocation.

On the positive side, however, a new society made up of freed slaves and similar social victims was a society already based too firmly in the ethics of the underclass, in the cause of minorities and the marginalized, and already too charged with the idea of human rights and of unrealized opportunities to limit it to the narrow constraints of political genealogy, chiefly lineage, and the other tools of corporate privilege. In fact, the chiefs personified the old order that promoted slavery, viewing civil society as fit only for the pluck. It was not apathy that chiefs feared, for they lived too much on the edge of political insecurity to be able to acquire or inculcate the habit of resignation. Uneasy lies the head that wears a crown, or, as one weary African crown prince put it, he would not be king if he could help it, because "king no happy; drink nothing until the man who brings it drink it first [to prove the drink safe]; eat nothing before the other eat first; never sleep twice in the same room; have his bed made in one room, and when it is dark he get up and make his own bed in another room; trust nobody; not trust his wife, nor his son, nor his daughter; he no want to be king."[11] It requires little imagination to appreciate the dangers lurking "within the hollow crown that rounds the mortal temples of a king," to understand chiefs' fearing a more powerful rival and the constant threat of being hustled into the bonds of servitude. The one sure protection against becoming a slave yourself was making slaves of others. Power was thus raised in vengeance and deterrence, with dynastic honor demanding that the sacred stool of honor weigh down on the necks of the vanquished, or be washed in the blood of the enemy, as one king bluntly put it (see Chapter 2). Chiefs and slave captains were joint partners in a common enterprise, however much they sought to outdo each other.

This point about chiefly agency had been earlier noted by the seventeenth-century traveler John Barbot, who said that the "trade of slaves is in a more peculiar manner the business of kings, rich men, and prime merchants, exclusive of the inferior sorts of blacks."[12] Anthony Benezet, the Philadelphia Quaker, cited Willem Bosman's observation that chiefs were averse to taking ransom for the individual who brought on a war, "though his weight in gold be offered, for fear he should in future form some new design against their repose."[13] Most important in this system was not just who was, or was likely to be, on your side, but who was, or might be, against you. The first rule of the old political morality was self-preservation, and the second, which fed the first, was distrust and retribution, the law of the survival of the fittest, with no second chance for losers.

To be esteemed, a chief needed slaves, whether that meant seizing other people, purchasing them, or receiving them as gifts or payment. You had to have power to be able to seize people, and power, too, to defend yourself against the neighbors whose people you seized. Similarly, you had to have the means to purchase slaves or to acquire them in other ways. Whatever the source, however, slaves so acquired had to be put to use, for example, as military conscripts or in domestic labor, civic projects, agriculture, mining, porterage, and trade. Slaves were also convertible currency. Such uses increased the demand for slaves, making slave capital an invaluable asset and also a source of competition and conflict. Whether at the point of origin or at the point of use, the institution of slavery fostered the ethics of gain, advantage, and domination with a built-in instability. The office of chieftain fed on slavery and on its attendant insecurity. That was why chiefs opposed abolition even when slavery was uneconomical. Its symbolic salience remained, steeped in hallowed genealogy. There simply was no viable symbol system with which to define and defend a chief's rule other than the power of life and death, of supreme authority, over the servile estate. Any ruler worth his salt had to have slaves, even if slave owning opened him to attack from jealous or aggrieved neighbors.

In 1824 the British consul general in Morocco approached the sultan on the matter of the abolition of the trade in slaves. In a reaction that any West Indian or Southern Christian slave-owning family would have shared, the sultan expressed amazement at the idea, saying that "the traffic in slaves is a matter on which all sects and nations have agreed from the time of the sons of Adam . . . up to this day." The sultan said he was "not aware of slavery being prohibited by the laws of any sect, and no one need ask this question, the same being manifest to both high and low and requires no more demonstration than the light of day."[14]

For the reasons identified above, it was important to the general anti-slavery cause that former slaves and captives led the drive against the slave trade. On the one hand, the antislavery movement in Europe and America would be greatly strengthened if a free colony in Africa were successful. It would provide powerful intellectual ammunition to those in Europe who wished to defend the humanity of Africans and their capacity to assume responsibility for themselves. Armed with such evidence, Western philanthropists could support their contention that blacks were not morally inferior and that slavery was a violation of their right to full humanity. On the other hand, a free colony would offer an alternative society in which Africans would be able to break out of the grim enslave-or-be-enslaved tit for tat of the indigenous code. A free, successful colony would show Africans doing well rather than threatening one another or their neighbors and in general advancing the common good by pursuing their own legitimate self-interest.

Antistructure

A free, thriving society in which caste and chieftain structure were excluded would represent a disruption of the old order. In challenging the power of "courtyard chiefs" and local authorities in order to redress the wrongs done their social victims, the antislavery movement was "antistructural" in that sense. Some writers have denied that there was ever such a radical break, arguing that missionaries and colonial officials became themselves structural alternatives that excluded, exploited, repressed, and stigmatized every bit as much as their chieftain antagonists. Thus colonialism and mission in this view made no qualitative difference whatsoever.

Yet, however true it may be that missionaries and administrators adapted and used chieftain structures to maintain order and secure allegiance, it remains the case that such adaptive reuse involved no return to the slave trade or slavery. Colonial administrations sometimes resorted to the corvée, and, as André Gide has pointed out with respect to the French Congo (*Travels in the Congo*), the corvée could rival the slave regime in cruelty and abuse. But such colonial abuses were ultimately vulnerable to attack of the sort mounted by antislavery, as Gide's revelations of the French Congo demonstrated. Thus, even if it wrapped itself in the mantle of chieftain prerogative, colonial oppression (or collusion with chiefs) could not immunize itself against the forces of African antislavery or against those of its sequel in the anticolonial movement. With the antislavery campaign, something new and permanent was attempted in African societies, and that represented a significant enough break with the old political morality.

It was not that in a free colony everyone would achieve success, or that such success would not itself create new orthodoxies that took on elements of the older structures. Revolutions are most vulnerable to what they oppose, and revolutionary virtue easily succumbs to the vices of the old system. Rather, we should see such success as being now open to those who were former slaves and captives, or to those most at risk.[15] It was the ethics of a second chance for such former slaves and captives and of reward for individual effort and personal enterprise, the stress put on individual responsibility and equality before the law, that gave this antistructural force a transformative power, the power to question old social and political dogmas by enlarging the ranks of the freed and free. Antislavery and antistructure combined to produce an identical effect. Freed slaves and ex-captives formed a successful society in which the driving force was personal initiative and enterprise. Children were raised on those values. Their personal example percolated through the rest of society and created a culture of individual expectations. It validated the teachings of parents and elders about people being able to rise from their lowly origins to achieve their ambition. Political genealogy based on birth, breeding, and titles had no room for such rapid social mobility and was, accordingly, superseded.

Given their inborn aversion to slavery, former slaves and ex-captives had a strong stake in making a success of a free settlement, and so, all being equal, they could be entrusted with its direction and leadership, allowing a crucial bridge in antislavery to be crossed.

I have focused on some representative Africans to try to develop the subject of leadership of antislavery and antistructure. In the eighteenth century Olaudah Equiano strove hard in England to promote antislavery, demonstrating the invaluable usefulness of African experience and agency. The obstacles Olaudah surmounted to get to where he did showed Africans could overcome tremendous odds to set a good example. They might do even better if they were gathered into a community of their own in Africa, as Olaudah believed. In any case, his enterprise helped to open the eyes of Europeans and others to what was possible with freed and recaptive leadership. Captured Africans who were rescued before they crossed the Atlantic, known as recaptives, played a huge role in this story.

In the nineteenth century stood the giant figure of Samuel Ajayi Crowther, an ex-captive who was rescued from a slave ship bound for Brazil and landed in Sierra Leone to join the colony of freed slaves. Crowther eventually returned to Nigeria, his country of origin, to lead the campaign against the slave trade and to establish satellite Christian communities among the dispossessed and downtrodden. As can be imagined, he crossed the paths of chiefs, not to say missionaries, whose interests he threatened. The figures of Olaudah Equiano and Samuel Crowther in their different ways sum up well the theme of this book by demonstrating the novel concept of recaptive agency in the shift of the antislavery strategy from Europe and America to Africa. At a time when Africa was still hidden behind a veil of deep obscurity, Olaudah rose to shed light on conditions there, conditions that were ostensibly precarious but still full of promise, he insisted. Olaudah's call for a Western-assisted productive indigenous enterprise also anticipated the notion of enlightened reciprocity between Europe and Africa, so that Europe would give something back in return for Africa's raw materials, what Lord Lugard, the architect of Britain's tropical empire, called the Dual Mandate. European assistance, however, easily led to economic exploitation and political domination.

It was colonial economic exploitation that would collide with Crowther's historic drive to promote antislavery and antistructure in Nigeria. Whatever the case, Crowther shared Olaudah's sense that African agents were indispensable to Africa's future. Both men were in the end overwhelmed by the juggernaut of European ascendancy, yet in their different ways they set the African course for antislavery and antistructure. Western philanthropists would feel vindicated by their achievements.

The American Factor

The story of antislavery with respect to Africa has traditionally been told from the point of view of Europe, in particular from that of Britain.[16] But Britain's role in the founding of Sierra Leone as a free settlement should be understood against the background of developments in America that had an important bearing on the success of the Sierra Leone enterprise. First, in Britain in the eighteenth century there were by some estimates no more than 15,000 blacks, whereas in America there were some 700,000 slaves and 59,000 free blacks by 1790, which by 1860 increased to 3.5 million, one of the largest communities of Africans anywhere outside Africa. It therefore stands to reason that America would constitute an important source of ideas—and stereotypes—about Africa, knowledge that was available nowhere else except in Africa itself.[17]

Second, the American Revolutionary War created an unprecedented movement among blacks to achieve their freedom. A good number of those who joined the Revolution on the side of America did so in the hope of obtaining emancipation. These blacks reasoned that if they fought for America's freedom from Britain and succeeded in achieving that goal, they would be rewarded in like manner with their personal freedom.

It was a similar motive that induced many other blacks to enlist on the opposing side with the British, thinking the promise of freedom offered by the British worth the gamble of casting their lot with the Crown authorities. Thus on both sides of the war blacks were galvanized into action to achieve their freedom. Of course, the British lost the war and were left in a quandary about what to do with the black loyalists to whom they promised freedom and land. This American factor eventually changed the arguments for establishing a free colony in Africa.

Third, many blacks in America wished to return to Africa to contribute to its peaceful development and economic security. Some of these blacks had written about their experiences in Africa and published their views in America and elsewhere, producing a much greater awareness of Africa and African issues among the public and in political and philanthropic circles.[18]

Fourth, colonization societies were founded in America to arrange for the repatriation of blacks to Africa, and although not many blacks left for Africa, the issue of emigration kept Africa before the attention of the public and created a network of information and personal contact. The American connection boosted interest in Africa and knowledge about conditions there.

Fifth, America adopted prevailing notions of freedom and applied them in a bold historic experiment in which the principle of political genealogy was publicly contested and rejected. In repudiating the old forms of society inherited from Europe, the Founding Fathers embraced an optimistic view of history based on deferred idealism. It gave warrant to future nostalgia, to the idea that tomorrow could be, and should be, better than today. The spirit of this peculiar nostalgia still resonated four score and seven years later in Lincoln's antislavery Gettysburg address ("a new nation, conceived in liberty . . . It is for us . . . to be dedicated here to the unfinished work . . . to the great task remaining before us . . . that this nation, under God, shall have a new birth of freedom; and that government of the people, by the people, and for the people, shall not perish from the earth"), just as it did in much of the social and religious language of American blacks in antebellum America.

The Founding Fathers adopted a novel and ironic instrument to achieve their purpose. They devised constitutional measures to take government out of the business of religion, and vice versa. The effect of such separation of church and state was to create a vibrant civil society of lay agency, individual enterprise, personal responsibility, and equality before the law. This arrangement challenged people to believe in progress and in the improvability of society, rather than to cling to the past and established structures, and provided an encouraging and useful model of what was required in Africa. It also appealed to former slaves who found in the American experiment support for their own campaign for freedom, for a new society conceived in antislavery and antistructure.

There is a subsidiary issue that persists in a good deal of the discussion about the Revolution, an issue relevant to the subject of this book. It was broadly framed in 1776 by John Adams when he said of the Revolution, "Idolatry to Monarchs, and servility to Aristocratical Pride was never so totally eradicated from so many Minds in so short a Time."[19] To define the issue precisely, we may say that when Americans embarked on their course, they did so not only against the structures and institutions of the old world, but in awareness of the effects of those inherited values on domestic relations, including the social dependencies of subjects, servants, and slaves. In America the subjects opted for political citizenship, the servants for organized unions, and the slaves for emancipation. Turning their backs on what one revolutionary leader called "the Vanity of Birth and Titles," Americans sought to remake their image by abandoning old world presumptions and, equally importantly, by wishing to free themselves of the burden of slavery. Consequently, Americans in Philadelphia in 1775 formed the first antislavery society in the world.[20] A nation based on birth and titles would feel no need to account for slavery and oppressed "Other-ness," but Americans for their part felt driven to the issue by the force of their own revolutionary logic: black enslavement would have to be explained and justified "in new racial and anthropological ways that their former monarchical society [in Europe] had never needed." Samuel Hopkins was adamant: the cause of the colonies and the cause of emancipation were indissolubly linked, and the words of Benjamin Rush echo the point. He noted in 1787, "The American war is over: but this is far from being the case with the American revolution. On the contrary, nothing but the first act of the great drama is closed."[21]

The issue often came before the American Colonization Society. In his address before the society Robert F. Stockton, the swashbuckling creator of Liberia, observed,

> We too sir, have a moral debt, contracted by our ancestors, formidable in its origin, and which has been daily accumulating. And if we desire that this young day's happiness may not be succeeded by a wretched imbecility; and that our constitution—the sublimest structure for the promulgation and protection of human rights the world ever saw—the very capital of human freedom, shall be first completed and then endure, through the lapse of ages, let us not presume on the tranquility of today . . . Let it not be said . . . that, in the pride of youth and strength of manhood, [America as a young nation] perished of a heart blackened by atrocity and ossified by countless cruelties to the Indian and the African.[22]

In that spirit the society challenged Americans to reflect "that this Republick, if not impeded by the depressing evil which it was the design of the Society to remedy, would, ere this, have become one of the brightest and most illustrious empires the world ever saw . . . The tree of liberty had indeed been planted; it had grown and flourished, and spread its branches far and wide; but there was a canker at its root, 'a worm that never dies.'"[23]

Americans were the first people in the history of constitutional government to define and evaluate themselves in the light of the demands of a different culture, to inscribe into their original national documents the acknowledgment of another culture. The different culture in this case happened to be African, and, in lieu of making good on that acknowledgment, the Civil War ensued as the final, vengeful phase of the Revolution, as Rush hinted. Americans eventually paid for the Western legacy of enslaving Africans with the "purple testament of bleeding war."

Meanwhile, in contemplating the Africa they knew so little of it was natural that Americans should see the continent in terms of the Africans they knew so well at close quarters and feel that their social proximity to blacks entitled them to prescribe remedies for Africa's problems. Viewing their involvement in the continent through the short end of the telescope, they saw themselves loom large in Africa's affairs. With the cultural barrier thus bridged by a leap of patriotic faith, Americans encountered Africa as a reflection of their own recent history and reduced it to a problem capable of solution, a continent, like America, gasping for deliverance from the choke hold of slavery. Americans felt that their history had a moral design repeatable in patterns of reassuring continuity, especially because America's influence on human events arose from altruism, not from old world vice. National liberty as America's most precious heritage was a little spark that overcame the darkness surrounding it and that now blazed so bright and so high as to light the world. Africa would vindicate America's noble intentions.

Yet the introduction of American ideals into Africa was something of a historical paradox. Freedom from slavery and from political domination inspired the establishment of free Christian settlements on the west coast of Africa, but it was in the wake of those free settlements that colonial administrations followed. The chronological fact of American independence preceding European imperialism in Africa finds a parallel in free Christian settlements preceding formal colonialism in Africa. That paradox was played out in early settler and recaptive resistance to official control. It goes a long way toward explaining why eventually modern African nationalism formed a realignment with a recaptive and charismatic Christianity, in other words, with religion as antistructure.

Apart from the historical paradox, American ideals were poorly applied in Liberia. In America's informal African empire, freedom and independence arrived on the scene with no public law behind them or indigenous roots for them. Liberia had no congressional accountability or oversight, no federal assistance or protection, no state rights, no territorial safeguards, and none of the vital indigenous African involvement that might have allowed these ideals to take root and flourish. Liberia was necessarily in Africa but preferably not of it. As E. W. Blyden observed with cruel irony, Liberia was a fake perpetrated on history. "We resemble," he said, "those plants which we call 'Life everlasting'—I do not know the botanical name—whose leaves, severed from the stem, appear to survive apart from the whole plant, with no connection with root or branch. They can be pinned up against a wall or anywhere and yet appear to be green. But we know that the condition is not permanent. Liberia is like that plant; and it is a wonder to many that it has appeared to live so long. We are severed from the parent stock—the aborigines— who are the root, branch and flower of Africa and of any Negro State in Africa."[24]

As well as having an artificial character, Liberia was a private colonization venture, and it came about from the belief that a scheme for repatriating freed slaves to Africa was a prerequisite for domestic emancipation, whereby the injustice of slavery would be remedied by a concession to race separation and removal. In fact, colonization, especially as a private idea, was impractical for the overwhelming majority of blacks, slave and free. The cost and enterprise involved was beyond their modest means, and the idea of their bondage in America being solved simply by their returning to Africa suggested, furthermore, they could be free and equal only when they left America. Not surprisingly, most declined the boon so prescribed for them, leaving Liberia flawed in concept as well as in design.

For the minuscule number of blacks who responded and left for Liberia, emigration burdened them with freedom at the price of abandonment and left them to choose either survival and the dark example of their menacing slave-enriched neighbors or an unpopular antislavery cause with certain reprisal from their hostile neighbors. Created as an outlet for American national slave pressures, Liberia found itself choking from the public antislavery requirements prescribed for it. The blacks who came did so personally to escape the twin handicaps of slavery and racism, and that gratefully, not primarily to win Africa to the general cause. Liberia suffered not from its being American or from its being uncommitted to antislavery, far from it, but from its being an informal, private remedy prescribed for a public social ill.

The Frame of Interpretation

In both its European and American phases modern antislavery had its roots in evangelical doctrine concerning the possibility of instant personal salvation and the gift of the Holy Spirit. By emphasizing instant conversion and equality before God, evangelical religion provided a welcome shelter for the outcast, the downtrodden, the excluded, former slaves and captives whose violation was approved by establishment structures and who carried on account of it a permanent stigma. The freedom conferred on and experienced by the seeker in the moment of conversion, and expressed in the open public assembly of worshippers, was one side of the coin of which the other side was the freedom that broke the chains of slavery and established the dignity of persons. A free and open religious community was of a piece with a free and open society. One simply could not live in the one without living, or wishing to live, in the other. Evangelical religion, freed of its Protestant denominational shackles and fired by a Franciscan-like passion for social justice, stirred this impulse of slave self-understanding and fused it with antislavery. The accounts, reports, testimonies, and autobiographies of slaves and captives attest to such combining of religious and social issues.

I shall describe in the following chapters the extent to which this conception of religion and society differed radically from medieval Christendom and its top-down view of history. That medieval scheme had been attempted in Africa for some three hundred years with little gain. Christianity was offered to chiefs and rulers in the belief that their conversion would achieve the collective goal of establishing a Christian society in Africa. When the offer was not refused, it was often accepted on temporal, self-serving grounds, to be repudiated when Christianity no longer served, or was seen to serve, the self-interest of the state. From about 1472 to 1785 European missions in West Africa went to chiefs and members of the nobility to seek their adherence to the church, surmounting extraordinary obstacles for the purpose, only to bounce back helpless from rulers' recalcitrance. Centuries of frustration did little to persuade missions to change their strategy, so deeply had the idea taken hold that Christian orthodoxy must be framed in political territoriality, and vice versa. Yet that equivalence was itself a fixed European cultural expression and as such was incapable of being transferred to the vastly different circumstances of Africa, whose political development and social evolution had few parallels with Europe. The stories of the dramatic conversion of kings, chiefs, and other local rulers became a rapidly fading memory, often with only a ruined chapel and the scattered fragments of a bell to show for the lonesome resolve of castaway priests. They were evidence, too, that the encounter of Africa with Christianity had reached an impasse and would require another approach.

It is this second route that the antislavery movement represented, a movement in which the humanitarian impulse spilled over into evangelical religion to empower slaves. Antislavery thus offered a bottom-up view of history. Outcasts, the downtrodden, and others derided as social stumps, because they lacked dynastic roots, were affirmed as the pillars of the new dispensation. The central institutions of society such as religion, education, law, government, business, and the family were stamped with the values of antistructure, the values, that is, of elevating freed slaves, ex-captives, women, and other despised members of society into positions of leadership and responsibility. Before this movement nothing similar in scale and deliberate purpose had been tried in tropical Africa.[25]

That new dispensation belongs centrally with antislavery. I have called it antistructure, and Victor Turner presents it as *communitas,* which describes the situation where people ordinarily excluded from holding office band together to form an alternative community that is for the moment freed of the norms and constraints of mainstream society.[26] In his usage Turner emphasizes symbolic action in the process of overthrowing the constraints and boundaries imposed by respectable society in defense of the status quo. Disenfranchised, the group occupies an enclave set loose from the fixed norms that control behavior and conduct and is, accordingly, imbued with superior merit.

In my view of antistructure there is an affinity between the historical circumstances of slave dislocation, or how that is memorialized in rituals of captivity and restoration, and the notion of a liminal territorial passage spoken of by Turner.[27] But I look for a historical and social achievement of the norms of *communitas* as the final resolution of alienation and transience. Accordingly, antistructure in my usage becomes not a matter simply of being temporarily suspended or indefinitely embedded in cyclical, isolated units of space and time, as in the style of revolutionary incubation, but a matter of securing for antislavery a permanent foundation in society and law. At that permanent point the concept of antistructure modifies Turner's thesis, though it conforms to his thesis in terms of decisive slave agency and the evangelical doctrine of instant conversion and regeneration by the spirit. I draw thus on Turner's analysis to marshal themes in antislavery and antistructure into a unified history. Ultimately, my approach joins Europe, America, and Africa together in slavery, and in antislavery as a sequential movement, with the gain and domination of slavery replaced by antistructure in terms of the repudiation of the norms of political genealogy and caste privilege.

In a book published in 1965 that strikingly anticipates Victor Turner, Michael Walzer describes the charged ritual observances of certain Puritan religious practices, observances calculated to achieve a sense of liminal separateness, to induce in the devotee a sense of "exile" from the world, a moral and temporal withdrawal designed to promote an ethical alternative to the corrupt status quo. One such Puritan, Richard Rogers, stirring with liminal expectancy and "full of pious worry and tense 'watchfulness,'" induced in part by his uncertain employment prospects, spoke of himself and his fellow Puritans as observing the fast and "the stirring up of ourselves to greater godliness," and espousing "the necessity of covenant making" as the basis of an association of "brethren" rather than of kinfolk, essentially an association of antistructure. Walzer explains: "Celebrating fasts with his fellow ministers, praying with them . . . working himself up to a pitch of piety—thus, though he [Richard Rogers] did not actually go into exile, he avoided the common course in his 'wary walking with the Lord.'"[28]

Insofar as the antislavery movement was concerned, this sense of finding oneself an outcast vis-à-vis mainstream society was the lot of many abolitionists, and it served to unite them with the slaves whose cause they defended. Theodore Parker, a Unitarian abolitionist, decried his fellow Protestant clergymen in New England for refusing to exchange pulpits with him, saying, "My life seems to me a complete failure socially; here I am as much an outcast from society as though I were a convicted pirate."[29] Parker and his fellow abolitionists were made to feel that they stood for a despised cause, so great was the gulf between the old theology and the new evangelical social activism.

Historiography

The argument pursued here is that the continuity of the old world structural tradition was broken with the collapse of the intellectual scaffolding for slavery and the slave trade. Under the spell of this collapse, confidence in the advantages of political genealogy, and the tradition-tempered etiquette of fealty and deference to which such confidence felt entitled, was shaken. The warrior ethos of the lord-man relationship (and its echo of the master-slave relationship) that distinguished the earlier epochs was no longer adequate in a culture of awakened expectations, personal freedom, social activism, and religious empowerment. Human motivation ceased to be a function of political pedigree, lineage distinction, gender status, civic pride, national glory, or military grandeur and became instead an issue of the striving for human freedom, equality, justice, and social reform. On and off the cotton, rice, tobacco, and sugar plantations, for example, slaves and former slaves were led in their religious meetings by spirit-filled witnesses, often with women and children cast in prominent roles. The experience spilled over into the larger society that was being transformed.

It is not enough to speak of this change simply as human progress, since, as the *Annales* school of historians contended, progress can mean only the latest round of struggle for power and influence—or what the successful public relations machine of the dominant class of a particular age puts out for popular consumption, as C. S. Lewis observed of the writers of the Renaissance.[30] Yet even in the *Annales* tradition the progress approach was inclined to stress institutional forms and to downgrade human agency in favor of general trends and systemic factors. Thus the laudable goal of the *Annales* school to reject the elitist and great-men view of history and instead to present history from below was vitiated, first, by their subordinating human action to structural factors and later, by a preoccupation with broad economic forces or sweeping global trends, as Fernand Braudel's seminal work on the Mediterranean shows.[31] The *Annales* school approached historical scholarship through multiple spatial boundaries rather than a core-periphery binary split, only to slip back and reinforce the inductive procedure of pressing general theories from descriptive, empirical work. In any case, this progress tradition in history succumbed to what it set out to repudiate and endorsed the elitist values of objective, structural influences in historical change. Plus ça change plus c'est la même chose.

In view of the mixed results of the *Annales* school, I prefer to speak of progress as a shift in social values and orientation that called people away from a defense of the primacy of privilege, breeding, rank, and order and toward an emphasis on human agents in effecting the demand for equality, freedom, and justice—in sum, toward a commitment to the ethics of good news for the poor, liberation for captives, and leadership by the oppressed themselves. This is the kind of normative history that Walzer called "a substitute establishment, 'in which things were compassed, which legally [or structurally] were never conceived.'"[32]

We may, therefore, refer to progress provided we allow for the fact that it was inspired by the spirit of the outcast and the downtrodden as well as by the refined sensibilities of the enlightened among the favored classes, and provided also we reject the indifference to the conditions of suffering and injustice of the underdog, and the disregard of the values of other cultures, that the progress tradition in the West has tended to foster.[33] In any case, with the epochal shift of antislavery goes a corresponding challenge to reshape and adapt the old and once valuable tools of structural analysis and reconstruction and place them at the service of antistructure, at the service of the community of ex-slaves, ex-captives, and their kinfolk in Africa and the diaspora. Within the limited confines of a book, that is what I have attempted here.

1

The American Slave Corridor
and the New African Potential

Writing from a deep sense of pessimism about what the slave trade represented for the future of Africa, the Igbo freedman Olaudah Equiano (in Igbo, Ekwuno), wrote in 1789 about slavery as a human rights issue, arguing that ending the trade in human merchandise would commence the real development and progress of the continent. He affirmed:

> Population, the bowels and surface of Africa, abound in valuable and useful returns; the hidden treasures of centuries will be brought to light and into circulation. Industry, enterprise, and mining will have their full scope, proportionately as they civilize. In a word it lays open an endless field of commerce . . . Torture, murder, and every other imaginable barbarity are practiced upon the poor slaves with impunity. I hope the slave trade will be abolished. I pray it may be an event at hand. The great body of manufactories, uniting in the cause, will considerably facilitate and expedite it; and as I have already stated, it is most substantially their interest and advantage, and as such the Nation at large. In a short space of time one sentiment alone will prevail, from motives of interest as well as justice and humanity.[1]

This view is echoed in many historical accounts. One such, with an American connection, is that of Theophilus Conneau (also called Canot). Conneau was born in 1808 in Florence, Tuscany, of French parents. His father served under Napoleon in the army that conquered Italy. The elder Conneau then followed Napoleon to Waterloo, where he died. Shortly thereafter, the young Theophilus entered the seafaring life, arriving in 1820 in Boston, where he enlisted in the business of a Salem merchant who had interests at sea. By this route Conneau made his way to the Cape Verde Islands in 1826 on a slave ship captained by a Spaniard from Majorca—"a poor sailor but good navigator . . . finely a poor tool for Commander of a slaver," Conneau observed wryly. The ship made landfall at the mouth of the Rio Pongo on the West African coast. In the process of obtaining slaves, Conneau made the acquaintance of a local woman, a mulatto member of a seraglio belonging to a slave trader from Philadelphia. The woman herself was the daughter of a mulatto mother and a white father who was an English missionary turned slave trader. After a particularly successful slave haul, the Englishman left without trace for America. Before he left, however, he christened his daughter with the biblical name Esther.[2] Such moral ironies, Conneau felt, riddled the whole culture of the slave trade, though he personally profited hugely from it. Out of a capital outlay of just over $39,000, for example, he made a profit in four months of over $41,000. He could, therefore, speak with authority about the practice, his own personal stake a suitable object lesson of the wider international guilt. Though he repudiated the slave trade, in fact Conneau returned to it in the 1840s,[3] a period that in an ironic way coincided with the appointment of the freed West Indian Dr. William Fergusson as the first black governor of Sierra Leone. Conneau confessed:

> To give a full account of the whole process and manner in which the Negro becomes a slave, it would require the work of many pages. Suffice to say that three quarters of slaves shipped are the product of native wars, which are partly brought about by the great inducement and temptation of the white man. I inculpate all nations, as all the principal nations have had a share in fomenting the slave traffic and introducing wants, desires, and luxuries, with a view to encourage the then humane trade. These wants, desires, and luxuries have become an indispensable necessity to the natives and the traffic a natural barter.
>
> England today sends to Africa her cheap Birmingham muskets and Manchester goods, which are exchanged at Sierra Leone, Accra, and the Gold Coast, for Spanish or Brazilian bills on London. France sends her cheap brandies, her taffeta reds, her Rouen cottons, and her *quelque-chose*, the United States their leaf tobacco, their one-F powder, their domestic spun goods, their New England rum and Yankee notions, with the same effect or the same purpose. Therefore I say it is *our*

civilized commodities which bring the cause of the wars and the continual, now called inhuman, traffic.[4]

It was from such eyewitness accounts that the antislavery movement obtained the evidence and authority to challenge the centuries-old practice of selling Africans as mere merchandise. Until the success of the antislavery movement in the 1830s, and sometimes even beyond it, Europe's image of Africa was a fanciful blend of the primitive and the grotesque, offering writers little greater challenge than to cater to the appetite. The tropics were thus a literary byword for extraterrestrial adventure, with stories "which merely deride or deplore the unfamiliar for the amusement of complacent readers at home."[5] This was the atmosphere that produced the figure of the "noble savage," "a literary convention that conflated the Iroquois and South Sea islander with sable Venuses, dusky swains, and tear-bedewed daughters of 'injur'd Afric.'"[6] Such stereotypes merely left people to proceed with business as usual. Yet that normal business was precisely what stood in the way of the antislavery movement, and so Olaudah Equiano and others decided to launch a campaign for abolition by drawing on the wealth of eyewitness accounts, testimonies, depositions, and repentant former slavetraders, to assail the racial caricature that fed the slave traffic. Slavery and racism were a deadly combination, demanding a strategy capable of dealing with both. (Liberia would prove the futility of splitting the two.)

But given the scope, time scale, and intensity of the slave trade, public policy on the matter needed to be boosted by the demonstrated capacity of Africans themselves, so that laws passed in Europe could find their effective application on the ground in Africa. Thus it is clear from Conneau's detailed account that, long after the act abolishing the slave trade in 1807, the traffic was booming not just in fast-speed schooners designed to evade capture on the high seas but in thriving, well-stocked coastal centers in Africa itself. The job, so hopefully but partially begun in Europe, ultimately required completion in Africa, and nowhere else.

The Historical Significance of Olaudah Equiano

This is where Olaudah Equiano comes in. Olaudah has remained something of a stand-alone figure in standard historical accounts of the subject, which is rather curious. He wrote passionately about the Africa he knew and cherished and about the pathos of the slavery he experienced personally and sought to dispel. All of that should have earned him the respect and appreciation of generations of readers. Yet that has not happened, or has not happened to the extent he deserves.

In moving relatively early to bid for African leadership of the antislavery campaign, Olaudah became the victim of his own success. In his book *The Life of Olaudah Equiano,* he produced an acute study of the social effects of slavery as a theme in the Western encounter with Africa at a time when interest in African social conditions had scarcely existed. There were contemporary writers who addressed the same topic, among them Job ben Solomon, called "the fortunate slave" because Job obtained emancipation and lived to tell the tale. But Olaudah's work was different from Job's in the crucial sense that Olaudah was not celebrating his escape from slavery. His burden was not personal relief but commitment to mobilizing a worldwide agitation to correct an injustice. Ironically, white philanthropists sympathetic to his cause wished to lead it themselves and managed to sideline him. His request in 1779 to be ordained and sent as a missionary to Africa was turned down by the bishop of London. In that request Olaudah signaled his leadership aspirations and was accordingly rebuffed. In 1783 in London he called on Granville Sharp, the antislavery humanitarian, to draw his attention to the fate of 130 Africans who were thrown into the sea from a slave ship so that the owners could fraudulently claim insurance compensation, an appeal that had an effect on Sharp and his fellow humanitarians.[7] And then Olaudah joined forces with another articulate ex-slave, the Fanti Ottobah Cugoano, who in 1787 wrote a book, with the possible collaboration of Olaudah, entitled *Thoughts and Sentiments on the Evils of Slavery,* a fierce, uncompromising attack on slavery and on the Europeans who promoted it in the name of Christianity. The book appeared in a French translation in 1788. Cugoano called slavery an injury and a robbery, saying there was not a trace in it of reason, justice, charity, or civilization. The Scots and the Dutch, he said, claim the Protestant religion and yet are among the worst specimens of "floggers and negro-drivers."

All these circumstances gave Olaudah and blacks like him a visibility of which the white antislavery establishment was jealous. Yet the cause was very much Olaudah's own, and so when his book *Life of Olaudah Equiano* was published in London in 1789, it was an instant best-seller. There were eight editions of the book in Olaudah's own lifetime, and in eight and a half months when he lived in Ireland campaigning in public for the cause, he sold nearly two thousand copies of it. When the book went into its fifth edition, he went to Scotland to sponsor it. The spectacle, then, of a well-educated African writing and publishing a fluent, lucid work of high intellectual caliber in which he took up the cudgels on behalf of black honor and pride jarred with the image of blacks as victims worthy of pity and protection but not of respect and partnership. Olaudah looked to Europe for partnership when Europe could offer only paternalism, and so he got little encouragement or recognition.

Although he was a patriot at heart, Olaudah would not indulge in collective self-pity or self-flattery or in pandering to stereotypes. He admitted that to people like him who wrote their own memoirs belonged the misfortune of discovering "that whatever is uncommon is rarely, if ever, believed; and what is obvious we are apt to turn from with disgust, and to charge the writer with impertinence."[8] That notwithstanding, the African roots of slavery he would not ignore, nor would he pretend that outside slavery Africans enjoyed an idyllic existence. "Our whole district," he testified on this point,

> is a kind of militia: on a certain signal given, such as the firing of a gun at night, they all rise in arms and rush upon their enemy . . . I was once witness to a battle in our common . . . There were many women as well as men on both sides; among others my mother was there, and armed with a broad sword. After fighting for a considerable time with great fury, and after many had been killed our people obtained the victory, and took their enemy's chief prisoner. He was carried off in great triumph, and, though he offered a large ransom for his life, he was put to death. A virgin of note among our enemies had been slain in the battle, and her arm was exposed in our market-place, where our trophies were always exhibited . . . Those prisoners which were not sold or redeemed we kept as slaves.[9]

The qualifications of Theophilus Conneau—that slavery was *partly* brought about by European cupidity and that not *all* slaves were such from the transatlantic trade—suggested Africans bore some responsibility, too. Olaudah admitted as much, saying that even though European goods incited Africans in the practice of slavery, Africans enslaved one another for other reasons as well, and his attitude in that regard found little favor with the generations of political activists whose cause was better served by focusing entirely on external enemies and on forces beyond the control of victim populations. The effort required to clean up the image of Olaudah and to make him acceptable to the vigilantes of political correctness was out of all proportion to the benefits to be derived from patient study of an articulate but complex man. It was much easier to let him languish in obscurity until a more self-critical generation could receive him.

Another reason Olaudah remained marginal is the difficulty of separating the antislavery movement from slavery as such; since Olaudah was prominent in the campaign for antislavery, it has been difficult to give him his due when the attention has been focused on slavery. Olaudah was interested in slavery only as motivation for antislavery. His scrupulous examination of the issues, his patient note taking, his unflinching field observation, all of that was not just an exercise in academic objectivity on the scale and scope of the slave trade but an effort to shift public opinion. He described with artless skill the details of the slave regimen and kept his nerve. In his work he availed himself of the mental habits of disciplined reading, evidence gathering, and tireless footwork to organize for action. Thus Olaudah brought the plaudits of learning, hard work, and commitment to the drive for abolition because he felt a native responsibility for antislavery. Yet his intellectual courage failed to find much appreciation among the educated Africans of later generations.

A final reason for Olaudah's isolation was his identification with Christianity. Olaudah felt that Christianity was relevant to African antislavery and that his own personal experience served as an object lesson. By his religion he transcended his situation and could as such analyze it with unflattering candor and keen insight. The gap between the virtues of humanity preached by religion and the evils of real life that religious people practiced, between the sanctity of human life as taught in Christianity and the cruelties of chattel slavery as committed in Christian societies, he saw clearly, to the incrimination of the beneficiaries of the slave system, African and European alike. Yet Olaudah would not yield his ground, as easy as that would have been, since whatever the ethics of Christian love and brotherhood, or of African kinship and community, he experienced only cruelty and disdain on account of his color and tribe. Thus, he spoke of standing without flinching before slave masters who humiliated or tortured him but from whom he would take away nothing of their god-given humanity except to invoke it to their guilt.[10] His view of Christianity as applied ethics led him to champion the cause of human rights in Africa; at the time few saw the connection, and the colonialism that intervened suppressed such ideas as foreign to African societies, as well as threatening to colonial rule. Olaudah wished to show how Christianity and antislavery could combine to effect, to show how the Christianity of ex-slaves and ex-captives could become a general liberating force. Thus his petition for ordination so that he could take antislavery to Africa revealed his desire to lead in that cause, a cause in which Ajayi Crowther, a future compatriot of his, would lead successfully.[11]

The other side of the colonial coin was the sympathy naturally reserved for Islam, and for chiefly lineages, enlightened or not. When in the 1730s Job ben Solomon, recently emancipated, burst upon the London scene, he was wildly greeted as a nobleman and "the High Priest" of Africa,[12] so congenial was the thought to those who grasped at Muslim Africa as the paragon of native innocence. Job was sumptuously received in London high society, "clothed in a rich silk dress, made up after his own country fashion, and introduced to their Majesties, and the rest of the Royal Family. Her Majesty was pleased to present him with a rich gold watch; and the same day he had the honour to dine with His Grace, the Duke of Montague, and some others of the nobility, who were pleased to make him a handsome present after dinner."[13] No honors on such a scale awaited Olaudah, though if we grant his own testimony, he had on the distaff side as much claim to them by virtue of his proximity to native wisdom and its high priestly duties.

James Ramsay (1733–1789), a friend and ally of Olaudah's, summed up the ideological barriers to the leadership aspirations of someone like Olaudah by observing that Olaudah's considerable abilities as a leader would be a stumbling block to his personal advancement, for the age was not yet ready to accept Africans, let alone ex-slaves, in that role. Ramsay said that Olaudah had defied superhuman odds to achieve freedom and to acquire the ability to read and write,

> and in vindication of the rights of his colour has not been afraid to contend in Argument with men of high rank [for example, Thomas Townsend, Lord Sidney], and acuteness of parts. But the extent of his abilities appeared very early, when Government resolved to return the

Negroes lately to Africa. Those to whom the management of the expedition was committed, dreaded so much his influence over his countrymen, that they contrived to procure an order for his being sent ashore. In particular, his knowledge of the Scriptures is truly surprising, and shows that he could study and really understand them.[14]

As Mary Beth Norton has documented, eighteenth-century England was far from hospitable to blacks, and the black loyalists who arrived in London expecting a fair deal were rudely awakened when they found little comfort outside the small circle of philanthropists. The public's attitude was that the blacks ought to consider themselves fortunate to be in a country that would not enslave them again; the country could not be faulted and instead should be commended, no matter how it treated blacks as long as it did not enslave them. The black loyalists were resented for coming "with a very ill grace to ask for the bounty of Government,"[15] even if the bounty was no more than a crust of bread. In Olaudah's case, in spite of his independent means, he found little welcome for his ideas.

These reasons account for why Olaudah failed to find general acceptance. He was an activist for antislavery at a time when the cause was not yet so defined, especially in terms of the multiracial partnership Olaudah was seeking. Eric Wolf, writing of the ambivalent effects of the slave trade on European and African scholars, sums up well the difficulty involved:

This basic point needs emphasis because a history written by slavers and their beneficiaries has long obliterated the African past, portraying Africans as savages whom only the Europeans brought into the light of civilization. That history denied both the existence of a complex political economy before the advent of the Europeans and the organizational ability exhibited by Africans in pursuit of the trade once begun. More recently, another approach to African history—with the signs reversed—has been put forward to deny the participation of African military and commercial elites in the enslavement of their fellows. Yet the task of writing a realistic account of African populations is not to justify one group as against another, but to uncover the forces that brought Europeans and Africans (and others) into connection with one another in the construction of the world. The human costs of the slave trade remain incalculable; but the economic and political causes and consequences for all participants are ascertainable.[16]

Thus, to proceed with Olaudah, as in deference we must, we should do so on other grounds, such as his effort to place Africa's encounter with the new world on strong human rights foundations, believing that a new Africa would emerge from the irreversible gains of abolition and emancipation, a new Africa freed of the old oppressive structures and institutions. Olaudah was unique in that he knew firsthand and so could speak authoritatively about the three worlds of Africa, Europe, and North America and about their bitter Atlantic connection.

Olaudah's characterization of the old Africa, while shorn of the romantic idealization of Swedenborgian mystics and of the sort of cultural innocence that concocted the noble savage, still falls short of the indigenous potential for anticipating Christianity that Crowther would claim. Olaudah himself spoke of a pervasive mood of pessimism in African religion, of a crippling sense of foreboding, with his mother presiding over the cultic rites. He wrote:

> [T]he natives believe that there is one Creator of all things . . . They believe he governs events, especially our deaths or captivity; but as for the doctrine of eternity, I do not remember to have ever heard of it; some however believe in the transmigration of souls in a certain degree. Those spirits which are not transmigrated, such as their dear friends or relations, they believe always attend them and guard them from the bad spirits or their foes . . . I was very fond of my mother and almost constantly with her. When she went to make these libations at her mother's tomb, which was a kind of solitary thatched house, I sometimes attended her. There she made libations and spent most of the night in cries and lamentations. I have been frequently terrified on these occasions. The loneliness of the place, the darkness of the night, and the ceremony of libation, naturally awful and gloomy, were heightened by my mother's lamentations; and these, concurring with the doleful cries of birds by which these places were frequented, gave an inexpressible terror to the scene.[17]

By contrast, in the passage cited at the beginning of this chapter Olaudah evoked a different mood when he called for a new entrepreneurial spirit within the antislavery movement to promote the productive exploitation of what he termed Africa's "hidden treasures of centuries." That view of the antislavery movement preceded by almost two generations the appeal of Thomas Fowell Buxton (and, later, of Dr. David Livingstone) for the "Bible and the Plough" to root out the trade in slaves. If we remember that as late as 1776, the year of the Revolution, there was not a single missionary in Africa at work to create a church or free African community, we shall see how farsighted were Olaudah's ideas. In 1776 Africa was a closed world, its peoples a mirage of savage tribes, accessible as a source of slaves, certainly, but otherwise relegated to a mystifying primitive backwater. By quite unexpected developments in North America, however, the shroud that hid Africa was torn apart, and what once looked like a most tenuous cause of African leadership in antislavery was bolstered.

Antislavery and Black Loyalists in the American Revolution

Faced with the revolt of the North American colonies in the 1770s, the British authorities actively sought to enlist black troops for the armies they commanded against the rebels. It was recognized that black enlistment would have to be procured with promises of freedom, an extreme measure worth contemplating in view of the corresponding seriousness of the crisis facing the authorities. And so it was that John Murray, the earl of Dunmore, issued a proclamation in Norfolk, Virginia, in November 1775, promising freedom to blacks joining the loyalist forces. He addressed his remarks to "all indented servants, Negroes, or others, (appertaining to Rebels) free, that are able and willing to bear Arms, they joining his Majesty's Troops as soon as may be, for the more speedily reducing this Colony to a proper sense of their duty, to his Majesty's crown and dignity."[18] In consequence, Virginians mobilized to combine the techniques of persuasion and sweet reasonableness with means forthright and punitive to stop enlistment. The Continental Congress also acted swiftly, producing instructions to mount an armed resistance to the order and commanding General Washington to take whatever measures he deemed appropriate to head off the instability the British declaration threatened. Virginia was handed a resolution to resist Dunmore, whose declaration, Washington charged, made him "the most formidable enemy America has; his strength will increase as a snowball by rolling."[19] Among the framers and signers of the Declaration of Independence several lost slaves to the British side: James Madison, Benjamin Harrison, Arthur Middleton, and George Washington himself. Slavery was a matter that touched the heart of the Revolution.

It was feared that Dunmore's proclamation would have an unsettling effect on slaves and, more seriously, would put dynamite under the whole servile structure and cause society to crash at its foundations, with consequences too painful to contemplate especially where whites were outnumbered. The likelihood of such a dreaded outcome increased with the attractiveness of the offer to slaves that in one bound they could shake off their hated shackles. A double threat was implied in this offer. Rebellious colonists would lose their slave workers and would be forced to stay home and take up the slack, leaving the British relatively free to occupy the field of conflict so half-heartedly defended. Moreover, slaves thus conscripted would swell the ranks of the loyalist forces, with the additional incentive of getting even with their abusive masters. All Dunmore needed to do, he boasted, was to set up the royal standard and the slaves would fall into line behind the British. Just the thought, he reckoned, would be enough to unnerve the rebellious sort. Such, indeed, were the stakes that few could afford to treat his claim as mere bluster.

Thomas Jefferson reported that Virginia alone lost some 30,000 slaves by Dunmore's measures. Reports began to bulge with rebel fears that Dunmore's appeal to the slaves was leading to a general slave insurrection and a considerable propaganda boon to the royalists. Dunmore, headquartered in Williamsburg, the colonial capital, was on hostile terrain, secure enough to issue threats but not so much so to ignore the antagonism caused by his pronouncement. When the time came to make good on his word, he abandoned Williamsburg and boarded the *Fowey* at Yorktown in June 1775, a signal that slaves could follow him there by actively enlisting as loyalists. It was a point of no return.

Rumors began to spread that slaves were on a stampede to join the British side, and, forewarned, the colonists launched a propaganda counteroffensive of their own to deter the slaves. Dunmore, it was correctly pointed out, had offered freedom only to the slaves of his enemies. As governor, he once refused to sign a bill of abolition. His present stand, it was charged, reflected an act of expedience, not of high principle, though it could be countered that Dunmore's critics were themselves scarcely acting any less expediently. In any case, the slaves who absconded were given an opportunity to change their minds. An amnesty was offered to those who returned within a specified time; otherwise punitive measures were threatened. Meanwhile Dunmore and his forces were driven off shore, where only the most daring, and luckiest, slaves could make it. But such was the draw that many tried. All who made it, perhaps no more than 800 total, ended up serving at sea, with all the limitations of a seaborne life. Such was the substance of what the sources enthusiastically called Lord Dunmore's Ethiopian Regiment.[20]

Commander-in-Chief Henry Clinton of New York in 1779 issued the Philipsburgh Proclamation also promising freedom "to every NEGRO who shall desert the Rebel Standard, full security to follow within these Lines, any Occupation which he shall think proper."[21] The expected universal stampede never took place, though the proclamation produced significant movement. Perhaps up to 100,000 blacks, or one fifth of the total black population, responded by walking over to the British side.

Yet the movement of large numbers of blacks conceals a complicated picture. Slaves were still such a valuable economic commodity that the British themselves could not resist the temptation to sell them in the West Indies. In fact, the line between slaves who turned up on the British side and those who were taken as legitimate spoils of war became blurred. Nevertheless, thousands of blacks responded to the appeal, although, as can be imagined, it did not endear Clinton to the colonies, inspiring a paper in New Jersey, for example, to poetic indignation.

Following the capitulation of Yorktown in 1782 and with it the evacuation of some 5,000 blacks with the British lines, the question of the real status of blacks who sided with the British erupted with particular force. The British official in charge of affairs in Charleston, South Carolina, for example, handed down an opinion reaffirming Britain's obligation to the blacks. He wrote: "There are many negroes who have been very useful, both at the Siege of Savannah and here. Some of them have been guides, and for their loyalty have been promised their freedom." These, he maintained, "could not with justice be abandoned to the merciless resentment of their former masters."[22] The British had faced a desperate situation at Savannah from the combined force of French and American troops and so, armed with promises of freedom, appealed to blacks to ameliorate the situation. The Revolutionists were defeated, but the governor, James Wright, found it difficult to disarm and reenslave the blacks, a dilemma that was in the end overtaken by events.[23] On 14 December 1782 the British evacuated Charleston with 5,327 blacks, half of them bound for Jamaica. From East Florida some 2,200 left for the Bahamas, over 700 for Jamaica, and 35 for England. In fact between 1775 and 1787 the black population of Jamaica increased by some 60,000, clear evidence that a significant demographic change was afoot.

In many slave communities there was a tendency to link the war with the specific cause for abolition. In 1774 blacks in Boston offered to fight for the British provided the British would promise to free them if they triumphed. The British took the proposal seriously enough to treat it as a matter for high-security discussion, though that very confidentiality suppressed information about its eventual outcome.[24] In 1775 a group of blacks organized in North Carolina to join the loyalists in the conviction that if they succeeded they would "be settled in a free government of their own."[25] In 1778 a slave named Tom, owned by one Henry Hogan of Albany, New York, was arrested and imprisoned for attempting to incite other slaves to bid for their freedom by joining the enemy side. In July 1780 news leaked of an impending slave plot in Albany County, New York, to burn the settlement and to flee to the British side. In Elizabeth Town, New Jersey, a major slave plot was reported brewing in 1779, aided and abetted by prominent local Tories.[26]

Such widespread and spontaneous outbursts of agitation among slaves indicated that there was widespread sentiment for abolition. Historical opportunity, in the form of siding with the British, was thought to be one way to advance the cause, as was legal action initiated by individual slaves. Thus in 1766 in Massachusetts John Adams backed the legal appeal of a slave woman who brought action in a court and prevailed. In 1769 another slave sued his master for his freedom in the Nantucket Court of Common Pleas and succeeded. In 1773 the slave Caesar Hendrick brought charges against his being "detained in slavery," as he put it, and won the case with damages and cost. In 1774 the slave of Caleb Dodge of Beverly, just north of Boston, initiated proceedings to obtain his freedom, which he did.

These individual suits were an important avenue of redress, and they were resorted to where practicable. Between 1640 and 1865, for example, a total of 591 cases came before the courts in fifteen states and the District of Columbia. Of those cases, 279 were won, 224 lost, and 88 unresolved.[27] Figures elsewhere show the same pattern. Of 670 suits for freedom in cases where slaves were claiming rights in wills that provided for their emancipation, 327 were won, and 248 lost, with 95 undecided.[28] Overall, the evidence proves that such suits were of limited value, important proof that the slave voice was never completely silenced but proof, too, that personal suits could not be an effective or universal answer to the problem. The enterprise and expense involved made personal suits an exceptional instrument, and the judgments rendered established no broad principle of universal freedom, with each individual case contested on its merits.

A more useful legal weapon was to invoke tort law. In January 1773 a group of slaves petitioned the General Court to grant them collective relief. "We have no property! we have no wives! we have no children! no city! no country!" they protested.[29] In June 1773 the legislature appointed a "Committee on the Petition of Felix Holbrook, and others; praying to be liberated from a State of Slavery." For their petition, the slaves sought the support of the governor, Thomas Hutchinson, but, to their disappointment, he declined, and the petition accordingly languished. Undaunted, the slaves drafted a second petition in May 1774 and sent it to the governor and legislature, describing themselves as "a Grate Number of Blacks who are held in a state of slavery within the bowels of a free and christian Country."[30] Their argument for freedom rested on natural law foundations. They were born free and had never forfeited that freedom by any compact or agreement of their own. On the contrary, they had been stolen from their parents, torn from their land, transported against their will, and condemned for life to be slaves in a country that claimed to be Christian. Their enslavement, they pressed, violated natural law norms, moral sentiment, and revealed canon. No species of law or truth could justify slavery. Their freedom should be restored, they insisted, not as a concession but as a right, and restitution by way of land should accompany it. The legislature debated the question but evaded it, stipulating simply that "the matter now subside." Thus the path of collective assignation, like that of individual suits, came to a desultory end, though the petition remained a crucial tool in the drive for freedom, as we shall see in a subsequent chapter.

Legislative activity persisted in another sector, that having to do with the foreign traffic in slaves. The matter was raised on numerous occasions in the New England legislatures. In 1766 Boston's representatives, Samuel Adams and John Hancock among them, moved for a bill to ban the importation and purchasing of slaves. Such a bill was eventually passed in 1771 but died when the governor withheld his signature. A commensurate bill was passed in 1774 but was thwarted when the House of Assembly was unexpectedly prorogued the following day. In 1774 Connecticut adopted a measure to ban the trade, strengthened by a measure that allowed the slave owner to manumit able-bodied slaves without becoming responsible for their subsequent maintenance. Rhode Island acted the same year but compromised its bold declaration that any slave brought into the colony would be automatically free with the concession that traders unable to sell their slaves in the West Indies might bring them to Rhode Island on condition that such slaves be reexported within a year. What it gave with one hand it took back with the other.

Vermont, not yet a member of the Union and a state without a large slave population to speak of, could afford to act the part of moral counselor to the nation, and so in 1777 it enacted into its Bill of Rights a clause that offered to ban slavery, only to qualify it with considerations of age, gender, law, debt, fines, and so on. It affirmed: "Therefore, no male person, born in this country, or brought from over sea, ought to be holden by law, to serve any person, as servant, slave or apprentice, after he arrives to the age of twenty-one years, nor female, in like manner, after she arrives to the age of eighteen years, unless bound by their own consent, after they arrive to such age, or bound by law, for the payment of debts, damages, fines, costs, or the like."[31]

Outside New England similar action was being taken against the trade in foreign slaves. Pennsylvania strangled it with a prohibitive tax, beginning in 1712 and continuing through 1715, so that by 1773 the amount charged reached the punitive scale of a per capita levy of £20. The measures were retained for the period 1761–1773. But New Jersey's attempts in 1774 to follow Pennsylvania's example failed. In Delaware the state constitution asserted that "no person hereafter imported into this State from Africa ought to be held in slavery under any pretense whatever; and no negro, Indian, or mulatto slave ought to be brought into this State, for sale, from any part of the world."[32] Virginia (1778, 1785) and Maryland (1783, 1796) provided for similar measures.

In the southern slave belt measures were being adopted against the foreign slave trade, but such measures were actuated by different motives. Virginia, North Carolina, and Georgia, for example, engaged in a struggle to repeal objectionable parliamentary legislation, and in that cause they adopted a policy of nonimportation of slaves. In that antiparliamentary struggle the Continental Congress also joined in 1774. In April 1776 Congress voted to reaffirm that policy for the same reason.[33] Jefferson wrote that in Virginia the foreign importation of slaves was halted by the outbreak of the Revolutionary War, saying "the business of the war pressing constantly on the legislature, this subject was not acted on finally until the year '78, when I brought in a bill to prevent their further importation. This passed without opposition, and stopped the increase of the evil by importation, leaving to future efforts its final eradication."[34] Meanwhile, a radical measure guaranteeing freedom to slaves after a certain date and holding that the children of slaves were to remain with their parents until they reached a certain age and were then to receive a practical education at the public expense, after which they were to be colonized under the protection of the United States, was later withdrawn on the ground that the public mind was not prepared for it.[35]

This was the context in which the antislavery clause, later expunged, surfaced in a draft of the Declaration of Independence, a clause that accused the king of England of conniving in violating "the most sacred rights of life and liberty in the persons of a distant people who never offended him." That language shows the slave question was being attached to the specific cause of the colonies in pursuit of a political aim rather than as an issue for the necessary reform of society at home.

Even Jefferson, as just quoted, said that in voting for the ban on slave importation he was not acting to abolish the trade as such. Rather, even if slavery was abolished in an indefinite future, Jefferson was not predisposed to accept the full implications of freedom for the slaves. On the contrary, he would contemplate emancipation only within the safeguard of deportation. He had studied the classics on the matter and learned a vital lesson. "Among the Romans," he noted in 1781, "emancipation required but one effort. The slave, when made free, might mix with, without staining the blood of his master. But with us a second (step) is necessary, unknown to history. When freed, he is to be removed beyond the reach of mixture."[36] It did not make much difference, Jefferson said, whether blacks were originally a distinct race or were made distinct by time and circumstances. The fact remained that their distinctness was a function of their inferiority vis-à-vis whites. It was thus more than likely that it was nature, not the condition of the blacks, that produced the distinction with whites. Jefferson called color "that immovable veil of black" which drew a sharp line between the races.

At an important conference convened in May 1783 at Orangetown on the Hudson River to discuss the matter of slaves who might be the property of Americans, these sentiments were very much to the fore. General Washington, flanked, among others, by George Clinton, New York's able war governor, parleyed with Sir Guy Carleton, the British commander-in-chief. Washington reminded Carleton that it was contrary to the terms of the provisional treaty, signed the previous November, to remove from the country blacks, or anything else, that might be considered the property of Americans. Carleton responded that the blacks who had taken advantage of the proclamations for freedom had the right to embark, admitting that some had already left under that understanding. Washington demanded compliance with the spirit and letter of the provisional articles, of which the seventh article stipulated that "His Britannic Majesty shall with all convenient Speed[,] and without Causing any destruction[,] or carrying away any Negroes or other Property of the American Inhabitants[,] withdraw all his Armies, Garrisons, and Fleets, from the said united States."[37] Carleton's interpretation of the seventh article amounted to an attack on the property rights of Americans, Washington charged. Carleton drew a fine distinction, saying that the article referred only to slaves who belonged to Americans, not to blacks in general. Thus, on this narrow interpretation, slaves who joined the British side were deemed free, in that by their action they ceased in a legal sense to be slaves and to be the property of Americans. Carleton insisted that "no interpretation could be sound, that was inconsistent with prior Engagements of the Faith and honor of the Nation, which he should inviolably maintain with People of all Colours and Conditions." If Britain took Washington's view, Carleton continued, his records would make full compensation possible, so that "the Slave would have his liberty, his Master his Price, and the Nation support [of] its honor."[38] To General Washington's dismay ("I have discovered to convince me that the slaves which have absconded from their masters will never be restored"),[39] Carleton responded that to abandon the blacks who had acted on Britain's word would be a "dishonorable Violation of the public Faith,"[40] and that Britain would be prepared to make monetary restitution in lieu of turning over blacks. Such blacks, however, formed only a small fraction of slaves.[41]

The Continental Congress, stymied by British reluctance to observe the terms of the provisional treaty on returning blacks, instructed General Washington to abolish the commission charged with negotiating with the British on the matter and to return to Philadelphia. Grievances over the question, however, continued to sour relations with Britain for over half a century, despite Alexander Hamilton's sympathy for the British position.[42] At any rate, with formal American resistance now out of the way, the embarkation process began desultorily. In August 1782, 4,230 whites and 7,163 blacks assembled in Charleston, awaiting departure instructions, which came only in March 1783 and even then affected only 259 white adults, 65 children, and 24 slaves, who left for Halifax, Nova Scotia. Many others left for Jamaica and East Florida in conditions of great hardship and uncertainty.[43] In New York matters proceeded more smoothly, and some 3,000 blacks left for Nova Scotia on 30 November 1783, collected, cataloged, and classified. To their ranks must be added a large number of nameless blacks carried in unregistered private vessels.[44]

Britain's determination to keep faith with its black loyalists created rather than resolved the issue of the final destiny to be assigned them. Life in Nova Scotia and other settlements such as New Brunswick and Shelburne diverged sharply from the high expectations that hope of freedom had nurtured. "Despite the relative insignificance of slavery in the province, and the difficulties involved in retaining a slave at all and then keeping him economically employed, still Nova Scotia was a slave society displaying the crude traits of all such societies."[45] Not surprisingly we hear of desperate pleas for freedom accompanied by demand for land. For example, in 1787 the government stopped the meager rations it was providing for the slaves in Halifax, and several owners turned out their slaves rather than provide for them. Two years later, the local Overseers of the Poor petitioned the authorities in Halifax to release the settlement from a "burden it cannot bear," with specific reference to the blacks of Birchtown, who were living "in the most distressing circumstances," with only the paltry rations from the overseers forestalling starvation.[46] To add to the gloom, reports proliferated that blacks were being carried off to sea to be sold in the West Indies. Even in Nova Scotia blacks were being sold for bushels of potatoes, so depressed were the economic conditions.[47] One gloomy assessment reported how the Nova Scotian blacks were "obliged to live upon white-mens [sic] property which the Govr has been liberal in distributing—and for cultivating it they receive half the produce so that they are in short in a state of Slavery."[48] Thus sharecropping aggravated the hardship. "It is," observed John Clarkson, "a Common Custom in this Country to promise a Black so much pr Day and in the Evening when his work is almost finished the White man quarrels with him and takes him to a justice of the Peace who gives an order to mulct him of his wages."[49] The problem of resettling the blacks, rather than being resolved, festered.

The Black Poor in London

The plight of those blacks who were taken to England was scarcely better, as the story of Peter Anderson makes clear. A sawyer from Norfolk, Virginia, Anderson arrived in England promised a pension, which he received in the sum of £10 following Lord Dunmore's timely personal intervention. He exhausted this amount quickly and was reduced to penury, appealing to the pension commissioners for assistance. "I endeavour'd to get Work," he pleaded, "but cannot get Any I am Thirty Nine Years of Age & am ready & Willing to serve His Britanick Majesty While I am Able But I am really starvin about the Streets Having Nobody to give me a Morsel of bread & dare not go home to my Own Country again."[50] By 1786 there were some twelve hundred blacks living in near destitution in London, taxing the slender resources of the Committee of the Black Poor.[51]

Carl Bernhard Wadström, a contemporary Swedenborgian with humanitarian interest in Africa, included in his *Essay on Colonization* an extract from the *Report of the Sierra Leone Company*. It paints a dispiriting picture of life for the London blacks.

> The blacks living in London are generally profligate, because uninstructed, and vitiated by slavery: for many of them were once slaves of the most worthless description, namely the idle and superfluous domestic, and the gamblers and thieves who infest the towns in the W. Indies. There are severe laws against carrying, or enticing slaves, from the Islands, without the knowledge of their owners. Yet some of those fellows contrive to conceal themselves, or are concealed by others on board ships on the point of sailing . . . In London, being friendless and despised, on account of their complexion, and too many of them being really incapable of any useful occupation, they sink into abject poverty, and soon become St. Giles's black-birds.[52]

The Committee of the Black Poor tried to devise a plan to relieve the growing distress of blacks on London's streets. In 1772 the estimates of the number of slaves in England put the figure at between 14,000 and 15,000. That year Lord Mansfield made his famous decision setting free a slave called James Somerset, and thereby setting in motion a powerful antislavery movement in England. Mansfield declared, *inter alia*, "The air of England has long been too pure for a slave and every man is free who breathes it . . . let the negro be discharged."[53] It happened that one of the members of the Committee of the Black Poor was Henry Smeathman. A man with pretensions to being a botanist, he had lived in Africa for four years pursuing his hobby of "fly-catching." It was his detailed plan that was presented before the committee. In the plan a settlement scheme would be established in West Africa, a settlement that would repeat the American experience in Africa. He wrote: "In short, if a community of 2 or 300 persons were to be associated on such principles as constitute the prosperity of civilized nations, such are fertility of the soil, the value of its products, and the advantages of such an establishment, that it must, with the blessing of the Almighty, increase with a rapidity beyond all example; and in all probability extend its saving influence in 30 or 40 years, wider than even *American Independence*."[54]

The Sierra Leone Resettlement Plan

In Smeathman's plan of settlement[55] the growing black population of London would be siphoned off and transported to Sierra Leone, where they would be put to productive work on the soil. A good and sound plan of public education would be instituted. The settlement scheme would, at a stroke, deal with a complex matter: it would remove blacks as a burden on English society; it would offer them land and the conditions necessary to their freedom; and it would, through useful labor, create the kind of legitimate industry required to repay the Crown for the costs of repatriation and to furnish an alternative to the continuing trade in slaves. Smeathman had hit on a winning formula. But he died in July 1786, before the plan could be put into effect.

After a couple of false starts, harbingers of worse to come, a batch estimated at 459 persons, including 112 white women prostitutes, drugged and bundled onto ships as partners to the black men, eventually left England. Anna Maria Falconbridge—married to a company agent, Alexander Falconbridge, who as a surgeon on slave ships abandoned that work to join Thomas Clarkson in the fight for abolition—said she was at first incredulous of the story. "Good heavens! how the relation of this tale made me shudder; I questioned its veracity, and enquired of the other women who exactly corroborated what I had heard." Nevertheless, she remained firmly convinced that the British government would not have countenanced what she called "such a Gothic infringement on human Liberty."[56] Later she met the white women in question, or such of them as had survived, "decrepid [sic] with disease, and so disgusted with filth and dirt, that I should never have supposed they were born white; add to this, almost naked from head to foot . . . I begged they would get washed, and gave them what cloaths [sic] I could conveniently spare."[57] Of these settlers about 50 died before final boarding, 24 were discharged, 23 absconded, and 34 died at sea. Eventually about 377 arrived in Sierra Leone in May 1787.

Olaudah had played an active role in the organization of the settlement effort in London, but just before the expedition set sail for Sierra Leone he was dismissed. The motive seems to have been jealousy of his influence. Olaudah admitted as much when he defended himself against aspersions on his character, saying he wished to inform the public

> that the principal crime which caused his dismission, was on information he laid before the Navy Board, accusing the Agent [of the expedition] of unfaithfulness in his office, in not providing such necessaries as were contracted for the people, and were absolutely necessary for their existence, which necessaries could not be obtained from the Agents. The same representation was made by Mr. Vasa [sic] to Mr. Hoare, which induced the latter, who had before appeared to be Vasa's friend, to go to the Secretary of the Treasury, and procure his dismission.[58]

The Sierra Leone expedition hardened into ill-will toward Olaudah, symbolized by contemporary remarks published at the time, such as the editorial in the *Public Advertiser* on 3 July 1787 to the effect that "what we asserted of Vasa the Black, some months since, and have proved what we expected, that the expedition would be carried on with more harmony by his absence."[59] In fact the *Public Advertiser* led a campaign of racial attacks and vilification against Olaudah, accusing him of advancing falsehoods "as deeply black as his jetty face."[60] In an anonymous attack in the *Morning Chronicle and London Advertiser,* Olaudah "is made in shape of a pig to bring up the rear" of the detestable ranks of abolitionists. But a sympathetic and knowledgeable correspondent objected that such scurrilous attacks ought not to be made "in a mask; while you yourself wish to fight in Masquerade, I have no desire to make the discovery."[61]

In any case, after some protracted negotiations with the chiefs, the London settlers, a rump of the "Black Poor," staggered onto land on 14 May 1787. They called their settlement Granville Town (after Granville

Sharp), capital of the Province of Freedom.[62] They chose Richard Weaver as their first governor. Weaver was a Philadelphian, apparently free-born. He went first to England in about 1779 seeking help. He and his wife were denied assistance by the claims commission and received only the daily allowance. He joined the expedition to come to Sierra Leone with hopes of improving his life.

The settlement was poorly sited, however, and the tropical abundance that Sharp and others promised the settlers turned out to be a pipe dream. The gravelly soil defied every strain of effort and optimism, and the tropical rainstorms, which in Sierra Leone amount to over one hundred inches in just three months between July and September, pounded and bleached the soil, sending out deadly malaria with the vapors. Richard Weaver wrote despondently: "We came too late to plant any rice, or anything else, for the heavy rain washes all out of the ground; and we must stay till next month, to plant a little rice."[63] In these forlorn circumstances death was a familiar companion, illness a common fate. The rains set in on 28 June, and the death toll rose. In all of June only 9 people died, but in July no fewer than 42 of the settlers were carried off. By 16 September 1787, 86 of the 377 immigrants had died while 15 had run away. Thus 170, or more than one-third of the original settlers, had died within about seven months, while 62, or nearly one-eighth, had run away or been discharged. The original numbers were reduced to 212 black men, 30 black women, 29 white women, and 5 white men, making a grand total of 276.

The survivors had to contend with grasping chiefs. Weaver wrote London asking for help to avert starvation. The settlers had bartered their stores, including muskets and clothes, for rice to survive, but had run out of anything more to trade. In despair, the settlers broke up into groups to work on passing ships or for nearby slave traders. Granville Sharp may be forgiven for his near despair at the sad state of affairs in Sierra Leone, and was at the point of admitting defeat. He wrote to William Pitt, the prime minister, that "all the surviving White people, the three surgeons, and the land-surveyor that was sent out last year at the expense of the Government, have actually entered the service of the slave-dealers, and that the greater part also of the Black poor are gone into the same detestable service at different factories in the neighbourhood, and some even on board the slave-ships."[64] To add insult to injury, some of the black settlers were sold themselves as slaves.

Sharp had reason, as he said, to grow "apprehensive that all the rest would be obliged to disperse in like manner, unless a speedy supply of live stock, with some recruits, could be immediately sent out."[65] Accordingly, a second batch of settlers, fifty in all, was dispatched from London to revive the settlement, but it was a drop in the bucket. Only thirty-nine embarked, of which twelve died of fever on the voyage, four stayed behind at the Cape Verde Islands, and two returned. This haggard remnant of humanity, what Sharp was used to calling "worthy passengers," "worthy inhabitants," twenty-one in all, tumbled out of the ship onto land, a stunning anticlimax of the plan to move the antislavery strategy to Africa.

Waiting for them was chiefly opposition. Local rulers disowned any treaty a predecessor had made with the settlers and issued an order to quit. Only under the shadow of gunboats would the chiefs prevaricate and offer revised terms of compromise. An official, without explicit authorization, would act on impulse and sign a treaty, judging rashness less risky than confrontation with the chiefs. After such a treaty, the settlement of Granville Town, with a total population of not more than two hundred, became official on 22 August 1788.

The agreement released pent up jealousies in the settlement. Weaver accused James Reid, elected to succeed him, of stealing the stores. Then Weaver, who had earlier fallen ill but had now recovered, signed the treaty with the chiefs in August 1788, only to find that John Lucas, governor in June 1788, had repudiated the terms in an earlier signing. The chiefs, exploiting the confusion, moved in to take advantage. The slave trade in turn benefited and increased as a result. Captains of slave ships grew emboldened and disputed the authority of the settlement. Thus challenged, the settlers acted with an implausible mix of force and threats to enforce treaty agreements. Such actions drew them deeper into costly entanglements while exposing them as less and less credible. Alerted, slave traders set up to pounce and exact revenge by inciting the chiefs, already at loggerheads with the settlement. In sum, a chain of antagonism was created, with any one incident set to ignite a widened circle of conflict. It strangled the settlement.

One such incident was a dispute involving an American slave ship whose crew had kidnapped some of King Jimmy's Temne people. The king retaliated by seizing a boat from another American slave ship, killing three of the crew, confiscating the cargo, and selling the boat to the French.

In November 1789 an American ship, the HMS *Pomona,* arrived in Freetown on a mission to deliver copies of Sir William Dolben's Act of 1788 regulating the slave trade. The captain, Henry Savage, immediately found himself at the center of a controversy between the settlers and Bowie, a slave trader on Bance Island.[66] No sooner had he settled that dispute than another surfaced, in which Bowie and the settlers made complaints against King Jimmy, who they alleged needed restraining so that he would desist from instigating hostilities against the settlement. Bowie also urged Savage to avenge the recent murders of three Americans. Savage's order to King Jimmy to report to the *Pomona* was ignored, but before he could decide on his next step, a young midshipman of the party he had sent out inadvertently fired into a thatched house and set it ablaze. The whole village went up in flames. In that highly volatile atmosphere Savage unwisely decided to send a second boat under the command of Lieutenant Duncan to apprehend King Jimmy. Before they could all embark, King Jimmy's people opened fire on them. Duncan, the sergeant of marines, and a settler were killed. In the next several days King Jimmy's people tried to prevent the *Pomona* from watering. One of the settlers, named Thompson, tried to get word out to King Naimbana but was shot dead as he stepped out of the boat. Savage subsequently got two of Naimbana's chiefs to come to the ship and instructed them to get King Jimmy to cease hostilities and to extract an understanding that Naimbana would hold a meeting of the chiefs to guarantee permanent peace. At that point, sensing further retaliation as foolhardy, Savage opted for a stay of execution and, accordingly, firing his cannon more in frustration than meaningful engagement, sailed away, leaving the settlers to the mercy of the chiefs. Instead of agreeing to establish a permanent peace, however, King Jimmy simply issued an ultimatum giving the settlers three days to evacuate.[67] It was not long after that that Granville Town was attacked and razed. Sharp did not receive the melancholy news until April 1790.

Antislavery and Early Colonization in America

The settlement was as good as doomed and, barring some miraculous intervention, so too, in fact, was the very idea of it. That intervention came in a timely fashion and from a quarter that, if not miraculous, was most unusual. The story of that second chance takes us to the United

States and its religious and humanitarian spirit. Even before black loyalists presented Britain with the problem of their final destination, there were individuals in the American colonies active in the cause of ameliorating the condition of blacks, slave and free. Quakers and Puritans worked tirelessly to spread antislavery sentiment, actuated by deep religious and moral scruples. The Reverend Dr. Samuel Hopkins, pastor of the First Congregational Church of Newport, Rhode Island, wrote in robust terms in his *Dialogue concerning the Slavery of the Africans* in 1776, arguing for emancipation. He urged the Second Continental Congress in 1776 to take urgent measures for the total and immediate abolition of slavery. He supported a scheme in which Christian blacks would be repatriated to Africa, where they could live as free men and enjoy the fruit of their labor. In April 1773 he approached a fellow clergyman, Ezra Stiles, a future president of Yale, about the matter. The two of them thought a group of thirty to forty blacks should be selected and trained accordingly. Two blacks from Hopkins's church were chosen consequently, John Quaumino, a freedman, and Bristol Yamma, a slave. Stiles thought the two "had good common natural abilities" but added soberly that they were "of slender acquaintance as to Letters." Undeterred, the two blacks left in 1774 for Princeton to stay at the college and receive further instruction from President John Witherspoon. Hopkins wrote to John Adams in December 1775, asking for funds to send the two to Africa. At the outbreak of the war in 1776 over $500 had been received from contributions, but hostilities ended any idea of proceeding further with the scheme. After the war Hopkins returned to the idea, and in 1794 under the aegis of the African Society of Providence James McKenzie was sent to Sierra Leone to prospect for a colony in the area.

The Quakers were prominent as pioneers of early abolition.[68] One of their most outstanding spokesmen was Anthony Benezet, a schoolmaster from Philadelphia. Benezet was born in 1713 of French Huguenot parents who fled to Holland shortly after their son's birth and thence to England, where they adopted the Quaker doctrine. Benezet subsequently emigrated to America and taught at a Friends school in Philadelphia. In 1770 he established an evening school for blacks. A fervent antislavery campaigner, perhaps the foremost of his day, he published several works against slavery. For example, writing in 1762, he excoriated slavery, saying, "Upon the whole . . . it must appear to every honest unprejudiced Reader, that the Negroes are equally intituled [sic] to the common

Priviledges [sic] of Mankind with the Whites, that they have the same rational Powers; the same natural Affections, and are as susceptible of Pain and Grief as they, that therefore the bringing and keeping them in Bondage is an Instance of Oppression and Injustice of most grievous [sic] Nature, such as is scarcely to be parallelled by any Example in the present or former Ages."[69] His writings had great impact on Thomas Clarkson, who was instrumental in organizing the antislavery lobby in England, with William Wilberforce as the parliamentary spokesman. Benezet also had an effect on Patrick Henry, who admitted even as a slaveholder that the practice, in his words, was "repugnant to humanity, inconsistent with the Bible,"[70] and destructive of liberty.

Benezet argued for the abolition of the slave trade, stating that the purported distinction between slavery and the slave trade was a spurious one, "a Plea founded more in Words than supported by Truth." From his educational work among blacks in Philadelphia, Benezet said he was convinced that the African had not only a right to freedom but a capacity for mental and moral improvement that would make blacks fit for the responsibilities of a free society. He rejected the prevailing view of the inferiority of the African race.

By canvassing such positive views of Africans, the Quakers put themselves on the cutting edge of eighteenth-century understandings of non-Western races and societies. The positive evaluation of blacks the Quakers were presenting was based on the facts, conditions, and circumstances of Africans living in the new world, not on fanciful concoctions of the Noble Savage theme. Firsthand knowledge and experience of new world Africans became a requirement for making judgments about the people, and it was the Quakers who mobilized as a group to advance that position so early. Thus Benezet wrote in 1788 that the accounts of travelers in Africa remained a source of much unreliable knowledge, because these travelers merely rehashed fabricated accounts, repeating errors from one traveler to another. It takes the report of only one trustworthy observer to expose the unsoundness of such travel accounts. One such report, Benezet said, was by Peter Kolben (1675–1726), a man of learning sent from Prussia to make astronomical observations in South Africa, who, "having no interest in the slavery of the Negroes, had not the same inducement as most other relators, to misrepresent the natives of Africa."[71] Mary Locke emphasizes the importance of such Quaker contribution and, in particular, takes the work of Benezet as representative of that cause. She offers her critical opinion that "there is probably no other man in the period of gradual abolition who did so much for the antislavery movement in America as Anthony Benezet."[72]

As for Dr. Benjamin Rush (1745–1813), a physician, a signer of the Declaration of Independence, and a close colleague of Jefferson, he was equally influential in humanitarian circles at home and abroad. His negative scientific ideas on race contrasted strikingly with his enlightened social views. He turned down an offer of a thousand guineas a year to practice medicine in Charleston, South Carolina, because, in his words, "he could not accept to serve where wealth had been accumulated from the sweat and blood of Negro slaves." He wrote on the subject in such robust terms and canvassed widely against slavery. Reacting to standard arguments that both the Old Testament and the New Testament are ambiguous on the question of slavery, Rush asserted "If it could be proved that no testimony was to be found in the Bible against a practice so pregnant with evils of the most destructive tendency to society, it would be sufficient to overthrow its divine Original."[73] His views influenced Granville Sharp.[74] It has been suggested that Tom Paine owed his radical ideals to both Benezet and Rush. Paine's first public essay, published in March 1775, was called "African Slavery in America," and in it he developed sentiments closely modeled on the writings of Rush. Paine's opposition to slavery was based on what he regarded as its inherent conflict with Christian conscience, a notion carrying more than a whiff of its Quaker source. It is a matter for debate whether political radicalism or religious idealism fired Paine to write in 1776 his epochal essay, *Commonsense,* but one may justifiably argue that the Quaker religious factor was a guiding light. One should also recall that the clause struck from the Declaration of Independence charged George III with violating, not so much the autonomy and economic interests of the American colonies, as "the most sacred rights of life and liberty in the persons of a distant people who never offended him, capturing and carrying them into slavery in another hemisphere, or to incur miserable death in their transportation thither."[75] It shows the scale of the Quaker religious achievement, and, indeed, in looking elsewhere for the continuity of the theme into the African setting, we find in the work of Olaudah Equiano an explicit reference to the ameliorating influence of Benezet and other Quakers who enabled "the sable race to breathe the air of liberty." The effect of the Quaker antislavery campaign was virtually to shut down the market for slaves in Philadelphia by 1715.

⟂In spite of such heroic efforts by the Quakers, there was a major structural weakness in their arguments. Their critics probably uncharitably charge that the Quakers could afford their antislavery stance because they had such little stake in slaves. Thus did Abbé Raynal argue, insinuating that "philanthropy was not a sufficient motive for the sacrifice of wealth."[76] Given the fact that slaves were a valuable economic asset, and that slavery was part and parcel of the prevailing worldview well into the nineteenth century, it is relevant if Quaker teaching discouraged Quakers from participating vigorously in slavery, resulting in a lower stake in the slave trade. If Quaker doctrine was effective as a deterrent, then it was also effective as a rallying force for antislavery. Philanthropy would thus be a motive as effective in counseling abstention as in calling for opposition. In other words, the charge of philanthropic principle being easily affordable need not stick to establish the structural weakness in Quaker arguments.

That weakness has to do with the Quaker pacifist tradition not allowing a decisive role for law and penal sanctions against the slave trade. The use of the magistrate's sword the Quakers rightly rejected in matters religious, but by forcing slavery through the bottleneck of stringent religious inquiry, by diligently "putting the cause to the Christian query," they deflected from it legal reprisals. With exemplary piety, they preached on the inhumanity of slavery and the slave trade, trusting in moral sentiment to dissolve the bonds of servitude. As Sir Harry Johnston remarked, the Quakers lit a candle that, though it flickered uncertainly for a hundred years, could not be put out.[77] Yet they forgot that mammon was able to ride conscience with easy rein, and that even if, like a headstrong steed, conscience should stumble and threaten to bolt, it would relent and respond to being massaged with worldly gain and advantage and then resume its course. Or, as the African proverb says, "The hand of money can make a bad road become a pleasant path."[78]

Thus, Quakerism championed the full humanity of the slave on the basis of the doctrine of universal innate human goodness, while persistent slavery proved a bitter contradiction of that doctrine. From that contradiction Quakerism seemed powerless to proceed against so endemic a public and political subject. Others would have to carry the fight into that muscular terrain. (George Fox [1624–1691], the founder of Quakers, had told slaves in Barbados that Christ died for them, too, but such Quaker teachings prompted harsh, restrictive measures against religious instruction for slaves.[79] In such a case the pacifist strategy was futile.)

The question we now have to consider is whether, and how, this American religious spirit remained with the African Americans who went to Nova Scotia and elsewhere and, furthermore, how and under what circumstances it was transmitted to Africa.

Concerning the situation of blacks in Nova Scotia, it was no secret to the authorities that they felt badly let down by conditions there. Their problem was how to fulfill the high hopes raised by the promise of freedom and economic opportunity for blacks. Whatever the solution, everyone concerned felt that only British jurisdiction would continue to assure the welfare of the blacks. Canada, while falling under such jurisdiction, had to all intents and purposes come up short on economic opportunity. Instead of a grateful society of freed blacks the authorities were confronted with simmering discontent, with disgruntled voices being raised against what was considered an untrustworthy officialdom.

Thomas Peters: Moving Antislavery to Africa

It was out of this ferment that new hope was born with the activities of Thomas Peters, who rejuvenated the idea of taking antislavery to Africa, which Olaudah, with all his setbacks, had also set out to promote. Peters had fled in 1776 from his master and joined the British, lured by the promise of freedom. Twice wounded in battle, he survived the war and then went with his wife to settle in Nova Scotia. Arriving in London in 1791, he bore the grievances of Nova Scotian blacks who felt cheated out of the promises made them by the British. Peters became an instant London celebrity and was warmly received by Granville Sharp and his fellow reformers. "His eloquence, his passion, his spirit, made him the rage of the newspaper world, the latest fashionable craze, and the nearest object of philanthropy."[80]

A few words are in order on the life of Thomas Peters. He was born in the 1740s in Nigeria as an Egba Yoruba. He was kidnapped in 1760 and sold to a French slave ship, the *Henri Quatre*. Peters arrived in French Louisiana, and soon after his French master sold him to an Englishman. By 1770 he had been sold again, this time to William Campbell, a Scotsman in Wilmington, North Carolina, the seat of New Hanover County, where Peters learned his trade as a millwright. The war approached

Wilmington early in 1776, and it was evacuated in February of that year. Peters joined the British side of the war to effect his freedom and enlisted in the regiment of the Black Pioneers. He was present at the British bombardment of Charleston in the summer of 1776, and was with the British when they moved north to take Philadelphia at the end of 1777. At the end of the war he and the other blacks were taken to New York City in preparation for their shipment to Nova Scotia.[81]

In Canada, where freedom proved no less elusive, Peters reasoned that he and his people "would have to look beyond the governor and his surveyors to complete their escape from slavery and to achieve the independence they sought."[82] Peters organized a petition among the blacks of St. John, New Brunswick, and Digby, Nova Scotia, and carried it personally to London for the secretary of state for foreign affairs, William W. Granville. The petition described the harsh conditions of blacks in Nova Scotia and New Brunswick, asking for an urgent plan to remedy the situation. The position of the blacks in Canada, which had been described three years earlier (in 1788) as desperate, with most of them "without Clothing" and numbers of them "destitute of the necessities of Life" and facing "the most keen Distress" with the winter cold,[83] had only grown worse and more alarming. The choice was between finding arable land in Canada, which was unlikely, or else emigrating elsewhere for the purpose. The petition brought immediate action, with the secretary of state initiating inquiries in Canada and asking that either the blacks be provided with useful land or else enabled to emigrate to Sierra Leone. The directors of the newly formed Sierra Leone Company accepted Peters's petition and "concurred in applying to His Majesty's Ministers for a passage for [the blacks] at the expense of government, and having obtained a favourable answer to their application, they immediately availed themselves of the services of Lieut. Clarkson, who very handsomely offered to go to Nova Scotia, in order to make the necessary proposals, and to superintend the collecting and bringing over such free blacks to Sierra Leone, as might be willing to emigrate."[84] The British government, what John Quincy Adams termed "our old Grandam Britain," it was agreed, would bear the cost of such emigration.

Encouraged, Peters returned to Nova Scotia with plans to organize the blacks for transportation to Sierra Leone, against a good deal of opposition from both blacks and whites, it turned out. The blacks were afraid of undertaking the hazards of a journey to a continent whence they or their forebears had been taken and sold into slavery, while the whites feared that emigration would deplete a source of cheap black labor. But nothing could stop the venture now. In August 1791 proceedings were set in motion to screen potential Nova Scotian black emigrants to Sierra Leone. John Clarkson, the younger brother of Thomas Clarkson, was chosen as agent for this task, and Peters became his indefatigable assistant.

, In interviews with the blacks John Clarkson was enormously impressed with their religious sense, with their vision of a better future for their children, and with their desire to seek a foundation upon which to build and transmit their heritage. One of these blacks was a slave named John Coltress, who came not to enroll himself personally but to send off his free wife and children. Clarkson said he found it heartrending to see Coltress put the Atlantic between himself and his family in order to ensure "a better life for them." Peters himself took personal responsibility in rounding up candidates for the enterprise. Finally on 15 January 1792 the freedom armada of sixteen ships spread sail. Clarkson wrote jubilantly: "I am now under sail with a fair wind and fine weather, having on board 1190 souls in fifteen ships, properly equipped and I hope destined to be happy." The whole enterprise had cost nearly £9,600, a sum borne entirely by the British government.

Two months later the party landed, haggard and buffeted by disease and weather. Sixty-five had died at sea and another hundred were too ill to disembark. But there was no mistaking the symbolic significance of the feat just accomplished. Here is one description of the landing scene in which Thomas Peters played a leading role:

> Their pastors led them ashore, singing a hymn of praise . . . Like the Children of Israel which were come out again out of the captivity they rejoiced before the Lord, who brought them from bondage to the land of their forefathers. When all had arrived, the whole colony assembled in worship, to proclaim to the . . . continent whence they or their forbears had been carried in chains—
>
> > "The day of Jubilee is come;
> > Return ye ransomed sinners home."[85]

Jupiter Hammon, an elderly slave, once wrote about liberty not simply as an expedient, feasible political project, though that would do, too, but as an ethical value that views the human being as a moral agent with responsibility for the challenges of history, a position from which it would be possible to effect the practical joining of the general cause of liberty with the specific imperatives of antislavery. Until then, human flourishing, what Aristotle called *eudaimonia,* would remain partial and incomplete. Accordingly, Hammon appealed:

> That liberty is a great thing we know from our own feelings, and we may likewise judge so from the conduct of the white people in the late war. How much money has been spent and how many lives have been lost to defend their liberty! I must say that I have hoped that God would open their eyes, when they were so much engaged for liberty, to think of the state of the poor blacks, and to pity us.[86]

Peters was ill with fever at the time of landfall, but he rejoiced openly at their safe arrival and the prospects that lay before them. He recovered early enough for his compatriots to elect him their speaker-general. He soon fell out of favor with his people, however, and was found hatching a plot to overthrow authority. Warned in advance, Clarkson called a public meeting of the settlers and before them threatened Peters as a mutineer. Peters was then accused of embezzling money owed to two orphans. In the subsequent trial before a jury, Peters was found guilty, made to give up the money, and censored severely. He made to mend his ways, attended the nightly prayer meetings punctiliously, and testified regularly. Clarkson, disinclined to ignore an early warning, also showed up, determined to neutralize whatever remained of Peters's influence. Disheartened by Clarkson's growing stature among the settlers, Peters made a final desperate gamble. He challenged the people at a public meeting to decide between him and Clarkson and was devastated when no one moved in his direction. "Isolated, threatened, sick at heart, Peters fell ill with the prevailing fever, and in the night of the 25th–26th of June [1792] he died."[87] His cloudy ending, however, did little to diminish his achievements as a pioneer and symbol of freedom.

Freedom and the Evangelical Convergence

This theme of freedom must be stressed again, particularly in terms of the Puritan roots of the idea of liberty and the distinctive American contribution and its far-reaching effects. For the English Puritans liberty was so important that, as John Milton expressed it, Christ the liberator made possible "our worthy struggle for freedom." Nevertheless, liberty for the Puritans was qualified by discipline and restraint, and it mattered little that it was self-discipline so long as it served as example by the elect few. Milton, who had a forceful pen in any case, broke a few reeds extolling the virtues of discipline. "The flourishing and decaying of all civil societies, all the moments and turnings of human occasions are moved to and fro as upon the axle of discipline. Discipline is not only the removal of disorder, but if any visible shape can be given to divine things, the very visible shape and image of virtue."[88] In this scheme liberty was a scapegoat for license, whereas the balance of American Pilgrim thought, as was later expressed by Mark Hopkins in the mid-nineteenth century, was on the side of the "liberty and rights of the individual," which have their source in "the value which Christianity puts upon the individual,[89] and fully carried out, must overturn all systems of darkness and mere authority." As Mary Locke pointed out, the principles of the American Revolution were not particularly American or particularly new, for they had been in the air at least since the English revolutions against the Stuarts and their exposition by John Locke. Similar ideas had been propagated by Montesquieu, and Scottish common-sense philosophy, such as that propounded by Francis Hutcheson, had also preached against the slave trade on the grounds of the original right of every person to his or her own liberty. "In America, however, the ideas of liberty and equality took root and flourished with peculiar vigor, and it is in America that they produced their fairest fruit. It is therefore with special interest that one looks for their effect on the condition of the slave."[90]

The peculiar effect of the general movement for liberty and equality on freedom for blacks found some of its most eloquent expressions in the eighteenth-century evangelical movement, with which slaves identified themselves. A slave who was attracted to evangelicalism attributed his attraction to the promise of freedom. "I had recently joined the Methodist Church," the slave reported, "and from the sermon I heard, I felt that God had made all men free and equal, and that I ought not to be a slave."[91] Francis Asbury, the pioneer Methodist preacher in America, gave hints that he saw and welcomed the new conception of society in which blacks would have an equal share. Traveling with Asbury was "Black Harry" Hosier, a free black who sometimes preached in Asbury's stead.[92] At the Baltimore Methodist Conference in 1780 a resolution was adopted disapproving of members' holding slaves and requiring traveling preachers to free their slaves. The stand was reaffirmed at the 1784 conference, though the 1785 conference rescinded the rule about slave holding.[93] At the 1787 Methodist Conference white preachers were urged to leave nothing undone "for the spiritual benefit and salvation of the negroes."[94] Asbury himself took note of the spread of evangelical religion among the Africans, observing, "these are the poor, these are the people we are more immediately called to preach to."[95] A Baptist preacher in Westmoreland County, Virginia, commented in 1789 on the spread of religion among the slaves, saying he was witnessing the signs of a spiritual revolution. "Oh," he exclaimed, "see God choosing the weak things of the world to confound the things that are mighty."[96]

Many Methodist churches reported having black members. Of the fifty-one churches represented at the 1789 conference, thirty-six reported having mixed membership. But such reports should not be allowed to hide the fact white Methodists were not all united on the matter. At Philadelphia's St. George's Methodist Episcopal Church in 1787 a white trustee of the church, in the hush of the service, challenged a kneeling Absalom Jones, a black, and ordered him and other black worshippers to remove themselves to the gallery, the symbolic back of the bus, out of the way of whites.[97] As David Brion Davis has pointed out, "Relatively few Negroes were accepted into eighteenth-century New England churches, and those few were often segregated both in worship and burial."[98] Protestant denominationalism was proving unpromising for antislavery.

Upsetting the Natural Order

The importance just noted of evangelical doctrine in antislavery has been well examined by Davis in his critically acclaimed study of slavery in Western society. He observed that in classical Western thought, slavery was the natural condition of some people as opposed to others. Thus could Aristotle claim that "from the hour of their birth, some men are marked out for subjection, others for rule."[99] In Aristotle's view the true slave was an organic extension of his owner's physical nature, with no will or interests of his own. Within the framework in which the West was able to imagine abstract states of perfection, slavery was a perfect form of subordination, the paradigm of ideal submission. Both Calvin and Luther shared that view, so that for them, too, Christian liberty had no effect on the accepted notion that some people are born free and others slaves.

In his stimulating study of political theology, the Oxford theologian Oliver O'Donovan makes a different case for slavery not belonging with the self-understanding of Christendom, arguing that when Christendom emerged it exposed colonial slavery as a recidivist movement and pushed it to the fringes of European society. Colonial slavery, O'Donovan continues, was not allowed to reenter Christendom's mainstream economic organization, which implies that colonial slavery was alien to Christendom.[100] Yet the fact remains, as Columbus observed, that slavery belonged with Christendom and would advance its universal colonizing drive. Besides, enslavement "in the name of the Holy Trinity," Columbus testified, was merely the perfect form of the submission that subjects owed to Christendom, with Spain at its center.[101]

Thus did old Christendom, and its Protestant sequel, modify the classical views on slavery without challenging them, offering slaves instead the pious prospect of freedom and equality in another life as reward for being submissive and faithful to their masters in this one. Thus did the Christian status quo offer a mere placebo for an otherwise acknowledged moral injustice: the slave and the master are equally subject to sin, but, since the master is deputy for the slave before God, the slave must serve the master "as unto Christ." In fact, from the fruits of the slave's labor, the master could make moral exculpation by offering himself "a holy and living sacrifice, pleasing to God."

By setting up God as the ideal heavenly master to whom was due unquestioned submission, theologians established an evasive strategy that turned human subjects into notional slaves and inscribed a defunct morality into the injurious relationship between slave and master. A theological warrant was furnished to guarantee in the social realm the preserving of the servile estate by making it part of our obedience to God, thereby condoning what Bernard Williams has called the "internalized warfare" of slavery and its illegitimate authority. Slavery had its moral sting drawn, with opposition to it neutralized by the old highbrow theology. The beneficiaries of slavery in church, society, and state were left untouched because the churches abandoned any enforcement of the code denouncing their conduct. This abandonment resulted in the widespread social procrastination and moral indifference that tolerated slavery. High-brow religion allowed the wheels to be knocked off any meaningful drive for abolition, ensuring that even a notional intolerance of slavery would dissipate in a fog of personal piety.[102] Even Hegel's contention—that the "problem" of slavery was that the more perfect the slave the more *enslaved* the master became[103]—was mere intellectual casuistry, since it meant that slavery existed only to bring unreflective white owners to a need for enlightenment. According to Hegel's argument, the masters, not the slaves, deserve our attention and our pity for not coming to their senses. Hegelian logic thus left the masters with slavery as their alibi, culpable for their moral lapse but not for their being enriched by it.

The German scholar Ernst Troeltsch agreed that such philosophical abstraction and theological idealization of slavery ended up inexcusably strengthening the institution in its social aspect. Philosophy and theology alike stressed "the responsibility of the master for the physical and spiritual welfare of his slaves, while the slave is exhorted to love and obey his master, since he serves God and not man. To this extent, at least inwardly, the nature of the slave relationship was neutralized by the claims of the ideal. Outwardly, however, slavery was merely part of the general law of property . . . which Christians accepted and did not try to alter; indeed, by its moral guarantees, [Christendom] really strengthened [slavery]."[104]

Ultimately, the antislavery movement ushered in a shakedown of the old world philosophical infrastructure whose support of chattel slavery was based on a top-down view of history. There emerged "a widespread conviction that New World slavery symbolized all the forces that threatened the true destiny of man."[105] Perhaps Davis means by that statement that slavery as human bondage was essentialized in the new world as a race matter pure and simple: whites could enslave blacks, but never vice versa, so that not even the free black was done entirely with the reputation of slave. In any case, Davis adduces as one reason for what he calls "this remarkable shift in moral consciousness" regarding the iniquity of slavery as an institution that corrupted the wellsprings of true religion, the new evangelical faith in "instantaneous conversion and demonstrative sanctification."[106] "The emergence of an international antislavery opinion," he continues, "represented a momentous turning point in the evolution of man's moral perception, and thus in man's image of himself."[107] Elsewhere Davis elaborates on this point, stressing that "men could not fully perceive the moral contradictions of slavery until a major religious transformation had changed their ideas of sin and spiritual freedom; they would not feel it a duty to combat slavery as a positive evil until its existence seemed to threaten the moral security provided by a system of values that harmonized individual desires with socially defined goals and sanctions."[108] It requires a moral breakthrough, as John Donne hinted, to grasp that although reason is God's viceroy, nevertheless it is easily seduced in matters of self-interest. It then shirks its duty to defend and instead is made captive. Consequently, it proves weak or untrue. The antislavery movement was a moral breakthrough in the sense of breaching reason's defenses and replacing them with a new ethic that would carry forward the story of human progress.[109]

William Wilberforce caught the spirit of this new ethic and its roots in evangelical religion when he asked:

Is Christianity then reduced to a mere creed? Is its practical influence bounded within a few external plausibilities? Does its essence consist only in a few speculative opinions, and a few useless and unprofitable tenets? And can this be the ground of that portentous distinction, which is so unequivocally made by the evangelist between those who accept and those who reject the Gospel: He that believeth on the Son hath everlasting life: and he that believeth not the Son shall not see life; but the wrath of God abideth on him?

Wilberforce went on to assert that the "morality of the Gospel is not so slight a fabric," that Christianity's practical precepts were no less pure than its doctrines were sublime, that Christianity called for reliance on the promises of God and for vigilant, unrelenting struggle against the works of sin, and that such an activist view of the world in the name of God was universal and uncompromising.[110] The committed practical life was the prerequisite of evangelicalism, not abstract speculation about doctrine.

This new ethic produced the momentous religious shift that Davis has described, and it led in due season to the related idea, then gaining general acceptance, that ex-slaves and indemnified Africans would necessarily be the cornerstone of a new society in Africa distinguished by the ethics of lawful enterprise, personal integrity, social responsibility, the dignity of labor, and the values of personal religion and free public association, a new society that would as such constitute the decisive culmination of antislavery and be a moral endorsement of it. It left the way open for a social experiment based on a bottom-up view of the world.

New Light Religion: Pushing at the Boundaries

Many of these ex-slaves in Africa had been converted to Christianity and had in turn converted Christianity to their worldview. The precise connection with John Wesley and with New Light religious ideas was important to this radical transposition of Christianity. Wesley had assured the blacks of Birchtown in Nova Scotia that he would provide for their educational needs "while I live," and the first Wesleyan missionary in the province, William Black, preached extensively among the blacks. Such efforts found allies in black Methodist preachers themselves, such as Boston King, a former shipwright, and Moses Wilkinson, whom we shall meet again in due course. The enterprise of these preachers and their flocks led them to join religion with the cause of social reconstruction.

The agent of such New Light ideas in Nova Scotia was Henry Alline, "neither college learned, nor authorized by the presbytery," an itinerant preacher from Rhode Island. He arrived in Nova Scotia in April 1776, proclaiming "liberty of conscience" and announcing that the Spirit of God was commencing a revival-type "troubling of the waters" (John 5:4). In his short life (he died in 1784 in New Hampshire at the age of thirty-six), Alline stirred the province and thoroughly shook up both church and state. He shunned established denominations, calling them "a crowd of professors"[111] led by "legal professors," those well-bred preachers and clergy who promoted the letter of the law but were deaf to its spirit. By contrast, New Light converts received their anointing from the Spirit and consequently took their authority from God, not from earthly powers. Alline's converts set up chapels as independent congregations in numerous parts of the province. Their radical social views attracted the attention of legal and ecclesiastical authorities. The New Lights repudiated the old-line religious and political consensus whereby church and state collaborated in the pursuit of a law-abiding, religiously respectable community of citizens, and instead demanded that the state be precluded from any role in religious and spiritual matters. The Church of England, as the established church, reacted to the New Lights by calling them political subversives and religious heretics. Thus, for example, did Charles Inglis, appointed bishop in 1787 after

Nova Scotia was created a diocese by royal decree, charge the New Lights with having "threatened to subvert all order and national religion," saying they were "almost to a man, violent Republicans and Democrats [in other words, Americans]," and hinting darkly that they were plotting "a total Revolution in Religion and Civil Government."[112] He alleged he could catch a faint odor of Thomas Paine's malevolent influence on Alline and his followers.[113] By raising the specter of sedition, Bishop Inglis justified adopting the political instrument to deal with a theological challenge. A national religion, he implied, was entitled to national protection.

To the blacks, however, Christianity as national entitlement rather than as personal conviction and social responsibility was a tool of oppression and exclusion, besides being an offense to conscience. In Bishop Inglis's denunciation of the New Lights as a political threat, we have an instance where New Light ideas were construed in terms of anti-structure. They were seen to appeal to outcasts and ex-slaves, and in such a society the perquisites of established office would be nullified. Anyone raised on such perks could not see revival religion except as popular insurrection, as inflaming the black cause with religious insubordination. As Rawlyk expressed it, drawing on Victor Turner's analysis, New Light exhortation caused people to experience "an anti-structural liminality," a ritual of status reversal, the means whereby devotees could break away from their "innumerable constraints and boundaries."[114] Inglis responded by composing special prayers and having the government authorize their use throughout the province, "to impress the minds of people with sentiments of reverence—both towards magistrates and their office . . . These sentiments will when duly impressed contribute much to the peace and order of society and produce a ready obedience to lawful authority for conscience sake."[115] Preaching in that scheme of things was not simply a sacrament of religion, not just a means for regeneration, but a rule of enforcement, in fact a branch of law. As Inglis said, the object was reverence for magistrates and their office, not the cure of souls, and so he had the magistrates empowered and soldiers deployed to restrict and arrest Nonconformist preachers and advocates. As a consequence, William Black, the Methodist preacher, had his meeting and congregation broken up and scattered by soldiers.

These hostile measures did nothing to dampen enthusiasm or restrain enterprising religious agents. For the blacks, religion and freedom were in any case too closely intertwined for them to give up one or the other. Since the authorities licensed religion as a national enterprise and outlawed that form of religion identified with antistructure, they assessed theological opinion in terms of its social significance only and required society to regulate it by legal force. According to this understanding, any genuine religious system stood by the force of social custom, with religion functioning to bind and promote society and to claim that a sense of civic duty was more important than personal religion. The New Lights were judged seditious, for they wished to overthrow authority in church and state and to replace it with a warmed-over personal religion. Alline had declared that it was Christ, not George III, who alone merited unquestioning obedience and that the spiritual warfare that he, Alline, was waging had primacy over the wars of nations. In the atmosphere of the events of the Revolutionary War, Alline's claims carried, or were made to carry, political meaning. His appeal to God and to freedom was accordingly dismissed as bogus. Stripped of their pious veneer, the New Lights were deemed a functional menace. Establishmentarianism inclines too easily to functionalism, and functionalism tires too easily of theology.

Inglis intervened regularly to arrest the slide toward Nonconformist deviation and its sharp tendency toward antistructure. When in 1791, for example, he visited a black community, he was shocked to learn that Joseph Leonard, the black preacher, had not merely been leading services and preaching and teaching doctrine, but had been actually dispensing the sacraments, baptizing children and administering the Communion. Inglis remonstrated with him. Leonard responded to the bishop's strictures by asking instead to be ordained and granted separation and independence from the whites. Leonard would thus take his religion with him into antistructure. Whereas the bishop thought Leonard's errors could be remedied with better instruction, Leonard felt it was not instruction he needed but separation and independence. Their conflict is a classic primer of antistructure, with Leonard's version of spiritual regeneration claiming rights that the officials insisted never existed, at least not so that social outcasts could receive unimpeachable warrant. Such conflicting views proved that "the more limited the options for approved participation in the cultural mainstream, the more refined and satisfying become the alternatives to those excluded from the approved norms."[116]

In that impasse Christianity continued to appeal to blacks by offering them a chance to stand before a God who welcomed them as the equals of anyone else, a pointed challenge the officials could not ignore, or suppress for that matter.[117] That was why blacks combined their project of freedom with their religious mission. They would travel to seek freedom, yes, but also to preach the gospel of human freedom and political reform. It is significant that the modern missionary movement began largely as the initiative of freed slaves and ex-captives and carried the message of abolition as the timely expression of the message of Christianity. In that scheme Christianity as religious doctrine was reconnected with the social cause of former slaves and became thereby a religion of antistructure. The system it subsequently encountered in Africa—of chieftaincy and hereditary privilege—it deemed as antithetical to the interests and goals of the new humanitarianism, with its irrevocable commitment to antislavery.

Colonialists, in turn, tried to soften or even to neutralize this commitment by seeking accommodation with chiefs and native rulers. This strategy led colonial administrators to attempt to divide Christianity's spiritual interests from its social and economic interests and to place the religion under conditions of private quarantine. In this way evangelical social teaching was split from the mainline denominations, which orphaned evangelicalism, leaving it without a natural ecclesiastical home. Fragments of the tradition survived as revival spasms on the fringes of polite society where denominations were centered.

Yet the Christianity of the blacks, freed of its upscale Protestant inhibitions, became a major carrier of evangelical ideas, a situation that both missionaries and colonial administrators deemed proof of unsound religion. In the end, colonial rule split Christianity's spiritual interests from its material interests, weakening the public demands of antislavery and leading to the eventual surrender of the religious initiative to chiefs and Muslim emirs whose interests were now served by the policy of "indirect rule" that the colonial administration introduced in the late nineteenth century. Administrators of the 1880s and later, confident of having effectively privatized Christianity, proceeded to drive a wedge between the proliferating communities of Christians along the coast and hinterland centers of native authority. Official policy adopted the view that being Christian and being African were contradictory and that Christian Africans should be suppressed as a public anomaly. That policy, aided and abetted by the general liberal distrust of missions, was assumed as the agenda of the modern national state. Thus, colonial success in muzzling missionary Christianity left administrators free to proceed against independent elements of African Christian revival as targets of legitimate suppression. Yet African Christianity, shaped by the antislavery movement, persisted as antistructure alongside official Christianity, and often within or beyor.d it.

And so, to resume our story and follow it to its conclusion, there were these African Americans back in Africa, far from being "thrown intirely [sic] out of the scale of notice," with the challenge to make liberty fruitful and multiply. They would build projects of social rehabilitation and ethical example on the foundations of liberty. Thomas Jefferson's grab-bag formula of "emancipate and deport" took no account of the social possibilities of liberty for blacks except in separation. For him, political liberty had its uses only in preserving existing social arrangements based on race pedigree, inherited status, and economic well-being. The blacks, by contrast, appreciated liberty for what it would do to the stigma of race and to the chains of enslavement. They had allies in many officials who were roused to include blacks in the scales of notice and to strive for the cause of freedom. For example, Governor Harrison of Virginia, determined to make good the promise of freedom to the blacks who worked to capture Yorktown, said that he would lay before the legislature a bill that would give "to those unhappy creatures that liberty which they have been in some measure instrumental in securing to us."[118]

It was with official assurances of a similar nature that a group of blacks, former slaves, renegade republicans, and wards of officialdom came to Sierra Leone as pilgrim saints. With their coming a turning point was reached. The Christianity they brought with them would take root and flourish in tropical Africa, not simply because they brought it but because in their hands the religion underwent a fundamental change. Christianity in their possession was cleared of the mists of ruling genealogies that earlier suffocated it in the stuffy chambers of chiefly etiquette. Typically in that chiefly environment a missionary personality would arrive laden with gifts of European merchandise and be ushered into an antechamber to wait his turn to be introduced to the chief or ruler. Failing that, he would return the next day, or more usually the next year or so, in a resolute, if by now a forlorn, effort to secure the ruler's conversion. Contact was rarely made except with local weaklings or on vague, illusory promises. If the ruler was really astute, he or she would extract favorable trade concessions in return for notional political access. It was not uncommon for rulers even to demand compensation for the offenses of other European traders—the tradition of collective responsibility was a versatile one, it turned out. Christianity simply languished in this cat-and-mouse game. And then, finally, the same slaves, or their descendants, whose capture and sale had supported and justified chiefly power, arrived back as bearers of the Gospel, their extorted status as slaves the most powerful incentive for their mission whose central premise was that no human being deserved to be made slave because no human being was made such by God. Milton might as well have been speaking for these blacks when he wrote, "No man who knows aught, can be so stupid to deny that all men naturally were born free." Who best to champion that cause than former slaves, or those likely to be enslaved?

One story, full of human pathos, makes the point memorably. Soon after arriving in Freetown, a Nova Scotian settler ventured out into the country, arriving in the village from where fifteen years previously he had been taken captive and sold into slavery. "An elderly woman seemed much affected by the sight of this N[ova] Scotian, and spoke to her companions with much agitation. At length she ran up to him and embraced him: she proved to be his own mother."[119] In such situations the authorities commented on the moving nature of the reunions and, when the aggrieved found reconciliation, on the importance of forgiveness as a force for social progress, recognizing that forgiveness of that order cannot be imposed. Thus, a local Muslim chief, otherwise commended for his "amiable character," allowed "Christianity to be good in many respects, [but] expressly objected to the forgiving of injuries, as a virtue unattainable, and therefore not to be required."[120]

Under antislavery, mission came to represent a structural adjustment of worldview in the transition from medieval missions to modern missions. How sweet is the name of freedom in a former captive's ear! I shall explore its implications in detail in subsequent chapters, but here it suffices to stress that the new kind of religious history embraced by antislavery involved a break with dynastic rights and their encasement in chiefly caste. In these new circumstances, we would have to forgo the habit of looking to chiefs and rulers as the symbols of legitimate order and stability and instead turn to those traditionally at their beck and call.

John Adams once observed that African Americans were "the most obscure and inconsiderable that could have been found on the continent," with reference to the role of Crispus Attucks, an African American, in the Boston Massacre of March 1770, when the British fired on a crowd in Boston, killing him and two others and wounding eight.[121] The story of such African Americans has been permanently inscribed into the annals of the American Revolution, and that is as it should be. However, the equally important aftermath of that story in the shifting of the antislavery strategy to Africa deserves no less attention.

If that strategy could succeed in Africa, it would deal a body blow to the slave trade and slavery and thus demonstrate the humanity of former slaves. By the same token, if the cause of abolition in Europe and the New World was destined for success, that is, if abolition was an idea whose time had come, as Quaker abolitionists contended in the 1820s and later, then a successful antislavery movement in Africa would give it transatlantic validity. Antislavery would as such become a universal movement of human rights, and the structures of gain, domination, and advantage that lived off slavery would be dismantled in the wake of the new social radicalism. Perhaps that was the cause that inspired the likes of Samuel Hopkins and Ezra Stiles; although they had Africa in mind, they could scarcely have imagined the full implications of the ideas they had set forth so innocently. Nor, at the same time, would they have banked on public authorities in America ducking out of any official responsibility for antislavery in Africa, as happened in Liberia subsequently. Yet the flickering idea of looking for a reciprocal link between new world antislavery norms and African leadership aspirations in time strengthened and spread, however checkered the course.

2

"A Plantation of Religion" and the Enterprise Culture in Africa

In the long, bleak centuries before the founding of a Christian colony in Sierra Leone, European missions in Africa focused on trying to convert rulers, chiefs, princes, and members of the nobility as the basis of church planting and expansion.[1] A similar structural model had been used for the conversion of Europe, an arrangement under which wealthy dukes, princes, and other nobles endowed churches, monasteries, and other religious foundations to spread Christianity, thus enabling the religion to rise by its social eminence. The political scheme that fostered this development of Christianity reached its climax with the Frankish king Charlemagne (d. 814), who, crowned as Holy Roman Emperor on Christmas Day, A.D. 800, was noted for baptizing the Saxons by "platoons." The shift symbolized by Charlemagne involved taking Christianity out of the sacristy and making it a royal theocracy as "Christendom," weaving it into the fabric of the state.[2] (Theodosius had created a Christian orthodox state but had stopped short of divine kingship, as Ambrose's successful challenge to his authority proved.) In that scheme the political ruler was seen as God's appointed agent, the herald and instrument of God's mission, like Bertha, queen of Kent, who kept "the flame of Christianity burning in pagan times," according to the guide for visitors to Canterbury. Political affairs and religious matters became intertwined, with the political strand generally determining the pattern of conformity to be established for the religious strand. It was an arrangement in which state authority held primacy over religious origin, with political orthodoxy offering a safe cleft for the church to hide itself.

Eventually, the great religious orders consolidated Christianity in the empire, skillfully integrating elements of primitive folk religion, Roman and Gallic practices, and ancient ideas of the ties between the living and the dead with the new Christian teachings. As Christopher Dawson has indicated, Europe owed its identity to the legacy of the Roman Empire, the classical heritage, and the Catholic Church.[3] This successful synthesis was transported to West Africa in the three centuries between 1470 and 1785 and attempted in the old kingdoms of Elmina, Warri, Benin, and the Kongo, among others, but without lasting success. Africa's political development, feudal or dynastic, had not advanced to the same degree or even along comparable lines to allow for a natural transition from Europe. Thus the experiment of Christianity as sociopolitical investiture failed, and whatever achievements remained of those pioneer centuries would be absorbed and reconstituted in the new phase.

As explained in the previous chapter, that new phase corresponds to the story of the Nova Scotian settlement in Sierra Leone, which provides the basis for demonstrating this primary, special religious view of history. Its immediate background was the American Revolutionary War and, by implication, the development of republican forms of society and religion. We might go further back and appeal to the English Puritan notions of individual liberty, personal industry, social discipline, civic activism, and moral reform as the source of American republicanism.[4]

The core belief of this view was simple: the individual, redeemed by God, was the root and branch of society, politics, and law. The congregation as the body of the gathered saints, what the Puritans called "the visible elect," inspired the open town meeting as the appropriate form of government, and the habit of regular church attendance and lay responsibility as the model for the conception of a social covenant between the governor and the governed. Furthermore, the language of open and equal access to God generated the discourse of participatory democracy: people who had a notion of their equal standing before God would not be inclined to normalize a political caste system among themselves, however strong the case or urge for cultural differentiation. And since the litmus test of human welfare was one's being persuaded of God's gracious and unconditional acceptance, then a political community worthy of the name would enshrine religious tolerance and freedom of conscience as inalienable rights of the person, sinner and saint alike. Thus began that decisive shift of understanding in which the end of human felicity was a matter supremely of God's sovereignty, which ultimately produced the novel and productive view that the state had no business in a person's relationship with God, that in fact the state shared in human sin and so might not pretend to divine infallibility.[5] Instead, the state should be held accountable for the people's welfare. In certain important spheres, such as religion, the state might be excluded from the people's lives, or otherwise step out of the way so people are free to worship God. Freedom and religion belonged together.

The intellectual roots of this understanding of religion and society lay in the efforts of some significant Africans and their descendants in Europe and the new world, some of whom, like Philip Quaque (1741–1816), William Amo of Axim, Jacob Protein, and Frederick Svane (d. 1769), were based in West Africa. These Africans called attention to conditions existing in African societies, drawing on reliable, verifiable information and up-to-date facts to appeal to European leaders and public opinion on the need to push for change. Slavery was the point at which Europe collided with Africans, and slavery it was that would also offer Africans the leverage for change and reform. Thus was mounted a systematic effort to marshal the relevant information and material evidence to move Europe to intervene beneficially in Africa's affairs. Africa would be understood for the first time on the basis of scientific knowledge, of data that could be verified, cross-checked, and, if need be, challenged. Thomas Clarkson (1760–1846), for example, applied this method in his antislavery campaign, carrying a wooden chest filled with specimens from Africa: samples of textiles, basketry, rope and metal work, and leather goods, along with commentary based on reports, statistics, sketches of slave ships, confessions by ship captains, logbooks, and so on, to mobilize public opinion and parliamentary support. In this context slave autobiographies were priceless since they preserved the integrity of the black experience without the polished hand of literary agents or the intrusion of zealous white preachers who considered themselves entitled to save and civilize. Those who supplied such hard evidence avoided exaggeration or fraudulent claims lest that damage the cause. Indeed, it is striking that the slave narratives seldom indulged in antiwhite animosity or in any desire for black vengeance—it was the slave system and its racism that needed overturning rather than whites that needed punishing. As a result, the autobiographies, while fully engaged with the evils of slavery, often understated the situation to mask the pain.

In any case, thus did the antislavery movement for the first time promote factual knowledge of African conditions driven by what was essentially an Africa-centered point of view, allowing Africa's view of things to inform and guide Europe's relations and knowledge of Africa. It became incontestably clear that the leading agents of this scientific engagement with societies in Africa would be the Africans themselves who were enslaved, or were likely to be, not the chiefs and rulers who enslaved them for gain, and even for ritual slaughter. For it was these chiefs who when they died, for example, brought up the sanguinary rule that as many slaves be killed as befitted the deceased chief's rank and power and buried with him.[6] The Asantehene Osei Bonsu, king of Ashanti, spoke for many of his chiefly peers when he linked warfare, political destiny, and the trade in slaves:

> If I fight a king, and kill him when he is insolent, then certainly I must have his gold, and his slaves, and the people are mine too . . . The great God and the fetische made war for strong men every where, because then they can pay plenty of gold and proper sacrifice. When I fought Gaman (1818–19), I did not make war for slaves, but because Dinkera (the king) sent me an arrogant message and killed my people, and refused to pay me gold as his father did. Then my fetische made me strong like my ancestors, and I killed Dinkera, and took his gold, and brought more than 20,000 slaves to Coomassy [Kumasi]. Some of these people being bad men, I washed my stool in their blood for the fetische . . . Unless I kill or sell them, they will grow strong and kill my people.[7]

The point needs reiterating here that Africa and Europe became inseparably entangled through the slave trade, their common histories forged in identical motives for gain and profit. The trade restructured indigenous political life and institutions and built up the state-forming impulse in otherwise segmentary societies. As Eric Wolf argues, "The demand for African slaves reshaped the political economy of the entire continent. It gave rise, in one common process, to new tributary states and specialized organizations of slave hunters, and it turned societies described by anthropologists as 'acephalous, segmented, lineage-based' into the predilect target populations of slavers."[8]

Antislavery and Antistructure

There thus arose from within the antislavery movement, and the missionary movement that was allied to it, a new conception of society.

Chiefs and rulers were at best questionable models for social justice and at worst the source of injustice. It should be remembered that it was the chiefs, Jimmy and Naimbana among them, who attacked and burned the settlement in November 1789, signaling an end to that first venture. The best hope for Christianity, not to say for civilization, lay in bypassing these chiefs or else reducing their role in the new social order, whether through conversion and incorporation or exile and distancing. It was not just competition with traditional rulers for power and authority in the old scheme that led missionaries and others to oppose chiefs. Rather, it was the fact that the old establishment view of history was in conflict with the new conditions whereby hitherto historical outcasts had a right to justice, equality, and personal improvement, new conditions that led to the irreversible demise of chieftaincy authority in much of Africa. Eventually, when that trend strengthened enough to express itself in free universal adult suffrage, it completed the process of consigning chiefs to the past, or else preserving them as diversionary social relics. Even when various colonial administrations tried expedient variations on the old theme, such as warrant chiefs, the die was cast. Boys and girls enrolled in schools and trained in professions or otherwise doing well by their own effort became a social force far more powerful than any chief, however distinguished with official festoons.

Few people at the time understood fully the implications of the new religious view of human empowerment or what it would do to hallowed institutions of caste and pedigree. For example, officials of the Sierra Leone Company were still operating on the premise that chiefly lineage, sanctioned with treaties and fortified with the Gospel, would carry all Africa before it. They adopted for an ally in this cause King Naimbana, whose son, John Frederick, age twenty-four and renamed Henry Granville, he gave to be educated in England "by a country clergyman certified by two bishops as respectable enough to instruct one who, it was hoped, would be 'as useful in Africa, as Alfred and the first Peter were in their respective countries.'"[9] Naimbana, ruler of the Koya Temne since 1771, regarded himself as the friend and equal of King George III, not an empty boast if you consider his intended meaning that he was not subject to anyone's orders, European or African. In any case, concerning his sons, he was acting more from expedience than from principle. To increase his odds, he had given another son to be brought up in Catholic France (he had ceded an island to the French in 1785), and a third he committed to be educated as a Muslim under a Mandinka cleric in the hinterland.[10] His religious eclecticism he summed up in his own personal habits. When John Clarkson and the Nova Scotian settlers arrived in Sierra Leone, for example, Naimbana, accompanied by his subordinate chiefs, paid him a courtesy call, "dressed in full state with a judge's wig, wearing a pendant lamb and cross set in brilliants" for effect.[11] Naimbana, to show he would be an adversary, promptly demanded payment for loss and injury suffered from an attack in November 1789, in which some Americans were killed. In fact, the settlers were at the receiving end in that incident, becoming the butt of reprisals from Naimbana's chiefly henchmen who burnt down Granville Town. A certain irony thus persists in Naimbana giving the name Granville to one of his sons. Chiefs were as such a factor of considerable ambiguity in the new policy formulated to produce an enlightened, just society in Africa.

The evidence on the ground, too, supported the view that chiefs had far more to gain from slavery, and from the structures that depended on it, than from abolition, or from the enterprise of slavery's victims. Chiefs and local rulers had been indispensable collaborators, their power the staff and comfort of slave traders. They gave structural shape to the slave system, dividing up the land into spheres of influence, organizing raids, ransoms, and markets, processing captives, signing agreements, providing security, and enforcing directives. Historians might argue that the slave trade corrupted chiefly power, diverting it from its original high purpose of community solidarity, military protection, and political security. Yet the close interdependence between chiefly authority and the slave trade suggests an original affinity. As such, the slave system bolstered chiefly power and produced permutations and combinations among indigenous interests. If power corrupts, then how much worse when corruption itself becomes power!

Consequently, these chiefs had no positive place in antislavery and so were kept out of the new social scheme with its premium on personal industriousness. The new design for society placed emancipated and industrious Africans at the heart of the enterprise. By their cumulative example of hard work, a sober lifestyle, honesty, social activism, self-denial, public benevolence, and public service, these Africans would establish a new kind of society established on equality, the rule of law, and individual enterprise. Shortly after arriving in Freetown, for example, Clarkson lost no time in moving to establish standards of respect and the rule of law. He ordered three European sailors flogged for being offensive to the Nova Scotians and for disobeying orders. Simon Proof, a Nova Scotian ex-serviceman, carried out the flogging in public.[12] The directors of the Sierra Leone Company reported that the Nova Scotians agitated to have a jury system established when the governor and council dismissed one of them for showing disrespect to his superiors. On that occasion they "applied to have a law established, that no Nova Scotian working for the Company should in future be turned off, unless after a verdict by a jury of his peers."[13] (Richard Burton derided Freetown juries as stacked with "half-reclaimed barbarians clad in dishclouts [sic] and palm oil" and "cankered" with tribal malice. The system was as such a setback for "the ruling race" and for progress.)[14]

In a detailed memorandum on social conditions in the settlement, Robert Hogan, the chief justice, wrote in 1816 that he spared no effort to

inculcate with the most anxious and unaffected earnestness in the minds of the [settlers] that they are all equally free, all intitled [sic] to the same encouragement and protection: all possessed of the same right, without distinctions, as well as liable to the same penalties for infringing [the rights] of others, and all alike objects of the paternal care and constant solicitude of the common government. A steady adherence to this principle, and the undeviating application of it to practice promise the most salutary effect, and with the aid of the measures which Governor McCarthy [sic] has already adopted and is preparing to put in execution for the good government and prosperity of this colony bid fair to prove for his administration here, the enviable honour of being ranked among the most useful of the investments employed by providence for the benefit of mankind.[15]

A later generation of escaped slaves, the recaptives, would participate in the same culture of equality, the rule of law and common citizenship. Thus when John Langley, an Igbo recaptive in Freetown, was assaulted in 1829 by his manager, Frederick Campbell, Langley brought action against Campbell in court and prevailed, winning monetary damages. Like the African Americans before them, the recaptives "learnt to cherish litigation as a guarantee of their rights: if socially inferior to Europeans and Settlers, they were their equals before the law."[16] Recaptives were socialized in that setting, leading them to associate British jurisdiction with freedom, justice, and equality.

In that new society, social structure, conceived in the image of the chief and embedded in political genealogy, would be overturned and leveled, its place taken by those trampled underfoot and now reinstated under a fresh patrimony. The authorities in Freetown befriended the chiefs and their subalterns to win their cooperation in the fight against the slave trade, removed recalcitrants, and installed amenable candidates. In all cases they tried to contain chieftaincy rule where they could not do without it.[17] It was that indigenous restoration, rather than foreign missionary suzerainty, that would assure the future of Africa. At any rate, that was the new conception of society, marked by trust in indigenous enterprise.

The conceivable alternative of a protected and supervised missionary enclave to hold ex-slaves and their families, however attractive in the immediate context, was not viable as a long-term solution. Enclavement was too contrived, and white missionary sponsorship too tentative, to have any meaningful organic future. Ultimately, indigenous agency and leadership were necessary, however unprecedented or unpalatable they might be.

It happened that this view of the new world order was vigorously promoted by blacks themselves, Africans or their new world descendants, and they did so by enlisting in the front ranks of the evangelical Christian movement and stressing its theme of personal responsibility. The leaders of the antislavery movement were all too aware of the radical social implications of the cause they were championing, and, accordingly, they appealed to the public not only as a reading public but as a new age, as a society that, in their words, was being turned "on its hinges to let in a new dispensation of learning, religion, and life." In such a society undergoing transformation the "African element [would] contribute largely to the causes that agitate mankind, and must have its place in the [final] product. The vital powers are attracted to it by the force of the charities that make them vital, and are amalgamating with that element to form a new basis for society." History would then culminate in a fresh and enlarged dispensation.[18] Transplanted to Africa, this heritage took root and flourished, crowding out the medieval notion of the ruler as the anointed stem in whom the benefits of faith and society converged to be spread to the subjects below. By implication, this view rejected the cult of human power, with its built-in resistance to change.

David George

Let us choose some well-known individuals as examples of what came to prevail in Africa. One was David George, a significant figure in the religious history of his people. He was born in Essex County, Virginia, in about 1742, of parents, John and Judith, who were brought out of Africa in bonds. He had four brothers and four sisters all born into slavery like himself. In an autobiographical piece published in a contemporary journal, he said he remembered as a slave boy fetching water and carding cotton, and then going into the field to farm Indian corn and tobacco until he was nineteen. He recalled many instances of violence against his family. His brother tried to run away and received five hundred lashes when caught. "They washed his [raw] back with salt and water, and whipped it in, as well as rubbed it in with a rag; and then directly sent him to work in pulling off the suckers of tobacco. I also have been whipped many a time on my naked skin, and sometimes till the blood has run down over my waistband; but the greatest grief I then had was to see them whip my mother, and to hear her, on her knees, begging for mercy."[19] His master's cruelty drove George to run away, and eventually he passed into the ownership of George Galphin at Silver Bluff, South Carolina.[20] He described his life there as that of a spiritual profligate: "I used to drink, but not steal; did not fear hell, was without knowledge [of good and evil] . . . lived a bad life, and had no serious thoughts about my soul," until one Cyrus, a black preacher, confronted him with the Gospel. His conscience awakened, he went through a "dark night of the soul," about which he testified thus (with his emphasis):

> I saw myself a mass of sin. I could not read and had no scriptures. I did not think of Adam and Eve's sin, but *I* was sin. I felt my *own* plague; and I was so overcome that I could not wait upon my master. I told him *I was ill* . . . I felt myself at the disposal of Sovereign mercy. At last in prayer to God I began to think that he would deliver me, but I did not know how. Soon after I saw that I could not be saved by any of my own doings, but that it must be by God's mercy—that my sins had crucified Christ; and now the Lord took away my distress . . . Soon after I heard brother George Liele preach . . . When it was ended, I went to him and told him I was so; That I was weary and heavy laden; and that the grace of God had given me rest. Indeed his whole discourse seemed for me . . . I was appointed to the office of an Elder and received instruction

from Brother Palmer how to conduct myself . . . Then I got a spelling book and began to read . . . I used to go the little children to teach me a,b,c. They would give a lesson, which I tried to learn, and then I would go to them again, and ask them if I was right? The reading so ran in my mind, that I think I learned in my sleep as really as when I was awake; and I can now read the Bible, so that what I have in my heart, I can see again in the Scriptures.[21]

George was eventually baptized by Brother Palmer, presumed to be the Reverend Wait Palmer, a Connecticut New Light preacher in the mold of Samuel Hopkins.[22] George lived in Savannah, Georgia, until the British took the town and his master fled. George eventually made his way to Charleston, and when the British decided to evacuate Charleston, he was given an opportunity to leave for Nova Scotia, which he took. After twenty-two days of passage he arrived in Halifax in 1782 just before Christmas. After six months of enforced idleness, he was allowed to move to Shelburne, where his wish to minister to the blacks of the town was opposed by the whites living there. "I began to sing the first night, in the woods, at a camp, for there were no houses then built . . . The Black people came far and near, it was so new to them."[23]

Earlier George had been active in religious pioneering, working side by side with George Liele, a black Baptist pastor who went out as a missionary to Jamaica and the Bahamas. George had become a regular pastor of the Silver Bluff Church, constituted in about 1775. He was also instrumental in setting up another branch of the Baptist church in Savannah in 1777. A man already softened by religious itinerancy and ad hoc opportunity, he extended his activities to Nova Scotia (where Liele kept in touch with him).[24]

It turned out that Canada was to prove no less testing. No sooner had he set foot in Nova Scotia than George set in motion plans to build a meeting house. He preached his first sermon at a spot cleared for the purpose before the building was finished, so eager was he to get to the point, as it were. "I was so overjoyed," he confessed, "with having an opportunity once more of preaching the Word of God that after I had given out the hymn I could not speak for tears." To his disappointment and further surprise, he found obstacles to his religious work when the town of Shelburne reacted negatively to news that he had baptized whites. A gang of forty to fifty strapping fellows, disbanded soldiers, marched menacingly to George's house and overturned it, threatening worse fate for the meeting house should he persist. Uncowed, David George would stand amid the ruins and at the appointed time hold forth on the Word, "till they came one night and stood before the pulpit and swore how they would treat me if I preached again."[25]

Such a fate did overtake him when one Sunday an angry mob stormed the meeting house, whipped David George, and ran him out of town, where he sought refuge in outlying swamps. Under cover of darkness George crept back into town to gather his family and to move to Birchtown, stalked by white opposition and black restiveness. The hostilities followed him to Birchtown, where the blacks now joined the opposition. He was forced down the river back to Shelburne, which he reached even though "the boat was frozen, [and] we took whip-saws and cut away the ice." His former meeting house in Shelburne had meanwhile been converted into a tavern (said the tavern keeper, "The old Negro wanted to make a heaven of this place, but I'll make a hell of it"), but it seems adversity refined the man. Under his unflagging leadership the faithful gathered for worship and prayer, their numbers rising through the One who gives the increase. His exploits brought him to the attention of the British authorities in Canada; the governor's private secretary, Jonathan Odell, issued him a preacher's license, and David George personally invited the governor himself to come and witness the baptizing.

It was on such a preaching tour that George suffered an accident, when his ship was blown off course and George, having no adequate clothing, suffered severe frostbite in both legs up to his knees. He had to be carried ashore when he returned to Shelburne. His travels were severely curtailed thereafter, though in preaching he continued to enjoy undiminished powers. One of George's parishioners testified to the preacher's eloquence, saying that when George began praying he was so astir with the spirit that "many tears like Brooks" ran "down his cheeks desiring me to call upon that worthy name that was like Ointment pour'd down upon the Assembly—My Soul was upon a Mount Zion, and I saw whosoever worked Righteousness accepted by him."[26]

By the time he was introduced to the Sierra Leone settlement idea, George had been living in fear of his life, or else of a rapid slide into economic servitude. Emigration to Sierra Leone as an explicit religious experiment he would have found attractive on grounds of principle alone, but when it coincided with arguments of personal safety it was irresistible. George had been presiding at a religious meeting when John Clarkson found him. Clarkson admitted: "I never remember to have heard the Psalms sung so charmingly in my life before"; according to Clarkson, seeing George in action convinced him that no business or person of rank was capable of deterring "him from offering up his praises to his Creator."[27] Clarkson made him, along with Thomas Peters and John Ball, supervisors of the evacuation and expedition. George signed up his own family of six, and forty-nine of his flock also joined him. Together they would follow Clarkson, "an unlikely white Pied Piper across the sea to the coasts of Africa," as one historian put it.[28]

The general background to the deplorable situation of blacks in Nova Scotia has already been introduced in the preceding chapter, but a few more details may be added here. Clarkson had undertaken a rapid survey of the conditions of blacks in Nova Scotia soon after arriving in the province. Appalled by what he saw, he turned from a neutral agent into an ardent propagandist. He promised himself "not to sport with the (Negroes') destiny," which he saw in a religious light.[29] When news reached Nova Scotia that the Sierra Leone Company was having difficulties with the chiefs, in particular with King Jimmy, calling into doubt the wisdom of setting out with a fresh batch of settlers, Clarkson, who was dining at Government House, bluntly denied the reports and cut short the governor with a lecture on duty. "The conversation dropped by the Governor's pushing about a bottle."[30] Thus singlehandedly, and by means deliberate and dubious, Clarkson moved to overcome official as well as popular opposition to the settlement scheme, and in that his greatest allies were the black religious pioneers.

After a passage of seven weeks "in which we had very stormy weather," they made landfall in Freetown in March 1792, with the high mountain, at some distance from Freetown, its peak blending with the clouds, appeared like a shifting mass to them. The settlers lost no time showing why they came, with George again stirring with the abounding energy of the entrepreneur. As he later wrote, "I preached the first Lord's Day (it was a blessed time) under a sail, and so I did for several weeks after. We then erected a hovel for a meeting-house, which is made of posts put into the ground, and poles over our heads, which are covered with grass."[31] George represented the general sense among the settlers of following ancient Israelite precedent, and they went ashore to the center of Freetown, singing,

Awake and sing the song
Of Moses and the Lamb;
Wake every heart and tongue,
To praise the Saviour's name.

An inventory of the skills and trades represented by the settlers shows perhaps the exaggerated faith in the limited means at their disposal, but it reveals, nevertheless, the bold outlines of the experiment to found a new society on African soil. The lists classify 12 as "qualified for particular trades," trades that fell into thirty-odd categories, including sawyers, carpenters, coopers, shoemakers, smiths, butchers, bricklayers, cooks, fishermen, tailors, weavers, and one each of a brewer, sail maker, and, pressing the limits of inclusiveness, chimney sweep. The roll included 127 described as "labourers acquainted with all tropical production,"[32] but 41 listed as "porters at wharfs and general labourers."[33]

There were 385 men and 825 women and children, a number that includes children born to the settlers since the embarkation from Nova Scotia. Up to April 1792 55 men (roughly 14 percent) and 57 women and children (7 percent) had died. The first rainy season brought widespread illness, with about 800 blacks laid up at one time and with Europeans far more vulnerable to the tropical fever. In the first few months the mortality rate was quite high, according to official reports. One such report announced that "of the 1190 free blacks embarked at Halifax in January, 1792, the following is a return of the deaths up to the 2d of September, 1792, which in the men and women have been principally old and infirm, and many of those who died on shore were landed in a diseased state. On their passage 35 men, 18 women, 7 boys, and 5 girls: total 65. Since their arrival, 28 men, 28 women, 21 boys, and 22 girls; total 99. General total 164."[34]

Of a different order but of equally lamentable gravity were the reports that some of the Nova Scotians left the colony to form alliances with neighboring chiefs and to engage in the slave trade. Zachary Macaulay, governor in August 1797, noted faintheartedly that "the Settlers were gradually contracting a more friendly disposition to the Slave Trade. At this moment," he testified, "there are two in the Rio Nunez, and three in the Rio Pongo, who are actually engaged in it; to say nothing of the number who, without carrying on a Slave Trade on their own account, are employed in the service of Slave-traders, and thus are aiding and abetting in carrying it on."[35]

In June of 1794 an insurrection broke out among the settlers, but it was put down without bloodshed, and six of the ringleaders were arrested and sent to England for trial. Then in September 1794 renegade French Jacobins attacked the settlement, causing widespread destruction to property. For protection, the government proposed what it called a Scheme of Premiums to encourage the settlers to move up into the mountains, where conditions for agriculture were also believed to be better. There were few takers. In September 1800 a new and most serious insurrection by the settlers threatened to overwhelm the colony. It was suppressed by the strategic landing of a large number of Maroons[36] with a military escort. Two of the insurgents were killed, thirty-five taken prisoner, of whom three were executed and thirty-two banished. A number of insurgents also abandoned the colony and melted into the native population beyond.[37]

These are not the sorts of events it takes to build a new Jerusalem, though if the settlement survived the drama and trauma of its early trials it would be entitled to a claim no less confident. As it was, the settlers had enough mettle to wish to defy the odds. History, in terms of proven practice or the advantages of personal circumstance, was not on their side, and many were the naysayers. With their sense of commitment, however, the settlers would invest themselves in the cause they felt worth promoting, whatever the risks and however precarious the future.

George quite naturally exchanged the role of preacher for that of political pioneer, gathering the concerns of the settlers and making representation before the authorities, who had rather specific ideas about what was in the best interest of the settlers. Zachary Macaulay had succeeded to the governorship of the colony in 1794, and he had little rapport with George, which may have colored his journal entries. In any case George appears as a defender of settler interest, and especially of what George called their "religious rights." The officials for their part were inclined to impute motives of republican conspiracy to settler restlessness, so fresh in their minds was the recent revolt of the American colonies against the Crown. "America" in colonial circles represented new world insubordination, and accordingly care was taken to scotch any ideas of republican sympathy. But such care did little to diminish the social power of a redeemed, emancipated, and industrious black community now permanently ensconced on the continent of its origin.

David George continued to demonstrate that fact by pressing on the religious and political fronts at the same time, arguing that his people's status before God as carrying no stigma had its earthly counterpart in liberty without prejudice. On George's visit to London in 1793, the colony chaplain, Melville Horne, sent a letter of introduction with him to John Newton as well as to other well-known philanthropists. Newton (1725–1807), a hymnwright, perhaps most famous for "Amazing Grace," had been a slave dealer on the West African coast until he underwent a dramatic conversion experience.[38] On his London trip George carried a petition on settler grievances and made contact with what Horne's letter described as "Christians of all denominations" as well as with the Baptists, trying to stir up interest for the cause in West Africa. When he returned to Sierra Leone he wrote to his English friends words of encouragement garnished with exhortation. "I want to know," he persisted, "how religion flourishes in London." In the same letter he sounded a theme that might be considered the hallmark of faith in the personal enterprise the settlers brought with them to West Africa. "I am very glad to tell you," he confided, "that the work of God revives here among our people, and I hope it will begin among the NATIVES OF AFRICA." In his view, the work of God revived the work of social rehabilitation and moral reform, with blacks at the helm, and God's spirit thus permeated the entire outlook of these settlers. Brought low by enslavement, broken by removal, and then stripped of any chance of personal recovery by the vagaries of multiple ownership, the settlers saw in the whole enterprise something of a second chance, which, if it worked out, would create a useful precedent for the rest of Africa.

Moses Wilkinson

With that note it is proper to introduce another pioneer settler, Moses Wilkinson, mentioned previously, under whom the settlers returned to the form of religion familiar to them, a form marked by the revival practice of prayer, testimony, and witness, all of it self-administered. The settlers spoke about being born again, often in the sense of setting good examples and leading by personal conduct. Wilkinson had been a slave in Nansemond, Virginia, from where he escaped, even though he was blind and lame. He was a fervent preacher and a stalwart defender of the religion he knew and loved. With a keen sense for the distrust the authorities felt for the "American" sentiment in religion, Wilkinson met head on official attempts to bring the settlers into line.

The authorities assigned official chaplains to the settlers as a precaution for ensuring familiarity with "respectable religion," with duplicate sermons to remedy deficiencies in the coarse native variety. In the establishment thinking, preaching and the pulpit needed to be placed under law. That way religious practice, suitably acculturated, would be brought into line with the pedantry of learned culture.[39] Religion was "the king's book and the king's proceedings,"[40] and should not be allowed to become what an English divine once termed "a shooting-horn to their vanity and gain."[41] Unless guided by law and controlled by regulation, the doctrine the settlers were propagating would "shrink up all religion into preaching," and thus incite sentiments of insubordination among the blacks. Preaching had a bad social reputation anyway, but its political implications made it a public nuisance. Thomas Hobbes had once regretted that the Puritan clerics had not "been all killed before they had preached," which would have taken care of the 1688 upstart revolution. That sentiment lingered in official suspicion of preachers.

Among the blacks, however, preaching was not simply religious ranting or cathartic discharge, though in the hands of the less gifted it could become mere show, throttle without torque. For the religiously minded, by contrast, preaching was an act of spiritual release, a celebration of freedom from bondage and oppression, both the human and spiritual kind. The experience of Olaudah Equiano illustrates vividly why speaking acquired the status it did among the blacks. He described how after his slave voyage across the Atlantic from Africa he arrived, still in chains, at a Virginia plantation in 1757. He was landed and ordered to go and look after a sick slave master in his house:

> when I came to the house where he was I was very much affrighted at some things I saw, and the more so as I had seen a black woman slave as I came through the house, who was cooking dinner, and the poor creature was cruelly loaded with various kinds of iron machines; she had one particularly on her head, which locked her mouth so fast that she could scarcely speak; and could not eat nor drink. I was much astonished and shocked at this contrivance, which I afterwards learned was called the iron muzzle.[42]

The iron muzzle had its symbolic parallel in the interdiction on slave testimony in free society, specifically in the courts and churches and in relations with whites.[43]

The conditions of slavery attacked the very fount of freedom by imposing restrictions and penalties on preaching, forcing the slaves to resort to secrecy and other evasive techniques in their religious gatherings—in secluded spots in ravines, in pockets of bush, and in isolated spaces in the woods, appropriately called "hush harbors."[44] One black preacher, for example, described how he preached to other slaves while the assembled meeting huddled under quilts and rags that had been made wet "to keep the sound of their voices from penetrating the air."[45] On a Louisiana plantation "the slaves would steal away into the woods at night and hold services," in which they "would form a circle on their knees around the speaker who would also be on his knees. He would bend forward and speak into or over a vessel of water to drown the sound. If anyone became animated and cried out, the others would quickly stop the noise by placing their hands over the offender's mouth." Another slave testified: "Some gits so joyous they starts to holler loud and we has to stop up they mouth."[46] The image of blacks stopping up one another's mouths after helping to open them dramatizes the potency of the power of speech. Thus the iron pot or kettle used to muffle the sound became a symbol of suppressed freedom.

The authorities attacked preaching as social anarchy. An Anglican clergyman of Salem, Massachusetts, derided the Great Awakening of the 1730s and 1740s as pandering to blacks and other social rejects. "So great has been the enthusiasm created by [John] Wesley and [George] Whitefield and [Gilbert] Tennent, that people talk of nothing but, 'renovating, regeneration, conviction and conversion . . .' Even children 8–13 assemble in bodies preaching and praying, nay the very Servants and Slaves pretend to extraordinary inspiration, and under the veil thereof cherish their idle dispositions and in lieu of dutifully minding their respective businesses run rambling about to utter enthusiastic nonsense." Another critic of the Great Awakening, Charles Chauncy, objected to blacks' flocking to revival meetings, indignantly exclaiming, "chiefly indeed young *Persons,* sometimes *Lads,* or rather *Boys;* Nay, *Women* and *Girls,* yea *Negroes,* have taken upon them to do the Business of Preachers."[47]

One John Thompson, born a slave in Maryland, testified in 1812 about the general effects on blacks of the Great Awakening. He said that his mistress and her family were regular worshippers at the nearest Episcopal church, which was five miles from the plantation. The preaching was above their heads, and so they were never better off when they left the church than when they went in, until someone brought revival religion and preached in a manner so plain and direct that even a simpleton could understand. The new religion caused a stir among slaves, making slave-holders anxious. Yet the new preaching style received increasing attention among the blacks because "it brought glad tidings to the poor and bondman [*sic*]; it bound up the broken-hearted; it opened the prison doors to them that were bound, and let the captive go free. As soon as it got among the slaves, it spread from plantation to plantation, until it reached ours, where there were few who did not experience religion."[48] Revival religion, then, inflamed the desire, and the obligation, to speak and testify, but slavery forbade it. Slave preachers often faced the whip or worse for preaching.[49]

Slavery as the effacement of the speaking person placed a premium on the power of speech as the attribute supremely of the child of God, that is, of the free person, and giving voice to thought was elevated to a redemptive act. To exercise the power of speech helped to enact the drama of redemption. In effect, for blacks who lived with the iron muzzle, speaking was like a territorial passage, a threshold act of ritual redeeming and renewing. They inevitably gave speaking a religious meaning: one preached and praised because one was religious, not in order to become religious. Thus, redemptive preaching, or for that matter, singing, stood at the heart of all their speaking. As W. E. B. Du Bois wrote, "the preacher is the most unique personality developed by the Negro on American soil."[50]

In this setting, the duplicate sermons offered with the intention to correct and instruct caused little offense to the settlers, merely allowing the worshippers to add them to the familiar form and increasing the time they spent at worship and prayer. Needless to say they were used to more lively things than the harmless specimens the guardians of respectable religion proffered.

One self-styled official chaplain, sent to safeguard the rules of respectable religion, testified of having been given a lesson himself. He described Moses Wilkinson's powers as follows:

Moses Wilkinson preached this evening from Isaiah iii: 11 and 12. He gave out his hymns and texts from memory. His manner was warm and animating . . . While hearing him I was led to admire the goodness and wisdom of God in the instruments which he frequently sees fit to use, to advance the interests of his kingdom. Many of the wise and learned in this world, if they were to see and hear such a man as our brother, professedly engaging in endeavouring to lead their fellow creatures from sin to holiness, would at once conclude it to be impossible for them to effect the object which they have in view. Experience, however, flatly contradicts such a conclusion. Numbers have been led by their means to change their lives, and are induced from day to day to pursue that conduct which conduces to their own happiness and to the welfare of those around them.[51]

Speaking of a similar experience in the United States, a white witness, A. M. French, wrote:

The real spiritual benefit of these people, instrumentally, seems to have been mostly derived from a sort of local preachers, Colored, and mostly slaves, but of deep spiritual experience, sound sense, and capacity to state Scripture facts, narratives, and doctrines, far better than most, who feed upon commentaries. True, the most of them could not read, still, some of them line hymns from memory with great accuracy, and fervor, and repeat Scripture most appropriately, and correctly. Their teaching shows clearly that it is God in the soul, that makes the religious teacher. One is amazed at their correctness and power. They say: "God tell me 'you go teach de people what I tell you; I shall prosper you; I teach you in de heart.'"[52]

From such personal acquaintance, the strange and the exotic seemed no longer remote, and so officials could overcome the fear of, and opposition to, black preaching simply from unfamiliarity. The settlers called such fervor "going into mourning" or, arousing official suspicion, "groaning for redemption" and "seeking liberty."[53] It dissolved all their inhibitions and stigmas, a genuine spiritual democracy of equal and open access where the spirit wafted on the lowly the breath of assurance. Many a preacher had communed on the passage of Isaiah, "Hast thou not known? hast thou not heard, that the everlasting God . . . fainteth not, neither is weary? . . . He giveth power to the faint; and to *them that have* no might he increaseth strength . . . [and that] they that wait upon the Lord shall renew *their* strength; they shall mount up with wings as eagles; they shall run, and not be weary; *and* they shall walk, and not faint" (Isa. 40:28ff). Prayer and worship offered sanction for a new society, and government responded by following the lead of religion. Many times the settlers suffered a tragedy: fire engulfed a dwelling or a chapel, death took away a pillar of the community, a shipwreck demolished supplies, the harvest failed, war in the interior disrupted trade, the fellowship split into factions, a trusted missionary turned into a thorn in the flesh, and still they remained unwearied, unfainting. As an old man in a quarter of Freetown known as Portuguese town testified to George Lane, who went to commiserate with him after a disastrous fire, "no trouble, no feel," meaning without tribulations and trials there can be no experience of divine grace.[54]

Another official chaplain was literally taken by his ears to witness the spectacle. One settler preacher, Prince Edward, had awakened from his religious inquiry and gone out to look for someone to share his revelation with. He found William Davies, an ardent young Welshman with pronounced scruples against settler religion. Edward burst into Davies's room and, finding Davies kneeling in prayer, "picked him up in his arms shouting 'I found him, I found him!'" Davies, beset with consternation, later recalled, "I asked him what he had found. 'I found Christ. I feel his pardoning presence. His spirit says, Go in peace, all thy sins are forgiven thee.'"[55]

The Countess of Huntingdon's Connexion

There were other pioneers and preachers who shared fully this view of religion and society, embracing without question its potentially liberating social and political consequences, and we should consider further some of these. John Marrant belonged to their number. He was born of free black parents in New York on 15 June 1755, and just before he turned five his mother removed him to St. Augustine, Florida, where he went to school. After a year and a half he moved to Georgia and then to South Carolina. There, in Charleston, he learned to play the violin and French horn; by thirteen he was an accomplished musician, much admired by audiences. He once described how he met George Whitefield, the revival leader, whose message fell on him like a thunderclap and knocked him out of his senses. Converted at Whitefield's hands, Marrant went in search of a missionary cause, running away from hostility at home and "travelling on for nine days, feeding upon grass, and not knowing whither I was going," except that the hymns of Isaac Watts sustained him. He found himself among the Cherokee Indians to whom he preached. "I prayed in English a considerable time, and about the middle of my prayer, the Lord impressed a strong desire upon my mind to turn into their language, and pray in their tongue. I did so, and with remarkable liberty," a performance that impressed the people enough to cause them to rescind the sentence of death and spare his life.[56]

Marrant was living in Charleston when it came under siege by rebel forces. Just before the town was abandoned, Marrant met his old friend, the king of the Cherokee Indians, who recognized him when he rode into town in the company of General Clinton. Shortly after that Marrant was evacuated to New York, from where he was pressed into service with the British. In an engagement at sea on 5 August 1781 Marrant was badly wounded and subsequently put on the invalid list and discharged in London, "where I lived with a respectable and pious merchant three years . . . During this time I saw my call to the ministry fuller and clearer; had a feeling of concern for the salvation of my countrymen."[57] The London merchant with whom Marrant stayed, John Marsden, along with his brother H. Marsden, spoke in their testimony of Marrant's honesty and sobriety, of his "being tender-hearted to the poor, by giving them money and victuals."[58] In regard to his vocational interest, Marrant received a letter from his brother in Nova Scotia in which his brother set out the need for a pastor to minister to the growing body of black Christians and asked Marrant to introduce himself to the community in Bath. When he received his brother's letter, Marrant approached Lady Selina Hastings, the countess of Huntingdon, who had come under the influence of John Wesley.[59]

The countess was no stranger to matters in America. In 1770, after the death of George Whitefield at Newburyport, Massachusetts, she took charge of the Orphan House at Bethesda, Georgia,[60] which Whitefield bequeathed to her. Around that time Phyllis Wheatley, "the black poetess," sent the countess a poem on Whitefield's death,[61] together with a letter offering a wax size image of Whitefield.[62] Her grandson was present in June 1775 at the battle of Bunker Hill at Boston and wrote to her about news of the action. After the meeting of the first Philadelphia Congress in 1774, the countess received accounts from her brother warning of impending war. In July 1775 there began to circulate reports that the countess was attempting to write what was called "a Plan of Government for the Americans," in which she supported the cause of the colonies.[63] In fact, she and her family did support the Americans: she wrote to her daughter in those terms and was allied for the purpose with her son, a Whig and a member of the Leicestershire Revolution Club. One of her preachers, Cradock Glascott, preached a sermon in London in support of the American struggle. In deference to her pro-American sympathies and her ideal of local autonomy, she arranged to have Bethesda transferred to American control.[64]

Thus by the time she met John Marrant she had felt thoroughly acquainted with the American question and been sympathetic to the cause there. She had John Marrant ordained at Bath in 1785 as a minister of her church, the Connexion, and enabled him to return afterward to Nova Scotia to found a congregation at Birchtown before leaving again for London, where he died in 1791. But he had passed on the torch to Cato Perkins, also a Charlestonian, who, with William Ash, another Charlestonian, established the Connexion in Freetown. Perkins was a companion of David George when the two visited London in 1793, during which visit Perkins met Lady Anne Erskine, an associate and a successor of Lady Selina, who had died in 1791. Lady Erskine extended some help to Perkins.

Another associate of Lady Selina was the Reverend Thomas Haweis, whom Perkins met. Haweis was an Oxford-educated son of a Cornish lawyer who happened to have cluttered himself with the coarse remnants of a long-running dispute about simony in Aldwinkle, a Northamptonshire village. In any case, the meeting with Perkins inspired Haweis to devise an imaginative escape from his troubles by contemplating a mission to Africa. Failing that, he became a founder of the London Missionary Society. Thus the cause for which John Marrant labored prospered greatly in Sierra Leone, and Cato Perkins's successors could preside over a branch of the church that now outstripped its parent. An official report of the Connexion described how the Sierra Leone Church first came to the attention of the English church in 1825 by means of a letter sent by John Ellis, a minister, through a settler woman. Nothing further was heard until 1839, when two blacks from Sierra Leone showed up in church, saying they had come to England on business and were taking the opportunity to make personal representation for the Connexion in Sierra Leone. Thus was established the relationship long sought by the settlers, though London was careful to note that the policy of association was based not on "control . . . but rather to advise, to inspire, and to help. In the matter of money," the statement continued, "what has been sent from England has been only a part of that required for the work. The larger portion of the expenditures has been met by the contributions of the people themselves."[65]

Perkins died in 1805, to be succeeded by John Ellis, who presided over the work of the Connexion without any further contact with the London branch. Then Anthony Elliott took over the leadership following Ellis's death in 1839, and under Elliott contacts with London were renewed. Elliott was born in Dartmouth, Nova Scotia, and was fifteen or sixteen when he arrived in Sierra Leone. He was licensed as a pilot to bring ships into Freetown harbor, but on New Year's Eve, 1813, he experienced a conversion; subsequently he became a preacher.

Elliott led the church in its expansive missionary phase, promoting the cause among the recaptives in the colony villages on the Freetown Peninsula. By 1835 he had established congregations at Goderich and Waterloo, and the following year groups were assembling in Campbell Town and Rokel. In the 1840s new meetings were being held in Igbo Town, Tombo, and Hastings, with others set up in other parts of Freetown colony. Thomas Ellis, a Maroon timber trader, opened a mission at Mabang, on the Ribi, and Bai Yinka, a chief of the Small Scarcies River, allowed Joseph Easton, a Huntingdonian preacher, to build a chapel and school at Rokonta. No wonder Easton boasted of how the work was prospering without European agency. "All hearts were glad," he wrote, "to see the Gospel carried by black men to black men, for the first time without any European being present."[66] There were eleven chapels, forty-eight preachers, and eighty-nine class leaders. In 1852 Scipio Wright, a local preacher, was brought to England and ordained into the ministry of the Connexion.

The Waterloo church of the Connexion, St. Mark's, was under the care of Henry Steady, a disbanded African soldier who was also employed by the Church Missionary Society (CMS) as a teacher in Waterloo. After he was dismissed by the society, he continued to live in Waterloo, working as a carpenter. Until 1843, when the CMS opened a mission in Waterloo (goaded into action following the launch of the 1841 Niger Mission, inspired, among others, by Crowther), religious life was under the care of the settlers and recaptives themselves.

Paul Cuffee

Religion and personal industry would make a successful combination in the person of Paul Cuffee, an African American Quaker from New Bedford and Westport, Massachusetts. Freed by his conscience-stricken Quaker master, Paul Cuffee (often spelled "Kofi," hence of Ashanti ancestry) was born under the name Slocum in 1759 in Dartmouth, Bristol County, Massachusetts, the youngest of seven brothers and sisters. His father was of African descent, his mother a native Indian, probably of the Wampanoag tribe. The name Cuffee (or Cuffe) was adopted by the family in about 1778. He received instruction early and by the age of thirteen was able to read and write. At sixteen he entered the whaling trade, his first voyage taking him to the Gulf of Mexico and a second to the West Indies. When the American War of Independence broke out he was on a whaling trip and was captured by the British and held in remand for three months in New York. After his release he gave up whaling and took uncharacteristically to agriculture in Westport. With life at sea still casting a spell on him, he gave in and built a boat with the help of a brother, David, to trade with towns on the Connecticut coast. That and several subsequent attempts to return to sea ended in failure, with Paul lucky on several occasions to escape capture by pirates. The end of the war found Paul still keen to pursue a career at sea. He fitted out an 18-ton boat to trade in codfish, and that laid the foundation for his future business success. Assisted by his wife's brother, he took again to whaling, making frequent trips to Newfoundland. He returned to Westport from these whaling trips and then went on to Philadelphia, where he exchanged his cargo of oil and bone for bolts and iron, with which he built a new 69-ton vessel, the *Ranger.* He ranged up and down the eastern seaboard and ran a particularly profitable venture in Virginia trading in corn. With success assured, Paul took on the maritime world and in 1800 commissioned a larger, 162-ton vessel, the *Hero,* which on one of its voyages rounded the Cape of Good Hope, a hint of things to come. In 1806 he fitted out two ships, one a 268-ton vessel, the *Alpha,* which traveled from Wilmington and Savannah to Gottenburg, Sweden, eventually returning to Philadelphia. In the other, the *Traveller,* he owned three-fourths interest. It was with this vessel that he crossed the Atlantic to Freetown, about which more later.

With the profits from his whaling business, Paul led an effort to establish a school for blacks in Westport, eventually building one from his own funds and offering it to the community. He was convinced that education offered the route to self-improvement for blacks, and he dedicated himself to promoting that cause.

This brings us to Paul Cuffee's religious background, and, thus, to the general theme of this book. His parents are recorded as having been regular attendants at the Westport meeting of Friends, where they would have been told that the revelation of the Divine Principle could enlighten "the soul of every man."[67] Paul himself joined the Friends in 1808 in what accounts describe as a sincere and faithful profession of faith. In the pithy words of his biographer, Paul "was considerate of little folks, for he presented them with Bibles and good counsel and endeavored to set before them an example of righteous conduct."[68]

In line with his religious interest, Paul strove for broader participation for blacks in the affairs of state and society, using his own personal advantages for the purpose. He and a brother, John, sent a petition to the General Court of Massachusetts Bay, on 10 February 1780, asking for the extension of franchise rights to blacks as the logical corollary to the fight for independence, in which blacks joined. Their petition argued for consistency of principle in that regard and for the need to change the situation of blacks,

> Having no vote or Influence in the Election of those that Tax us yet many of our Colour (as is well known) have Cherfully [sic] Entered the field of Battle in the defense of the Common Cause and that (as we conceive) against a similar Exertion of Power (in Regard to taxation) too well known to need a Recital in this place.[69]

The petition as an extrapolitical remedy has a long history, going back at least to the 1628 *Petition of Right,* in which Charles I assented to the declaration of rights and liberties of the people as presented to him by Parliament. In that form the petition was a branch of patronage and addressed as such to the ruler as superior authority, whatever material qualifications might have been implied in concessions granted in the entreaty or supplication. In the words addressed to Archbishop Ussher by Michael Robarts of Jesus College, Oxford, he was "a petitioner to your grace for favour."[70] As used by the blacks, both in America and in West Africa, the petition thrived as a bill of grievance, an appeal to assert rights and seek remedies deemed just and proper. It expressed the individual rights of the petitioners and fit with the Puritan doctrine of the divine right of personhood, which, as Milton put it, held that we "are made in the image and resemblance of God." In this view the petition was not merely appeasement or propitiation of superior authority, but a tool of justice. It was the American blacks who in West Africa employed the principle of the political petition on a regular and sustained scale, with

James Wise and Samuel Brown among the most accomplished and polished at that epistolary art.[71] Wise, for example, combined legalistic sophistication with literary flair, reporting accurately on settler demands, carefully sifting the unreliable from the trustworthy in the petition, pointing out the legal hazards of dealing with a chapel trustee who as attorney also held a brief to the dispute, and ending with a warning couched in understatement: if you give in "there will be room for vainglory."[72] Both Wise and Brown, among others, were prominent in resisting official attempts at asserting control over the settlers. The petition as a regular medium of communication became, in the context of political agitation, an outlet and a conduit for grievances, and thus an important documentary source of historical issues, attitudes, concerns, and major actors.[73] James Wise was active early in the process, for the missionary John Huddleston was writing in February of 1822 of Wise being a leader of a Young Turk faction determined to oust the missionaries from control.

To return to Paul Cuffee, he had in 1808 expressed an interest in doing something tangible to help improve conditions in Africa, by which time a settlement had been established in Freetown. Zachary Macaulay, the governor, had written on behalf of the African Institution, an antislavery organization, to encourage him.[74] On 27 December 1810 he set out for West Africa from Philadelphia, where he had gone from Westport. After he arrived in Freetown the following year, he visited Governor Columbine, a girls' school, and a Methodist service and went to Bullom to meet old King George, whom he regaled with Quaker materials and some choice advice about the abhorrence of slavery and the need to adopt a sober, industrious life. In his meetings with local chiefs, Cuffee was careful to observe the rules of court etiquette but not to leave himself open to chiefly demands. In one case he noted dryly that the gray-headed grave chief he met was not content with the courtesies extended to him, comprised mainly of religious materials and ethical advice, and was delaying his departure till he got some rum. "I Served him With Victuals But it a peared [sic] that there Was rum Wanting but none Was given."[75] Cuffee's official reception by the governor was cool, and he was not allowed to land "6 bales of India goods," for fear of competing with local trade. The governor also discouraged Cuffee from making contact with the Nova Scotian settlers whom he said he found "the most troublesome." There were 982 of them at the time.

Invitations to visit London from William Allen and William Wilberforce had reached Cuffee. To prepare for that he gathered views in the
colony on the slavery question and composed a petition with the title
"Epistle from the Society of Sierra Leone, in Africa, to the Saints and
Faithful Brethren in Christ" and took it with him to London. In July
1811 he arrived in England in his ship the *Traveller,* making landfall at
Liverpool. One of his first tasks was to help obtain the release of a slave
named Aaron Richards, with a petition on the matter to the Board of
Admiralty, established under the terms of the 1807 act abolishing the
slave trade. He was able to draw on the support of Thomas Clarkson. In
London he visited Wilberforce in the company of William Allen and
subsequently went to Parliament. He also met Zachary Macaulay, since
retired as governor of Sierra Leone. He had occasion to meet William
Bootell, a slave trader, who invited Cuffee to his lodgings, and Captain
Pane, another slave trader. The African Institution, whose president was
the duke of Gloucester and whose directors included Wilberforce and
Allen, convened a meeting to which Cuffee was invited. When he left to
return to Freetown in September 1811, he carried with him the views of
the African Institution. He reached Freetown in November of that year.[76]

Cuffee's intention in going to West Africa was to establish a trading
base at the source of the slave trade and, with others, to work from there
to undermine the slave traffic. He also wished to use the transatlantic
link between America and West Africa to bring that about: tropical produce, obtained through scientific cultivation, would be carried in ships
owned by blacks to America, and the profits used to establish more
African Americans in West Africa, and so the cycle would be repeated.
But the authorities in Sierra Leone saw this plan as unacceptable encroachment on their economic interests and blocked it. Charles Mac-
Carthy (soon to be governor of the colony), for example, reported on
Cuffee's arrival in Freetown, saying Cuffee was "permitted to sell every
article except some tobacco and naval stores which would have proved
prejudicial to the British trade, for these he found a market at a short
distance from this colony."[77] On his trip back to Freetown from England
Cuffee offered passage to a missionary of the British Methodist Church as
well as to three schoolteachers. They all made it to Freetown. Before
returning to America Cuffee helped found the Friendly Society of Sierra
Leone and later wrote to its secretary, James Wise, "I instruct thee to
endeavor that she, the Friendly Society, may not give up her commercial

pursuits, for that is the greatest outlet to her national advancement.—I foresee this to be the means of improving both your country and nation."[78] Meanwhile Cuffee set out for the United States on 4 April 1813, arriving after a fifty-four-day voyage. Thomas Clarkson, in a notice of 28 January 1814, referred to Cuffee's Friendly Society, saying it existed "to devise means of disposing of [the settlers'] produce on the most advantageous terms, and of promoting habits of industry among each other. This association continues but," he urged, "it cannot carry its useful plans into execution, without assistance from England."[79] Cuffee arrived in America, and his fame followed him.

His ship had brought British cargo with it, which was in contravention of existing embargo laws. Cuffee negotiated on the matter, meeting President Madison in Washington for the purpose. He was made an exception.[80]

Cuffee continued to make representation on the issue of slavery, challenging what he called "enlightened Methodists," for example, how they could fail to see the evil of making merchandise of a brother. He took the message to the New York Methodist Conference. The theme had been set forth in the "Epistle of the Society of Sierra Leone," which demanded that the saints held in bondage be liberated, that blacks be freed of "the galding [galling] chain of slavery, that they may be liberated and enjoy liberty that God has granted unto all his faithful Saints."[81] Among the signatories were James Wise, Moses Wilkinson, Joseph Brown, and John Ellis.

A study of his letter to William Allen in London shows that Cuffee was thinking very much in the language of the new society. He spoke about the place religion occupied in Freetown, mentioning that four meetings are held on Sunday and two on other days. He said there were two Methodist churches, one Baptist, and one without denominational affiliation, which was run by "an old woman, Mila Baxton who keeps at her dwelling house."[82] He described the measures taken for poor relief, with an organization convening for the purpose once every month, with people appointed to take responsibility for those needing care. A general meeting was held every six months.

Cuffee then went into detail about the necessity of a sober life, and how the habit of regular meetings would promote "all good and laudable institutions . . . and increase your temporal and spiritual welfare." He harped on the theme of sobriety, steadfastness, and faithfulness, so that the community would be served by good examples in all things, "doing justly, loving mercy, and walking humbly."[83] He admonished against "following bad company and drinking of spiritous liquors" and against "idleness, and encouraged [all] to be industrious, for this is good to cultivate the mind, and may you be good examples therein yourselves." Those who work and serve should be "brought up to industry; may their minds be cultivated for the redemption of the good seed, which is promised to all who seek after it."[84] He returned to an address he gave to free people of color in Philadelphia in 1796. "They are advised to attend to religion, to get an elementary education, teach their children useful trades, use no spiritous liquors, avoid frolicking and idleness, have marriage legally performed, lay up their earnings, and to be honest and to behave themselves."[85] Idleness was the great Puritan vice, and so it remained for Cuffee and the brethren. The importance of setting a useful, industrious example was remarked on by a traveling Quaker minister, Stephen Grellett, who reported from Liverpool at the time of Cuffee's visit there, describing Cuffee as "a black man, owner and master of a vessel . . . He is a member of our Society . . . The whole of his crew is black also. This together with the cleanliness of his vessel, and the excellent order prevailing onboard, has excited very general attention. It has, I believe, opened the minds of many in tender feelings toward the poor suffering Africans who, they see, are men like themselves, capable of becoming like Paul Cuffee, valuable and useful members of both civil and religious Society."[86] Thus, for the blacks, idleness was not just a personal vice, the mark of fallen man, but a matter of social organization and economic enterprise.

In a memorial he addressed to the U.S. president and Congress in June 1813, Cuffee made clear he wished to see established in Africa a model society based on new foundations altogether. The fundamental rule to be established in Africa would be the rule of equity and justice, requiring the cessation of the trade in slaves. A new society in Africa thus conceived would require raising a new foundation conducive to producing wholesome and practical fruit. What they needed in Sierra Leone, Cuffee pleaded, was a sawmill, a millwright, a plow, and a wagon on which to haul loads so that people would not have to carry loads on their heads. He pledged to Congress that he would commit his own resources to promote the improvement and civilization of Africa and help avert from its people the curse which the slave trade had brought. He would lay before the American public a challenge "in the expectation that persons of reputation would feel sufficiently interested to visit Africa, and endeavor to promote habits of industry, sobriety, and frugality among the natives of that country."[87]

On 7 January 1814 the memorial was presented to Congress on Cuffee's behalf and referred to the Committee on Commerce and Manufacturing by the Speaker of the House. The Senate passed a resolution authorizing the president of the United States to allow Cuffee to leave for West Africa with a cargo of goods, but the measure was rejected by a majority in a final vote in the House on the grounds that it would let British goods elude the blockade imposed by Congress. A similar request in London was turned down as too risky given the current state of navigation laws still dealing with the consequences of the Anglo-American War of 1812 and the Napoleonic Wars.

Cuffee would not be stopped, however, and, with the help of Quakers in Westport, he fitted out the *Traveller* again and set sail in November 1815. The *Traveller* was carrying a cargo of tobacco, soap, candles, naval stores, flour, iron to build a sawmill, a wagon, grindstones, nails, glass, and a plow. There were thirty-eight passengers, eighteen heads of family and twenty children, common laborers who wished to till the soil. On board was a Perry Locke, a licensed Methodist preacher, "with a hard voice for a preacher," commented Cuffee delicately. (Cuffee reminded Locke in Freetown that Locke had complained in America of being deprived of his liberties and was again murmuring because he was called upon to serve as a juror. "Go and fill thy seat and do as well as thou canst," Cuffee told him.)[88] Another passenger was Anthony Survance, a native of Senegal, who had been sold to the French in Saint Domingo and who escaped to Philadelphia during the Revolution. He learned to read and write and studied navigation, though, in spite of his effort, life at sea ill suited him because of his susceptibility to seasickness. Cuffee did not think he would make a good mariner. He joined the voyage at his own expense with hopes of making it eventually to his home in Senegal.

The party dropped anchor in Freetown on 3 February 1816, much of the crew by then weary from the journey, and Cuffee himself beset afterward with landing difficulties. He was required to pay heavy customs duties for his goods. It was not going to be the profitable venture he had hoped for, but for consolation he met Governor MacCarthy and the chief justice, who both received him cordially. Yet nothing could hide the fact that Cuffee had ceased being a welcome visitor to Sierra Leone. William Allen was at first mystified by the change, puzzled as to why a person of such exemplary character, industry, and self-effacing demeanor as Cuffee should be vilified in Sierra Leone. He noted in his diary on 27 December 1813: "Much taken up, day after day, with examining witnesses on the State of Sierra Leone . . . I feel it a duty to stand by the poor black settlers—they have few to take their part."[89] At long last, he said, he found the reason for the antipathy to Cuffee. "I think we shall be able to prove," he wrote in 1814, "that the principal thing attended to by the white people of Sierra Leone, at least by many of them, has been getting money, and that in the shortest way. The mystery of poor Paul Cuffe's ill usage is now unravelled."[90]

In Cuffee's own estimation, economic motives alone were not sufficient to justify the high risks of investing in Africa, though he admitted that "trifling trade" would be necessary to make long-term involvement viable. Rather, he felt that the slave trade was a great stumbling block to the claims of full humanity to which everyone was entitled, including slaves. He realized, too, that the old power structures in Africa depended too profoundly on the slave trade to cooperate in its destruction. But so also were the European commercial interests. "It appeared to him in a very clear light of view" that the efforts being made to raise a productive class of Africans were being undermined by their heavy debts to European traders. "I had to encourage them to exert themselves on their own behalf and become their own shippers and importers that they may be able to imploy their own citizens for at present their colony is stript of their young men for as soon as they are discharged from school they have no business to go into and they enter on board foreigners so the Colony is Continually stript of her population [sic]." It was an acute social analysis from which chieftaincy rule emerged no less culpable. "I May also add further that in conversing with the African chiefs that it was with great reluctance they gave up the slave trade saying that it made them poor and they Could not git things as they used to git when they traded in slaves."[91] Thus the profit motive in trade and the corrupt nature of chieftaincy office had to be remedied by the new ethics and politics of antislavery and antistructure.

Cuffee would not travel again to Africa. Instead he devoted his energies to the cause of American colonization directed to Africa. Robert S. Finley, a Presbyterian minister from New Jersey and later president of the University of Georgia, had been rallying public opinion for a settlement for free blacks in Africa. He made contact with Cuffee, writing, "The great desire of those whose minds are impressed with the subject is to give opportunity to the free people of color to rise to their proper level and at the same time to provide a powerful means of putting an end to the slave trade, and sending civilization and Christianity to Africa."[92] Finley's entreaty resulted in the founding of the American Colonization Society in 1816. Cuffee advised the society to look outside Freetown, probably wishing to avoid conflict with the authorities there.

Another figure of national importance who approached Cuffee for advice and counsel was Samuel J. Mills. Mills is credited with founding the American Bible Society as well as the American Board of Commissioners for Foreign Missions, two organizations that would become pillars of the new society Cuffee and his friends were promoting in Africa. When Mills wrote to Cuffee desiring to know the conditions of life in Africa, Cuffee described to him what he observed of the slave trade and the need to patrol the continent's coastline to discourage the traffic in slaves. He called to Mills's attention and to that of Finley the work of the African Institution.

The Friendly Society, which had meant so much to Cuffee, was starved of the goods it needed from America and went into rapid decline. But Cuffee would have agreed with the sentiment, offered here in a hard sell, that, as a correspondent expressed it, good behavior tied to honest, diligent industry ("in which a few horses would be an assistance") in Africa would likely be rewarded "with yams, cassada [sic], plantains, fowls, wild hogs, deer, ducks, goats, sheep, cattle, fish in abundance, and many other articles, good running water, large oysters."[93] Cuffee himself died on 27 July 1817, a much accomplished figure in the new world and European understanding of the new society that was being created in Africa.

In a memorial notice of the board of managers of the American Colonization Society, Paul Cuffee was recognized for his clear and strong judgment, his informed opinion, his commitment and dedication, and the hands-on experience he had of life in West Africa. The tribute to him ended with the point that any future engagement with Africa would have to be based on partnership of an uncommon order, one in which fact and knowledge would replace prejudice and aspersion, an order that must be evaluated in terms of its "usefulness to the native Africans and their descendants in this country."[94]

Cuffee's public exertions and personal industry as well as his proven contacts with Africa and with philanthropic bodies concerned with the continent were a powerful stimulus for the awakening of the social and humanitarian impulse in America. New England papers, for instance, cited him as proof that overseas outreach was viable, an idea that the Haystack Prayer meeting in 1806 in Williamstown, Massachusetts, which galvanized America's missionary resolve, had helped to keep before the attention and sensibility of the public.

Other pioneers who took the idea of "America" to Sierra Leone included Henry Washington, a former slave of George Washington.[95] He came to West Africa, he said, to improve his situation by applying to the soil the scientific techniques he had learned on his former master's farms at Mount Vernon, Virginia. There was Luke Jordan, a former slave on a Virginia plantation, and an Aaron beside Moses Wilkinson. There was the aforementioned James Wise, whose urbane epistolary brilliance and long career gave the settlers an effective outlet for their views and opinions. We can add to the list numerous others, including those who settled in Liberia from 1820 on: Daniel Coker, a pioneer organizer of the African Methodist Episcopal Church, who in 1816 came out to Freetown, where his path crossed that of James Wise; Lott Carey, a former Virginia slave who converted in 1807, purchased his freedom for $850 in 1813, and, with that example of personal responsibility in his arsenal, embarked for Liberia, resolved to see the cause prosper there, too; Elijah Johnson, Carey's companion; and so on. (Chapter 5 examines the Liberian side in some detail.)

In any meaningful assessment of the new society being created in Sierra Leone, economic factors would play a major role, as Paul Cuffee's career proved. So also would political and legal questions, including the use of the petition to address local grievances. Yet deeper than the settlers' attachment to trade, politics, and law, as Fyfe maintains, "lay their love of religion." He continues:

> They observed Sunday scrupulously, turning out in their best clothes for church, the men in gingham coats and nankeen breeches, the women in muslin dresses and turbans, or beaver hats (worn by both sexes). Religion coloured their speech: the letters they sent Clarkson complaining of Macaulay's government abounded in biblical phrases. Anderson sent him a barrel of rice grown on his own farm with the words, "it is said Thou shalt not mushel the ox that Treadet out the corn and If so how much More Your Hond ought to be estened More them an ox."[96]

Anna Maria Falconbridge, herself the radical epitome of a liberated woman long before a movement existed to promote the cause, testified in identical terms:

> Among the Black Settlers are seven religious sects, and each sect has one or more preachers attached to it, who alternately preach throughout the whole night; indeed, I never met with, or heard, or read of, any set of people observing the same appearance of godliness; for I do not remember, since they first landed here, my ever awaking (and I have awoke at every hour of the night), without hearing preachings from some quarter or another.'[97]

Many of the settlers attended an early morning service every day before work, "so that whether or not they worshipped devoutly, the sound of hymns and prayers was ever on their lips and in their ears."[98] The company authorities, taking a rather measured, even skeptical, stock of Nova Scotian life and prospects, admitted the importance of religion for the blacks:

> The character of the N. Scotia blacks, who may be said to constitute the colony, it will be proper fully to describe . . . Marriage being general among them, the evils attending it's [sic] disuse are, in a great measure, avoided. Drunkenness and swearing they are by no means addicted to. Their attention to the Sabbath is great; they then abstain entirely from work, dress in very good (and some in very gay) attire, repair with their children to church, where their deportment is represented to be strikingly decent and serious.
>
> From this sketch it appears, that the Nova Scotians are superior to the generality of the same class in England, in the practice of the duties mentioned; but this is certainly the most favourable view of them. To give a just idea of their character, it may be proper to notice their religion . . . Besides being punctual in their worship, many of them profess much regard to religion, in other respects . . . There are five or six black preachers, of their own body, who have considerable influence; and the discipline they preserve in their little congregations, is supposed to have contributed much to maintain general morality among them.[99]

In spite of such good evidence, the authorities remained skeptical, suspecting the settlers of emotional excesses whipped up into frenzied outpourings by preachers who, furthermore, dabbled in a crude, volatile mixing of politics and religion.

From the settlers' point of view things looked very different, indeed. As religious leaders of their people, the preachers were seldom paid for their religious labors. They acted *pro bono*. Anthony Elliott, for example, pastored his flock while he lived off his pilot's fees, and was often out of pocket over the expenses of the church. The congregations themselves built the churches or meeting houses, vesting their control in a board of trustees. European missionary officials regarded these congregations and their meeting houses with suspicion, ostensibly because their leaders were illiterate and thus incapable of dispensing sound doctrine, but more tellingly because the congregations fostered a style of lay leadership that competed well with Crown authorities for the loyalty of the people. If these congregations proved viable, then they would imply declining public confidence in the influence of establishment doctrine—in fact, they would make self-reliance the proven alternative to missionary and colonial control.

The truth, of course, was that mission and colonial rule could co-opt this spirit of religious enterprise to guide and constrain. Thus did the officials of the early settlement recognize that the service or prayer meeting was the best and most effective time to rally public opinion. Similarly, if an issue of public order required addressing, the authorities would invoke religion and appeal to the moral conscience of the colony and its high missionary standards. When agitation was threatened, the authorities would remind the people that they represented the blessings of Christianity on the continent. When a settler was tempted to enrich himself or herself by profiting from the trade or exploitation of slaves, officials would appeal to the norms of ethical example and remind the people that such behavior would cede vital ground to those enemies who preached the inferiority of the black race. The appeal was effective in each case, and, to acknowledge that fact, Clarkson modeled his farewell address on the lines of the homegrown settler homily.

The prayer meetings became vintage community fare. Thus in 1794 when the French Jacobins invaded Freetown, making effective government virtually impossible and scattering the settlers far and wide, the prayer meetings continued. The governor at the time, Zachary Macaulay, "reaching Pa Demba's one exhausting Saturday, notes, 'as there were a good many settlers here, we had the pleasure of joining together at night in the worship of God.' All the time the Nova Scotians predominated in the colonial population, the meeting-houses were the vital centers of public opinion and communal action, and the preachers to a large extent the key to government."[100]

If we dwelt on the formal structures of the colony's government, on the ordinances, the administrative machinery of state, the governor, the chief justice, customs and excise, parliamentary regulations, and so forth, then we would overlook the informal institutions and agents that were the backbone of the settlement. For example, although in the main these pioneers did not receive an official paycheck for their religious work, they nevertheless exercised real influence in the colony. They shaped and defined the terms of public and private morality that distinguished the settlement. They were not only major players but powerful symbols of the cause of that new society whose foundations were laid in the struggle for human dignity and the hope that all may share eventually in the fruits of a sober life and honest labor.

The Voluntarist Impulse

In the medieval conception, Christianity was territorial faith, a religion woven into the fabric of state, society, and language. The establishment of the faith required its adoption by the ruler and the nobility, with the rest of society following suit. In that scheme, territorial conquest was necessary to Christian expansion just as political patronage was essential to religious custom.

This medieval arrangement of religion as territoriality was brought to Africa and attempted on a huge scale over several centuries. It failed. By definition, Christendom was not an exportable arrangement. It was too bound up with conquest and quarantine, too invested in political caste and military guarantee, too steeped in social pedigree and the language and culture of princes, nobles, and the learned few, and too vulnerable to calculations of structural continuity to survive unendowed and undefended in remote Africa. Former outcasts, ex-slaves, illiterates, and other oppressed members of society were strangers to the habit and custom, to the natural deference and unquestioning obedience, that any hereditary institution, political or ecclesiastical, required for its maintenance. Squeezed between the forces of antistructure spawned by antislavery and the effects of dislocation and resettlement, venerable Christendom lost its appeal, and so was shirked.

It is that circumstance that brings us to the point where, with the eighteenth-century American religious pioneers, we reach a vital break with the medieval notion of Christendom and its imperial European adaptation. The Puritan religious was an autodidact who would not be bound by customary formulas and hierarchical controls. The Puritan stressed faithfulness to the word of God, not because, as the authorities in Freetown came to fear, he was opposed to order and authority, but because the word represented freedom from slavery to corporate privilege and caste patronage.[101] When, for example, David George spoke of being "at the disposal of sovereign mercy," he meant not escape into anarchy and idleness but acknowledgment of a new basis of society at the heart of which would be the individual, self-reliant, self-disciplined, and self-taught. So he testified about teaching himself to spell and read. Similarly, George Liele testified: "I have a few books, some good old authors and sermons, and one large bible that was given to me by a gentleman: a good many of our members can read, and are all desirous to learn; they will be very thankful for a few books to read on Sundays and other days."[102] To acquire the tools for a useful life, one did not need the old corporate structures. The work of God, as George explained to his friends in London, revives just as well by humble and lowly means as by any other, if not better. He was alluding to new forms of association of underdogs, former slaves, and ex-captives, on whom the Spirit had bestowed divine favor. A mighty work was afoot in Africa, and it would be productive of much good, George assured. His faith recalls the remark of the nineteenth-century American evangelist Charles Finney, who said that a revival was not a miracle but the right exercise of the powers of nature, though Finney, neither modest nor tentative and ever the entrepreneur, was thinking here of method, strategy, and technique, not of transcendent power or miracle. Equality of opportunity for Finney was a creed for the evangelical entrepreneur, who equated growth with progress and salvation with success.

In the same revival company belongs Anthony Elliott, the prominent settler religious leader, who had no formal schooling. Like most of the preachers he was a self-educated man.

Yet, though his church retained the inspirational tradition of Cato Perkins, it did not lapse from orthodoxy. The Fifteen Articles of Faith of the Countess of Huntingdon's Connexion were observed; the Anglican liturgy was normally used, the congregation joining fervently in the responses without guidance of the parish clerks still found in English churches. If the services were often excited and emotional, particularly when conversions took place, they retained their European form, the emotional manifestations probably closer to contemporary revivalism in England and America than to worship in the later Ethiopian churches.

Like all the Colony churches they enforced stricter discipline than was usual in churches in England. Backsliders were tried at the Leaders' Meetings, and if found guilty were formally expelled, only readmitted on repentance. Daily services were held at 5 A.M., many members attending regularly before work. Some attended an evening service too.[103]

Christianity and Antinomianism

As will be described more fully in the next chapter, Sir Charles Mac-Carthy, the governor of the colony from 1815 to 1824, raised a Roman Catholic but now the servant of a Protestant monarch, preferred that Africans be baptized as soon as they had adopted European ways. He was still operating with notions of corporate Christendom, with political and cultural assimilation as sufficient qualification for Christian membership. William A. B. Johnson (d. 1823), a German missionary of Hanoverian background who came out in 1816 via London,[104] was in charge of religious life in the mountain village of Regent, and he defied MacCarthy in spite of the latter's threat to report him to the archbishop of Canterbury. MacCarthy relented,[105] having tried but failed to reduce the church to the terms of a colonial concordat as a safeguard against antinomianism,[106] the doctrine of personal exemption from the moral law on account of having been saved by grace.

It is, thus, unfair and misleading to stigmatize settler or recaptive religion as antinomian, as the authorities tended to do in Freetown. The preachers stressed justification not by faith but by the Holy Spirit, by the action of what David George called "sovereign mercy." Many of them were illiterate, and "inevitably they put inspiration (which they could claim to have received) before interpretation of doctrine (which they were not equipped for)." To Macaulay's charge that David George was "using the Holy Spirit as an excuse to cloak evil-doing . . . it could have been answered, if God speaks to men through the Holy Spirit he may just as well speak to the illiterate as to the literate. David George could have called Macaulay a Pelagian—though he was doubtless too polite to do so."[107]

But antinomianism was actually an otherworldly doctrine, more in tune with gnosticism than with the activist tendencies of the settlers. They considered their activism the result of regeneration by the Spirit, which invests human effort and action, even of the least of the brethren, with dignity and a good example. In his study of the phenomenon, John Blassingame concluded that when the slaves testified to being filled with the Holy Spirit they intended no otherworldly escape but rather an honest facing of their earthly troubles. Their religious experience enabled them to transcend human degradation and to obtain the security with which to endure pain. "Their joyful noises to the Lord indicated they valued the ideals of personal honor, godly living, strict morality, integrity, perseverance, faith, freedom, and family life."[108] Such an ethical understanding was implied in the testimony of one of David George's parishioners that, as she saw it, whoever worked righteousness was acceptable before God. This was, according to the record, a generally acknowledged doctrine. George Liele put it down as accepted teaching. "I agree," he affirmed, "to election, the fall of Adam, regeneration, and perseverance, knowing the promise is to all who endure, in grace, faith, and good works, to the end, shall be saved."[109] It was not enough to claim to be saved: works of righteousness, the fruits of wholesome society, were necessary, as the testimony of Liele proves.

The religious path, thus, runs parallel to that of social action; society may be formed in the image of those who, as Paul Cuffee put it, are preeminent for "doing justly, loving mercy, and walking humbly," and who, furthermore, keep "out of idleness . . . for this is good to cultivate the mind, and may you be good examples therein yourselves." As Blassingame rightly pointed out, for blacks on slave plantations and elsewhere, God was no mere abstraction "but a Being who took an interest in the lowly slave and interceded in his behalf. He was the God of freedom to whom slaves prayed for deliverance from bondage. They poured out their troubles to Him and saw visions of Him."[110] Minds possessed of the things of God must also "be cultivated for the redemption of the good seed" of industry. All this promoted religion as social responsibility rather than as gnostic self-exile. The resemblance, then, of antinomianism to the doctrine of regeneration masks a genuine difference: antinomianism taught self-absorption and indifference to the world, while regeneration demanded attention to society. The one was inclined to human autonomy, the other to hope of a second chance in life. It is only the dust thrown in our face by the wind of controversy that makes us lose sight of the difference.

There was another dimension to the charge of antinomianism, and that was the official view that the settlers, unversed in the vital points of theological learning, became too tolerant of religious difference. As such, they were too vapid to apply stringent tests of doctrine sufficiently to exclude religious mixing. The new chaplain of the colony, the Reverend John Clarke, a Scottish Presbyterian from Edinburgh, joined by other Presbyterian schoolmasters, confessed to being astonished "at the Nova Scotians' lack of intolerance. Baptists and Methodists attended one another's services, and expected them to do the same, showing an example of Apostolic simplicity. Clarke was soon preaching in David George's chapel."[111] Their Calvinist hackles raised by such unsanctioned fraternity, however, the Scotsmen charged that so-called Apostolic simplicity was merely a cloak for corrupting the grace of God into lasciviousness. The question of authority was at stake, too, with the Scottish missionaries wanting to take control of settler religion, in particular the pulpit, but finding that they were taking aim at a moving target.

In considering the pulpit as an itinerant habit, we should view it in the dynamic, improvised setting of black religious preaching and distinguish it as such from Hobbesian notions and establishment suspicions of the practice. In the conditions of slavery, slave owners saw preaching in a dialectical light: either it fomented insurrection and rebelliousness or it taught submissiveness, either it tended toward radical revolt or it inclined to blind acquiescence, and without question there is evidence enough in slave sermons to support both positions. But this formulation allows us too easily to repeat stereotypes and, furthermore, dissuades us from taking cognizance of the broad tradition of black preaching. It fails to illuminate our understanding. For that we may turn to Albert Raboteau's judicious summary of the evidence.

The weight of slave testimony suggests that the slaves knew and understood the restrictions under which the slave preacher labored, and that they accepted his authority not because it came from the master but because it came from God. They respected him because he was the messenger of the Gospel, one who preached the word of God with power and authority, indeed with a power which sometimes humbled white folk and frequently uplifted slaves. For a black man and a slave to stand and preach with eloquence, skill, and wisdom was in itself a sign of ability and talent which slavery's restrictiveness could frustrate but never completely stifle.[112]

The settlers and the recaptives between them introduced new forms of religious association and mission with considerable impact on European styles and forms. For example, the religious class organization, in which members are grouped into classes under a lay class-leader and which had been revived in English Methodism after being banned in the sixteenth century, was transferred to Sierra Leone and practiced there by the settlers and recaptives. As a result, the "system was adopted by all the religious bodies in Sierra Leone (even the Anglicans), and spread the Gospel more widely than any direct missionary instruction could have done. Converted recaptives, appointed class-leaders, could instruct unconverted countrymen from their own distant homelands in familiar ways a Settler or European would not have known."[113]

On its own terms, then, settler religion established Scripture as the principle of the new society of independent initiative, lay leadership, and adherence to a code of personal integrity and accountability. The verdict of Charles Lyell on what he as a European saw of slave religion in the southern United States could apply with equal justification to settler and recaptive religion in Sierra Leone. He spoke of the favorable impression made on him, convincing him of merit in the black cause. He had observed, he said,

> a body of African origin, who had joined one of the denominations of Christians, built a church for themselves—who had elected a pastor of their own race, and secured him an annual salary, from whom they were listening to a good sermon scarcely, if at all, below the average standard of the compositions of white ministers—to hear the whole respectably, and singing admirably performed.[114]

In that black cause government and authority were depersonalized: the chief was banished from their midst; the king was removed behind a wall of ineffectual local officials and kept further at bay by the insistence on religious autonomy; missionaries were smothered by a blanket of petitions going over their heads; and meanwhile the different skills of schoolteachers, mariners, preachers, millwrights, sawyers, coopers, carpenters, tailors, fishermen, secretaries, merchants, builders, and others joined in a common defense of the general cause. The blacks identified that cause with the promises of God, or with "trustin' de Lawd," and drew confidence—specifically, confidence in the unfolding design of Divine Providence—from having been spared the brand and the muzzle. Things would be attempted in the name of this general cause that would be forbidden or otherwise unimaginable in respectable society where breeding and pedigree ruled the roost.

We should recall that in New England high society, for example, "the abolitionists stood for a despised cause," and that those "who came out of the agreeable circle of New England aristocracy, were made to feel that it was a choice between the slave and the friends of their youth." One defender of the old theology was Moses Stuart, professor of Hebrew at the Andover Theological Seminary, who justified slavery using the New Testament; another was Hopkins, the Episcopal bishop of Vermont, who came forward as "a thick-and-thin defender of slavery."[115] Most mainline Protestant churches condoned or supported slavery, including Methodists, Baptists, and Bible and missionary societies, so persistent were the habits fed by the old structures. The old theology as a pillar of liberal society shared its reactionary outlook with the respectable New England colleges then basking in the glow of an ascendant enlightenment. Longfellow and Emerson, for instance, reported that students in Cambridge disrupted antislavery lectures with shouts and hisses and other "vulgar interruptions." The president of Dartmouth College similarly extolled slavery as an institution of God in accordance with natural law.

It was this old theology and its high-minded notions that evangelical theology challenged. The efforts at freedom, religious instruction, education, economic improvement, and political self-reliance represented for blacks a radical departure from hallowed precedent. As George Liele stated, even when circumstances were not auspicious, it was important to keep the cause in mind. The "FREE PEOPLE in our society," he wrote, "are but poor, but they are willing, both free and slaves, to do what they can. As for my part, I am too much entangled with the affairs of the world to go on (as I would) with my design, in supporting the cause: this has, I acknowledge, been a great hindrance to the Gospel in one way; but as I have endeavoured to set a good example (of industry) before the inhabitants of the land, it has given general satisfaction another way."[116]

In the general dispensation so conceived it was more important to be familiar with the word of God than with the pillars of high society. The fellowship of the Gospel was meant in this sense of the good cause, for it implied the public reconstruction of society without aid of social pedigree or class origin, and it pointed people toward an open, innovative society of freedom and equality, not to the old forms of the chiefly entourage, the tribal clique, or the nocturnal cabal. Voluntary public association, not the secret society, would be the model form of assembly and of society, its deliberations worthy of the support and loyalty of free citizens. The secret conclave belonged not to that public order, even though Masonry would later rise and thrive.[117]

There was little precedent for what these African Americans were attempting. When they arrived in Africa they were blissfully ignorant of conditions there, and their sense of religious inevitability, their sense that, given the invincibility of the Creator's purpose, their cause would prosper, became their shield and anchor amid the obstacles and tribulations of resettlement. By our more abstemious standards all of that seems extravagant, even unreal. But in their testimonies and prayers the settlers reflected often on their experience of hardship and disappointment, balking only at sullen resignation or scheming militancy. They did not come to seek vengeance, nor to nurse a sense of injury, but rather to strike a blow for freedom. In their religious life on the plantations, on the road, in fellowship groups and company societies, they had steadiness of purpose and none of the wild gamble that would drive adventurers in a forlorn cause.

In dark despair Agamemnon urged upon the ancient Greeks, his bewildered compatriots, to undertake one more final journey toward deliverance with the words: "Let us flee to our own country." On the eve of their departure from Nova Scotia the settlers had indulged dreams of providence and abundance, and spoken of how they would soon "kiss their dear Malagueta," a reference to the Malagueta pepper that for them was like "grains of paradise."[118] What they found instead was a challenge to faith and endurance such as they had never imagined. As Anna Falconbridge put it graphically, it was customary in the settlement to greet the morning by asking, "how many died last night?"[119] The prevalence of death led to desperate measures to stem its tide, with preventive remedies being adopted, such as purges, emetics, or even bloodletting, all to little avail.

For these historical flotsam and jetsam, religious teaching would overcome the odds of history and offer a second chance. The day had arrived when, to quote Samuel Brown, men and women "have been awakened, struggled into liberty, by the exercise of faith and prayer, and rejoice in a full assurance of the sons of God,"[120] when people, to cite another contemporary, have become "mighty able to divide the word of truth"[121] for themselves and others.

In the context of such a social experiment, and following the abolition of the slave trade in 1807, multitudes of Africans were skimmed off the slave ships bound for the new world and brought to Freetown, where they were set free, ready to be absorbed into the original Nova Scotian community. By that channel a stream of immigrants from hinterland Africa flowed into the settlement, creating a lively confluence of cultures and languages and propagating the view of Christianity as the religion of an ex-slave, half-literate, or completely illiterate, predominantly underemployed, historically uprooted, and politically despised community of blacks. The new evangelical Christian movement, or this version of it, was the exception to the law of the survival of the fittest.

The new society thus created in Sierra Leone involved a change in philosophy from looking to princes and rulers and the nobility, the fittest of the fit, to focusing on social rejects and economic victims who might be reclaimed, trained, and equipped to lead useful, industrious, and exemplary lives, a restoration program that opened the way for people at the bottom of the social heap. This change was without precedent, and it affected much of Africa and shaped its history into modern times. In fact, it created that history, and to understand it we must turn our gaze from the corporate Christendom of old Europe to the voluntary association of the new world.

3

Abolition and the Cause
of Recaptive Africans

Under the terms of the act of 1807 abolishing the slave trade, a Vice Admiralty Court was established in Freetown to ensure the effective implementation of abolition. The Royal Navy would set up a patrol along the West African coast, and the slaves it captured on the high seas would be brought to Freetown, where their status as slaves would be established in law before they would be set free. The procedure was called being "condemned," for it permitted the authorities to invoke the right to seize enslaved Africans as forfeitures to the Crown, allowing their captors to receive as compensation a bounty for each slave. The experience gained from dealing with the Nova Scotian settlers was called upon to tackle the issue of resettling recaptured Africans. A valuable precedent had been established with the Nova Scotians, and a viable colony had taken root on African soil, vindicating the official hope expressed at the time that the Nova Scotian experiment would "produce many important consequences, and give, in some measure, a new character to the whole undertaking."[1]

Consequently, the recaptured Africans were brought to Freetown to be rehabilitated in that favorable Nova Scotian milieu. Such was the confidence of the officials that Freetown would transform this new batch of dislocated Africans from mere exposure and general influence of the Nova Scotians that no concrete steps were taken to see to their welfare. The recaptured Africans were simply let loose on society and left to find their own way. None of them, offered now a second chance, had a clue where to begin, the idea of a second chance for losers being that unprecedented.

110

The lack of an official plan to deal with what was bound to be a major influx of recaptives represented a failure of administrative foresight. The slave ships that plied the sea lanes between the West African coast and the Western Hemisphere had cargo drawn from all over the continent, with the result that the recaptured Africans who landed in Freetown came from a wide range of backgrounds. They had in common only their plight as refugees on their own continent, recently snatched from the jaws of calamity. They would be resettled under the aegis of the religious and humanitarian supervision extended to them. In 1807 the population of Freetown colony was 1,871, including 95 military personnel. In the census of April 1811, the population was around 3,500, with most of that increase coming from the landing of recaptured Africans. In July 1814, it was 5,520. In a report drawn on 31 December 1818, the number of recaptured Africans was put at 6,406. Between 1819 and 1820, 943 re-captured Africans landed in Freetown. The census of 1 January 1822 put the total civilian population of the colony at 15,081 of which 1,590 had landed from slave ships in the previous year. The accompanying table supplies the figures for the Christian population only. Sometimes there is a variation in the numbers, due mostly to how the colony area is defined. Thus the official report in the annual "blue books" put the number of recaptured Africans in the surrounding village settlements on the Freetown Peninsula for 1826 at 10,123, and for 1827 at 11,891. But the report also lists as a separate category "Coloured Inhabitants of Freetown and its Vicinity including the Liberated Africans who have left their villages," for which the number was 3,500 each for 1826 and 1827, suggesting an estimate. There is, in addition, a category of soldiers, called the King's Troops, comprised of 480 whites and 820 natives in 1826. In the June 1831 census, the number of recaptured Africans in the Freetown district was put at 22,783, excluding Europeans, with the city of Freetown proper showing an additional population of 7,839.[2]

These figures, needless to say, represented only a fraction of the slave-borne trade at the time. For instance, during 1810 alone it was estimated that some 80,000 slaves were being illegally shipped, mostly to markets in Brazil and Cuba. By mid-century the numbers had multiplied, with Brazil, Cuba, and the United States the chief markets in the Western Hemisphere.[3] The increase is reflected in the figures of recaptured Africans in Freetown by that time. Allowing for necessary uncertainty in the figures, by 31 December 1840, some 67,000 recaptives had landed in

Christian population by district, Sierra Leone, 31 December 1818, 8 July 1820, and 1 January 1822

Parish or district	Principal town	Year founded	Population		
			1818	1820	1822
St. George	Freetown	1787	4,430	4,785	5,643
St. Charles	Regent	1812	1,177	1,218	1,551
St. Patrick	Kissey	1817	860	1,033	1,069
St. Andrew	Gloucester	1816	356	563	697
St. James	Bathurst	1818	222	469	393
St. Peter	Leopold	1817	308	469	420
St. John	Charlotte	1818	205	268	420
St. Thomas	Hastings	1819	—	195	171
St. Michael	Waterloo	1819	—	353	519
Arthur (sic)	Wellington	1819	—	456	547
St. Paul	Wilberforce	1812	203	409	595
St. Henry	York	1819	—	297	494
St. Edward	Kent	1819	167	296	418
Leicester	Leicester	1809	69	78	30
28 native villages	—	—	1,141	1,468	1,964
Islands in river	—	—	213	115	—
St. Ann	Gambia Island	1820	—	37	—
Banana Islands	—	1820	—	—	150
Total			9,565	12,509	15,081

Source: R. R. Kuczynski, *Demographic Survey of the British Colonial Empire,* 3 vols. (London: Oxford University Press for the Royal Institute of International Affairs, 1948–1953, repr. Fairfield, N.J.: Augustus M. Kelly, 1977), vol. 1, p. 156.

Sierra Leone of whom about 60,000 were settled in the colony alone. These Africans, who had the good fortune to be rescued and brought to Freetown, were in the beginning crowded into ramshackle mountain districts of the colony, unexpected, untaught, unchurched, and unled.

Sir Charles MacCarthy: Christendom Revisited

It was Governor Sir Charles MacCarthy's bold administrative plan, known as the Parish Scheme, that took on such human misery and eventually created order out of chaos by parceling out the recaptives among supervised village-type "parishes," most of them under an appropriate patron saint, with government and mission collaborating in the work of resettlement and rehabilitation. Thus Catholic institutional forms upheld the structures of Protestant colonial rule, structures aimed at reforming character and promoting a sense of identity among the recaptives.

MacCarthy wrote a memorandum in which he offered an assessment of the political development of Sierra Leone, saying the colony had changed significantly from 1808, when it became a Crown possession and was only a single settlement of not more than 2,000, to 1816, when there were twenty settlements of about 17,300. Progress could be noted among the inhabitants, he contended, "who are rapidly advancing towards English manners and ideas, and are accumulating considerable permanent property." This new circumstance made the original charter for the colony inadequate and of little use. MacCarthy recommended revoking the existing charter and granting him as governor authority to establish commissions. He also recommended establishing a supreme court and reorganizing the administration of justice. The regulation of marriage belonged to such reorganization.[4]

MacCarthy's understanding of "English manners and ideas" extended to matters of ecclesiastical jurisdiction. Accordingly, presented with a chance to place state resources at the service of church and society, MacCarthy set up to draw on Christianity for the cause of civilization. The real qualification, he felt, for being a Christian was assimilation into the cultural customs of Europe. As soon as Africans were able to prove that they had learned enough of Europe's culture, they should be admitted into the church. When presented with contrary evidence—when reminded, for example, that European traders kept their distance from missions and, in spite of their being European, opposed missions bitterly in centers of Christian impact—MacCarthy would not see the point, so convinced was he that European culture and administration were the requisite means for producing the polished natives of Christian profession. Christianity remained for him the king's religion, and the Bible the king's book. Worship must reflect this national character and inscribe it into the simple native habit. Rather than look to the heart for proof of moral regeneration, as he was urged, MacCarthy looked to cultural habits for marks of civilization. This view of religion as cultural necessity was the vital impulse of the old Christendom, and it had primacy over the theological necessity of salvation. The method of cultural apprenticeship, of instructing Africans in the art of respectable religion and impressing on their tribal herd instinct the duties, manners, and responsibilities pertaining to civilization, was the prescription for sound religion. Christian conversion for MacCarthy meant instituting establishment rules in obedience to hereditary power.

William Davies, a Welsh Methodist missionary recently arrived in the colony, was something of a kindred spirit with the governor, with regard to whom he testified: "We meet with every encouragement from his Excellency the Governor, Col. Macarthy [sic]."[5] Davies gave the following account of MacCarthy's view of things:

> I have often heard him observing, after coming into my house, "Davies, such and such a man, that lives in such a house, is one of your members, is he not?" "How does your Excellency know?" "Why, he has white-washed his house, his fence around the premises is good, his garden is clean and productive." "Your Excellency is right—he is a member, and Christianity alone can civilize: for godliness is profitable for all things, and when they get religion they will be industrious."[6]

MacCarthy described himself as a worldly man, with no pretensions to religious piety. It was enough, he felt, that he acted in accordance with the dignity of his office, an agent and representative of enlightened rule. He saw no reason why such an establishment view of Christianity should not be promoted in Africa, so that Africans who received the blessings of civilization would reckon themselves fortunate to count the church as their ally. On one level, MacCarthy looked for a unified structure of church and state, a pair of complementary functions vested in a single authority, as in classical Christendom. On another level, however, he understood only one way of going about this: through an orthodox Christian state into which were subsumed the functions of the church. Christianity could spread only if it followed the lineaments of political establishment, that is, if the religion expressed the ruler's will and mission.

The field of Christian mission in this scheme was defined by the territorial scope of the ruler's authority. Thus MacCarthy battled gallantly with the Church Missionary Society in London against establishing a mission base outside the Freetown colony where Britain's suzerainty had not yet been established. He campaigned as well for the closure of the Susu mission. He did not speak of divine rulership, but his reasoning that only rulership such as he knew it could act validly in the religious domain, that the territorial sphere was the proper boundary for the religious sphere, and that the will of God was properly expressed in the wishes and pleasure of the earthly prince, that reasoning propelled him toward that conclusion, or at least toward the view that the establishment order was the best and most reliable representation of God's will for society. For MacCarthy the goodwill of Great Britain became the designated channel of the blessings of Providence for the people of Africa. It was an elaboration of the doctrine *cuius regio eius religio,* meaning tell me your ruler and I will tell you the rest.

As a faithful servant of Britain, MacCarthy could contemplate with supreme equanimity a group of happy, well-ordered villagers offering a successful alternative to the ramshackle sprawl of settlements into which hapless recaptives were herded. At the heart of the arrangement would be a village superintendent who would be judge, magistrate, adjudicator, confidante, town planner, master builder, storekeeper, bookkeeper, intermediary, moral instructor, and consul. He would "see to the making of bricks and the erection of woodwork."[7] He would also keep school and evangelize the flock. In a memo of 15 June 1816 MacCarthy elaborated on his vision:

> I have explained . . . my views as to the means most likely to forward the Civilization of Africa, more particularly of the Colony and of the numerous classes of captured Negroes who under the Blessing of Providence are indebted for their emancipation from a cruel slavery to Great Britain only.
>
> I conceive that the first effectual step towards the establishment of Christianity will be found in the Division of this peninsula into Parishes, appointing to each a Clergyman to instruct their flock in Christianity, enlightening their minds to the various duties and advantages

inherent to civilization—thus making Sierra Leone the base from whence future exertions may be extended, step by step to the very interior of Africa.[8]

In the model community of MacCarthy's design, Christian orthodoxy and cultural quarantine were interchanged to produce a holy domain protected by rule and sacrament, even though such cultural norms had no resonance with settler and recaptive piety. What Africa needed existed in its full measure elsewhere, not in pious dreams of life in another realm, but in the tried and proven world of baptized Europe. MacCarthy was an evangelist for "Europeandom," and he was keen for that reason to secure the collaboration of Christian missions. As a consequence, he embarked on an ambitious scheme to import from Britain the material symbols of civilization, expecting missions to follow him into quarantine.

> Bells, clocks and weathercocks were ordered from England for church towers, forges for village blacksmiths, scales and weights to village markets. Quill-pens and copy-books, prayer books and arithmetic books were ordered for schools, with tin cases for the children to carry them in, lamps to read them by. Hats were ordered for the men, bonnets for the women, shoes for all; gowns and petticoats, trousers and braces—buttons, too, with needles, thread and thimbles, soap and smoothing-irons, even clothes-brushes, nothing was forgotten.[9]

It was efforts such as these that inspired MacCarthy's chief justice, Robert Hogan, to write, "of this I am certain—that religion and civilization, which, as the necessary consequence of religion is but the name for it, must effect here, what they have uniformly wrought in every other part of the world, a concomitant improvement in arts and sciences, and a correspondent elevation of the human character and race. This great work is in progress: the finger of providence appears to have traced out the line to be pursued for its grand consummation."[10] The great shortcoming in all this was that missions could not provide on so lavish a scale and at such distance, nor, for that matter, could government, and so the plan was abandoned. Yet the fact that it was conceived at all, and pursued with such purpose and energy, indicates that the phantom of a triumphalist Christendom still cast a spell on many in high places.

It could be argued that what ultimately saved MacCarthy from a particularly severe case of recidivism into Christendom was the opposition of missions and, more tellingly, the opposition of settlers and recaptives themselves. The point was made with some eloquence by his encounter with the colonial chaplain W. A. B. Johnson, a German of Hanoverian background who came out to Sierra Leone in 1816 after serving a church in London. MacCarthy had complained that Davies was unwilling to extend baptism to those Africans who had demonstrated enough acquaintance with European manners and customs until such Africans had shown marks of real spiritual regeneration, and hoped Johnson would be more sensible and see matters differently. MacCarthy was simply at a loss to understand why being *civilized* was not an adequate and sufficient ground for taking the Christian name, and he told Johnson so. If missions were not in the business of producing "Black Europeans," and, as Charlemagne did with the Saxons, baptizing converts by the "platoon," then what, in heaven's name, were they in Africa for? Johnson kept a record of their meeting.

> His Excellency the Governor came here today. He had led the conversation while we were in the garden to baptism. He wished I would baptize more people. I told him that I could not, unless God first baptised their hearts. He said the reason so many were baptised on the Day of Pentecost was that the Apostles despised none. I replied that they were pricked in the heart, and that I was willing to baptise all that were thus pricked in the heart. He thought baptism an act of civilization, and that it was our duty to make them all Christians. He spoke in great warmth about these things, and I endeavoured to show him through Scripture passages the contrary. He gave it up at last; calling me and the society a set of fanatics.[11]

The stakes were high enough for MacCarthy to deem it worth the effort to make a second attempt at changing Johnson's mind and, while at it, to throw in a little spice of religious rivalry, too. "The Governor said a great deal about baptising all the people, which I refused. He said much about its necessity, but I kept to the word of God. He said that the Apostles, on Pentecost day, baptized 3000 at once. I replied that they were pricked in their hearts, and *as many as believed* were baptized . . . He could not answer this, but said that he would write to the Archbishop of Canterbury concerning the matter . . . and would send those refused to Mr. Davies, for he thought Mr. Davies' baptism as good as ours."[12] One can imagine MacCarthy's utter consternation when Johnson refused to endorse singing "God Save the King" because it was customarily sung over a beer mug, though Johnson would mollify the disconsolate governor with his willingness to endorse saying "Honour the King" because, he claimed, that had apostolic warrant for it. The English lord who, asked what his religion was, replied he did not know until he saw the last act of Parliament, would be a person after MacCarthy's heart—such being the sensible course that Christendom had laid and that Johnson, alas, was failing to honor. But a transplanted Christendom in the new Africa could only mutate, or else wither, from its protective official custody. Thus the structures MacCarthy was busy setting up were being altered into radical strains of antislavery and antistructure. Or, as Johnson put it in language weighty with New Light meaning, society would yield to those who have been pricked in the heart or were so predisposed.

The answer of officials, both earlier and later, if they could not get the ear of individual missionaries, was to fix on the chaplaincy to preside over the religious life of the settlement. The settlers were congregating, often twice a day, morning and evening, to pray, testify, and witness. A passing sea captain noted in his diary in 1794 that the Nova Scotians "appear very Religious attending Services by 3 o'clock in the Morning and till Eleven at night, four, or five, times per week."[13] Officials considered this unsound religious practice and chose to smother it with restrictive measures and to replace it with an alternative sedate Sunday worship. The Nova Scotians took that as a signal to leave the chaplaincy church, sending out a message to others that sanctions would be taken against those who stayed. The response in the Methodist camp was immediate, with most of them withdrawing

> from the Church entirely, and their attendance would have exposed them to ex-communication. As it was important to remove this obstacle to their improvement, the Rev. Mr. [John] Clarke [the chaplain] obtained leave to preach among them. He first called on Moses Wilkinson who gave him a long account of a revival of religion, which he said had taken place, last autumn, when it was usual for numbers of his hearers, especially children, to be struck down by the powers of his preaching, and to roar out in agony.[14]

This was the background to William Davies's implausible project to implant correct notions of religion, to see that the colony produced what Henry Alline and his New Lights would have derided as a breed of conformists. Davies was emboldened by having in MacCarthy an ally in the cause of king, country, and God but had miscalculated the depth of settler feeling on the matter. For one thing, he came under fire from the settlers and recaptives for having become a salaried agent of the state.

For his part, Davies, as a Welsh Methodist, was keen to prove his loyalty to government and thereby remove any odious hint of Nonconformist stigma. He was aware that in 1811 a bill had been introduced in Parliament to impose severe penalties on Nonconformists. The law was later relaxed with the passage of the Trinity Act of 1813, which removed the stigma of illegality from Nonconformist religion. Nevertheless, the effect of the 1811 measure was to put Protestant dissenters on notice that they were only a tolerated collection of sects still under the watchful eye of the law. They continued to be subject to loyalty tests until 1828, when the Test and Corporation Acts breached the Anglican constitution to give Nonconformist worship the recognition of the law. Until then Nonconformists carried with them a sense of questionable loyalty, which among Welsh Methodists and Baptists produced the sentiment of a "Little England beyond Wales."

Davies was smarting from such official discrimination, and it says something for the political atmosphere of the time that he felt his attitude needed little justification beyond claiming that he was a loyal subject of the king. When he outlined his differences with the settlers and recaptives, he turned the charge of disloyalty against them. He was confident his audience would recall how the American colonies recently revolted against the Crown and how America concluded a second war with Britain in 1812. Men and women, we know, can speak only the language of their age and generation, but, because of his personal history, Davies' voice had singular resonance with his time and place. Furthermore, he had a personal incentive to become an official oracle. American republican spirit was public enemy number one, he felt, and that was what he was up against. He seemed shamed by his Nonconformist heritage but grateful not to be blamed for it. And so, implausibly, he set out to place religion on a favorable political footing in order to reclaim it for king and country. He was proud that government had taken notice of him; proud that it had paid his salary, appointed him to public positions, decorated him, and proud, too, beyond words, that the administration continued to consult him regularly. He would gladly let it be known that he had the governor's ear. A social climber now in elevated company, he found that only the refusal of blacks duly to conform stood in the way of his becoming a complete establishment man.

The explanation for black intransigence, in Davies' view, lay in blacks' having embraced unsound religious doctrine. That was the source of their erroneous notion of the political community as one without a king, an error that produced a culture of political ingratitude. In his own words, Davies nailed his colors to the mast of the Christendom on which America, for one, had disreputably turned its back. The irony was lost on him that under the terms establishing Christendom, his own Noncon-formist tradition had been stigmatized. Yet in his forlorn plea for a trans-fer from Freetown he admitted in so many words that he was the wrong man in the wrong place at the wrong time. He deserved to be put out of his misery.

In January 1817 he wrote a letter admitting that he could do no more useful work in the colony, chiefly because he was receiving a salary from the state. He neglected to say he had also all but repudiated the Noncon-formist cause. He pleaded to be sent to the West Indies instead.

> The Leaders of the Society in Free Town have declared against me and have refused me the pulpit, I am too *plain* for them, and truly I have found them a proud and stiff necked generation. I understand they are going to accuse me of lording it over them, of being too proud for a Methodist Preacher, and of paying too much attention to Government, the truth in this respect is, when we arrived here we found Methodism very low indeed, in the esteem of Government and the European Gen-tlemen in the Colony, My dear Departed Jane's and my own conduct some how or other pleased the most respectable part of the community, in consequence thereof some got jealous, Most of our Leaders as far as I can judge are of the American republic spirit and are strongly averse to Government, I am a Loyal subject to my King I wish to do the little I can for the support of that Government especially in a foreign part w[h]ere there are not so many able advocates as at home . . . I am now the Senior Alderman in Free Town and a justice of the Peace. I objected as much as I could to both without absolutely giving offence to the Governor which it was not my duty to do, for His Excellency has been and continues to be a father to me, and I feel it my duty to obey him as far as I can consistent with religion, which teaches me to fear God and Honour the King.[15]

Davies was subsequently employed by the government as a superin-tendent of one of the recaptive villages, receiving £150 annual salary. Still, his troubles with the settlers were far from over. "We were sorry to find Mr. Davies and the Leaders and Trustees not united," confessed a fellow missionary despondently. "I have used my influence to have Mr. Davies back to his work and office in the Town but all to no purpose," he concluded.[16]

There was nothing new in this situation: the settlers and other blacks wished to have no official interference in their religious and civil affairs, though the officials were slow to appreciate that view. Thus, for example, did Zachary Macaulay proceed in July 1796 to enact measures to regulate marriage among the settlers, who then mobilized a petition drive to rescind the promulgation. A total of 128 signatories were appended to the petition, which was duly delivered to Macaulay in the name of "The Independent Methodist Church of Freetown." Among other things, the petition declared:

> We consider this new law as an encroachment on our religious rights ... We are Dissenters, and as such consider ourselves a perfect Church, having no need of the assistance of any worldly power to appoint or perform religious ceremonies for us. If persons in holy orders are allowed to marry, we see no reason why our Ministers should not do it. Our meeting-house we count as fit for any religious purpose as the house you call the church. We cannot persuade ourselves that politics and religion have any connection, and therefore think it not right for a Governor of the one to be meddling with the other.[17]

Such official views about religion represented a significant gulf with settlers and recaptives. McCarthy's Christendom policies showed how slow officials were to grasp the force of the sentiment for church-state separation. Nevertheless, confronted with the Christendom formula of religion as political orthodoxy, the Sierra Leone settlers and recaptives, in spite of their varied backgrounds, were united in their view that the Europeans sought to use politics to circumvent religion.

This policy of political assimilation as religious prerequisite (or substitute) was widespread in other parts of Africa, too, where it produced comparable responses. Here, for example, is the trenchant statement of one Christian African who was born in Mozambique and became a missionary in Nyasaland, now Malawi. The irregular English medium still managed to preserve the poignancy of the native idiom.

> Poor Resident, he thinks too much of his skin and not of his heart. What is the difference between a white man and a black man? Are we not of the same blood and all from Adam? This startles me much—is Europe still Christian or Heathen? . . . The three combined bodies,

Missionaries, Government and Companies, or gainers of money—do form the same rule to look upon the native with mockery eyes. It sometimes startles us to see that the three combined bodies are from Europe, and along with them there is a title "CHRISTENDOM." And to compare or make a comparison between the MASTER of the title and his servants it pushes any African away from believing the Master of the title. If we had power enough to communicate ourselves to Europe we would advise them not to call themselves "Christendom" but "Europeandom."[18]

Recaptives and the New Society

All of that notwithstanding, MacCarthy hastened to answer the clarion call of duty that was beckoning to him in the unmet needs of the recaptives. With the help of agents like Davies, he took charge, farming out the recaptives to newly created villages on the Freetown Peninsula, each village directed by a clergyman. There would be a chapel, with required attendance, which on other days would also serve as a school. Before 1815 there were three such villages: Leicester, founded in 1809; Wilberforce (formerly Cabenda), established in 1810; and Regent (formerly Hogbrook), founded in 1812. Before 1820 ten more villages were set up, among them, Kissy and Gloucester in 1816; Wellington, Hastings, and Waterloo, in 1819; and Charlotte and Leopold (the latter renamed Bathurst) in 1817. Between 1828 and 1829, over 8,300 recaptives landed in Freetown, and two new villages were founded to absorb them: Murray Town and Aberdeen.

These villages became the human crossroads of Africa. A separate village, called Congo Town, was founded for Africans from the Congo; the Bambara of Mali gathered at Leicester; at Gloucester there were Wolof from Senegal, Mandinka, Susu, Temne, Mende, Fanti from Ghana, Igbo, and people from the Congo; at Bathurst there were Wolof, Bassa, and others from the Rio Ponga in Guinea. After the disbanding of the Royal African Corps in 1819, some free slaves and recaptives were pensioned off and settled in Freetown, many of them going to a village named Gibraltar Town (a number of the servicemen had served in Gibraltar). At Regent village the population included Bulom, Kono, and Susu from the colony area; Bassa and Gola from the Kru coast of Liberia; and Ibo, Efik, Kalabari, Yoruba, and Hausa, all from the Bights of Benin and Biafra in Nigeria. Mende recaptives were called Kosso and settled in Kosso Town. Then there was Fula Town, a prosperous area of east Freetown where Fulbé traders went to settle and do business. The missionary linguist Sigismund Koelle, who arrived in Freetown in December 1847, was able to document over 120 different language groups among the population. It was the first scientific linguistic enterprise ever undertaken on such a scale, long before the study of comparative linguistics became an academic staple. A different linguistic principle, also first undertaken in Freetown, was that pioneered by Hannah Kilham (d. 1832), who held that it was essential to teach children in their mother tongue at primary school and to strengthen their learning by using material from their own background, before introducing them to European languages at the secondary school level. Thus literacy in English should take into consideration the special needs of second-language users.

The Fulbé represented Islam, which received official encouragement from most governors. A teacher of Arabic from Timbuktu earned a comfortable living working in Fula Town. Later in the nineteenth century an impressive mosque was constructed there, lending an oriental flavor to the local landscape. Fulbé caravans from deep in Fula country in the Futa Jallon came down to trade in the colony and lodged in Fula Town. In 1841, for example, Freetown Muslim recaptives, many of them Yoruba (also called Aku), led a commercial and educational delegation to Futa Jallon to meet the militant Muslim leader al-Ḥájj 'Umar al-Fútí (d. 1864), returning to Freetown as affiliates of the Tíjániyah confraternity of which al-Ḥájj 'Umar was apostle. Muslims started religious street processions at this time. In 1876 the governor, Sir Samuel Rowe, threw a party at his official residence for Muslims, over seven hundred in all, to celebrate the end of the Ramadan fast. In deference to his guests, he made sure no alcoholic beverage was served.

Into these recaptive villages the Nova Scotian settlers introduced the arrangements that would ensure, in David George's phrase, that "the work of God revives" in Africa. For the recaptives the choice between MacCarthy's religious establishmentarianism and the heartfelt experience of the settlers was a foregone conclusion, and nothing better clinched the point than the ripples of "revival" that stirred ordinary hearts. Here is an unflattering depiction of revival outpouring in the Christianity of the colony, with hints of its primitive African antecedents. The settler preachers in these newly created villages carried on the Nova Scotian tradition of appealing to the spirit rather than to reason. Some could not read. Converts testified by what was called "Seeking and Finding," becoming convinced of salvation by physical signs—visions or convulsions. Worship was emotional: hymns begun to hymn-book tunes might end with tunes from the recaptive members' far-off homelands, accompanied by clapping and dancing . . . Recaptives sought religious enlightenment eagerly, rejoicing together over conversions.[19]

By contrast, another writer portrayed revival religion as a piece in the pattern of cultural continuity, as a bridge between the Nova Scotians and the teeming African recaptives flooding into the colony: "The revival spirit which had once touched the Nova Scotians and done much to mould their religion invaded the new Churches, and something of what was seen in Nova Scotia in the 1780s reappeared in the 1810s and 1820s, in a more pervasive and lasting form, in Freetown and the Mountain District."[20]

Thus, in terms of the collaborative responsibility between mission and government for the well-being of the recaptives, the Nova Scotians carried the lion's share of the religious portion. Similarly, when government took action to establish schools, chapels, and other institutions in the villages, it was the recaptives who provided crucial leadership and the order and responsibility necessary for success. For instance, the village companies and benevolent societies that were established evoked the cooperative model of Paul Cuffee and his Quaker allies. And, where they struck root, these companies served to encourage the reappearance of practices that once abounded in pre-Christian Africa, if now with the ritual forms of antistructure induced by dislocation, restoration, and rapid transition. Recaptive social life soon absorbed the imprint of antislavery and antistructure. But the underlying fabric of African life and values was preserved. In this respect, Yoruba recaptives, apt to be construed as cultural Young Turks, provided illustration of adaptive responses to the momentous changes. They added new motifs to old stock, improvised at the points of interactive encounter, made modifications to the fabric of settled thought and practice, and thereby provoked new fashions and styles without unraveling the whole tapestry of tradition and custom. One writer described the Yoruba element as follows:

Despite many Companies [in the recaptive villages] having been changed into Christian Companies, the churches remained suspicious of bodies connected with the pre-Christian past. Some felt it scandalous that Burial Companies should be able to compel their members (on pain of fine) to attend wakes with heavy drinking, and further ceremonies a week or so after the burial, according to old Yoruba custom. Egungun devils still danced. In addition to these old practices brought from their recaptives' homeland, Bulom women introduced the Bundu [Secret] Society at Wellington and Hastings and persuaded women to join or send their daughters. Male circumcision also continued.

Thus in this Christian community the godly were often affronted by drumming and dancing, drunken wakes, thinly veiled pre-Christian practices, incompatible with the standard of propriety to which the respectable members of society gave homage.[21]

A significant new religious culture developed in Freetown, with the Nova Scotians and the recaptives as agents of adaptive forms of Christianity. The familiar elements of Freetown Christianity that European officials recognized there led to their expectation that a wholesale adoption of European institutions was possible and necessary and that colonial and missionary superintendency was essential to remedy defects and furnish corrections. Yet the local religious grammar—of observing indigenous rites and customs, venerating the ancestors, adhering closely to the old mortuary rites, establishing friendly and benevolent societies and companies, and even speaking the peculiar pidgin English, a hybrid Afro-English called Krio—suggests the emergence of a distinctively African form of Christianity, an eclectic blend infused with local flavor. Accordingly, elements that were the backdrop of African American and West Indian religion—either in "hush harbors" on southern plantations, on the fringes of New England high society, or in mountain cells in Jamaica—moved boldly to the foreground in Sierra Leone and there, reattached to their roots in local African life and custom, received public warrant. Blacks shared a common religious understanding and often, by way of pulpit exchanges, the practice of a common religious life. A lively religious spirit stirred in this common heritage and in hints of its primordial African past.

Thus revival religion had a natural kinship with traditional Africa, though it appeared to signal a rupture with the standard Christianity officials preferred. Or so it was feared. Yet, even respectable Christianity benefited from the revival connection, and that connection breached the Christendom walls that MacCarthy was committed to raising.

The Example of Samuel Ajayi Crowther

The person who made the crucial conjunction between the religion of the settlers and the mass of the African people was a Yoruba recaptive, Samuel Ajayi Crowther, the foremost churchman of nineteenth-century Africa and a pioneer of the cause in his native Nigeria. I postpone to a later chapter an assessment of his contribution to the new understanding of religion and society in Africa and deal here only with an outline of his life and career. Born around 1806, the year before the abolition of the slave trade, Crowther came from the Yoruba town of Oshogun, where he was captured by invading Yoruba Muslim forces who sold him as a slave to a Portuguese slave ship in Lagos. By a series of remarkable coincidences he was eventually rescued, in April 1822, by the British Naval Squadron and brought to Freetown, where he came under missionary instruction.

After his enfranchisement he was taken to Bathurst village, and in 1826, he went to the Islington School in London. He returned as a teacher to Bathurst and subsequently moved to Leicester, where a training school had been established for recaptives. With his wife, who came from a Yoruba Muslim background, he went in 1829 to Regent and eventually to Wellington. Back in Freetown he preached to Yoruba recaptives at Kissy, attracting interested Muslim inquirers. Crowther's own views on Islam were uncompromising, but he was no blind crusader. In fact, as a mark of Muslim appreciation and respect for his statesmanship, he was accorded in Nupe the Muslim title *Lemamu,* from the Arabic *al-imâm,* a clerical office. Crowther was conciliatory toward Muslims. He advised his fellow missionaries to remember that "a Mohammedan can never be brought round by his religion being quarrelled with, and abusively charged with falsehood and imposition; but by kind treatment he may be led to read and study the Christian's Bible."[22] It is a tribute to his generous spirit that he bore no rancor toward the religion of those who invaded his town and enslaved him.

Crowther (the name was adopted from his English missionary sponsor) rose rapidly to positions of responsibility and influence, his relatively young age notwithstanding. He was endowed with unusual native intelligence and with a great flair for languages. Faced with a growing population of Nigerian recaptives in Freetown and their remarkable talent for religion and commerce, Crowther and a few of his compatriots conceived the idea of mounting a mission to the slave ports of Nigeria.

And so at their own initiative and expense a party of sixty-seven passengers set out on 1 April 1839 for Badagry, where "they proposed not only to trade but to bring their countrymen their new religion, to proclaim in a centre of the slave trade over 1,000 miles off a Gospel they trusted would sweep it away. They asked for a missionary to help them. But the initiative was theirs, the plan conceived by Africans in Africa, not round a missionary society table in London."[23]

The idea of establishing a new mission in Nigeria, or anywhere else, alarmed both the Church Missionary Society and the British government, so chary were they of deeper entanglements in the heart of what was still regarded as the Dark Continent. When in 1841 a rather timorous CMS was forced to enter Nigeria, Crowther was drafted to join the expedition. In the end the European members of the expedition suffered a horrendous casualty (to be described in the next chapter), a tragic confirmation of CMS fears. Just at this time Henry Venn (d. 1873) became general secretary of the CMS, and his views on native agency coincided almost exactly with those of Crowther and other recaptive figures in Sierra Leone.

Crowther's leadership was momentous for African Christianity: his translation of the Yoruba Bible was the first such translation into an African language. In addition to Yoruba, Crowther wrote in the Igbo, Hausa, and Nupe languages. On his visit to London in 1851 at the instigation of Henry Venn, Crowther had interviews with Queen Victoria and Prince Albert, and such was the effect of his meetings that he was able to move a reluctant British government to intervene in Nigeria against the continuing slave trade. British policy at this time was set by Lord John Russell's government, and it was against further expansion in Africa, though in other respects Russell's cautiousness was overcome by the dominant personality of his foreign secretary, Lord Palmerston. In the African territories, however, Russell was backed by his colonial secretary, Earl Grey, who enunciated the policy by stressing that

> Parliament is, I think, right to be very sparing in its grants for purposes of this kind, not merely for the sake of avoiding undue demands upon the people of this Country, but also because the surest test of the soundness of the measures for the improvement of an uncivilized people, is that they should be self-supporting; and great advantage arises from throwing those who are to carry plans of this kind into effect upon their own resources. The people also, for whose benefit such measures are attempted, are rendered more sensible of their value when the pecuni-

ary means required for their adoption are furnished by themselves. For these reasons, I considered myself bound to adhere to the rule of not proposing to my colleagues, that Parliament should be asked to increase the usual grants for the civil establishments on the West Coast of Africa; and though I was most anxious for the adoption of measures of improvement, which could not be accomplished without considerable expense, I thought it right, in this part of the African continent as well as in Natal, to proceed with those measures only, as their cost could be provided for by means of local resources.[24]

Stung by the tragic failure of the 1841 Niger Expedition, Earl Grey proceeded to enunciate the rule that colonial policy would not license reckless overseas territorial acquisition and that religious expansion would not be allowed to create a pattern out of step with political realities. It was a sentiment MacCarthy would have appreciated for his own reasons. Against the background of such official reluctance Crowther was commissioned to lead the missionary expansion beyond Sierra Leone. Ordained in London in 1843, he was authorized to resume the Niger Mission and, in effect, to become the leader of the outreach to Nigeria. (A detailed treatment of this subject must be postponed till the next chapter.)

Few events have changed the religious picture of Africa as significantly as the Niger Mission. With Sierra Leone as the launching stage, the Anglicans, the Presbyterians, and in the 1890s the Roman Catholics all entered the delta because Crowther's heroic exploits had demonstrated that it could be done. And from those beginnings we can trace the emergence of renewal movements both within and outside the church, as the dramatic career of Garrick Braide (d. 1918) makes clear. Thousands of Africans began to enter the church, and although numerical expansion even in those days was impressive, in retrospect such expansion was only a trickle compared with the massive influx in the second half of the twentieth century, at the rate of 6 million annually, or 16,500 every twenty-four hours.

A few more names among the recaptives may be useful here. John Langley, an Igbo and old friend of Crowther's, was mentioned in the previous chapter. He played a large part in raising the necessary funds to launch the Niger Mission. One recaptive Yoruba woman went to Abeokuta, leaving her husband at Hastings in Freetown, only to meet her original husband from before her captivity. She settled down with a flourishing business of her own as a dye trader. Other famous Nigerian members of the recaptive community included James Johnson and John Christopher Taylor. Johnson acquired the sobriquet Holy Johnson on account of his religious eminence. He was a companion of Crowther, whom he succeeded as the de facto leader of the cause in Nigeria. He was consecrated assistant bishop in 1900 by Archbishop William Temple. Johnson was to play a critical role as the catalyst for modern African nationalism. He wrote to great effect on the unique African contribution to the story of Christianity and was an ally of Dr. Edward Blyden, perhaps the foremost black intellectual of the nineteenth century (to be described more fully in Chapter 5). Johnson died in 1917.

John Christopher Taylor was an outstanding recaptive who served in the Niger Mission as a close associate of Crowther. Born of Igbo parents in Freetown, Taylor was a pastor at Onitsha and founder of the Akassa mission on the Niger. He was a careful and methodical scholar. He did a translation into Igbo of the New Testament and the Anglican Book of Common Prayer between 1860 and 1871. Another leading recaptive was Henry Johnson. He was trained at Cambridge University and ordained in 1866. He also spent some time in Palestine studying Arabic. He wrote a primer on the Mende language. He was archdeacon of Niger between 1879 and 1890. In 1886 he published a comparative vocabulary of the Niger and Gold Coast (Ghana) languages.[25] Recognized for his linguistic ability, he received an honorary master's degree from Cambridge University.

The Strange Career of John Ezzidio

A recaptive African who embodied the spirit of the new society as well as anyone else was John Ezzidio, a Nupe rescued from a Brazilian slave ship who arrived in 1827. The ship in which he was being carried was intercepted on the high seas and brought to Freetown with its surviving cargo of 542 captives. All of them were freed in October 1827 and resettled in Freetown. Ezzidio, then in his teens, was apprenticed to a French shopkeeper, M. Beyaust, who gave him the name Isadore, which was transcribed "Ezzido" and became "Ezzidio."

Ezzidio learned the ways of business from his apprenticeship to Beyaust, after whose death he entered the employment of an English firm, eventually becoming manager of a European shop. He was a self-taught man, having acquired the rudiments of reading and writing and progressing to the stage where he became an effective communicator and correspondent. He proved his personal enterprise when he resigned from a European trading house to start his own, using his savings as capital outlay.[26]

To advance in his trade Ezzidio had to break into the monopoly of European firms: their agents and petty retailers controlled the logistics of distribution along the capillary-like network that reached deep into up-country. Ezzidio needed capital, and since there were no banks as such, real estate became one tried and proven way to build capital. Ezzidio obtained a parcel of land in 1839 and built and furnished a house. In 1841 he purchased from the Jarretts, a Maroon family, a piece of property on George Street for £100. (The house was subsequently destroyed in a fire in 1896.) In 1842 Ezzidio visited England, where he was introduced to wholesale firms in London and Manchester, which opened up business opportunities for him and allowed him to cut out the whole class of middlemen. The value of the goods Ezzidio imported annually from England was put at between £3,000 and £4,000, shipped directly to his shop on George Street. The goods he imported included clothing, haberdashery, groceries, ironmongery, black suits, patent leather boots, muslin dresses, ladies' hats and silk bonnets, hams, cookies and tea, and port and sherry, all of which shows there was a growing middle class in the colony with a rising standard of living.

Ezzidio embodied this entrepreneurial middle-class culture, a living symbol of ex-slaves and ex-captives rising to positions of wealth and influence by dint of personal ambition, hard work, sobriety, and honor, and without much formal education, or chiefly mediation and endorsement for that matter. In 1844 the governor of the colony, Dr. Fergusson, a West Indian army doctor and the only governor of African descent till after independence, appointed Ezzidio an alderman. In 1845 the appointment was upgraded to that of mayor of Freetown. It was a powerful signal that the recaptives had made it in society.

A mercantile organization was started in the 1850s, to function as a sort of chamber of commerce. Known as the Mercantile Association, it became the forum for political opinion on the affairs of the colony after the office of municipality was allowed to lapse. The association, begun by European merchants, included Ezzidio and other prominent Africans. In 1862 Governor Blackall introduced legislation to divide the Governor's Council into a Legislative and an Executive Council, allowing for unofficial representation on the legislative one. The merchant community was invited to send a representative. By secret ballot the merchants, consisting of twenty-four Africans, fourteen Europeans, and one West Indian, chose Ezzidio, who was voted in with twenty-three ballots. The voting split neatly along racial lines. It was a historic event, as he was the first African to be so elected to a responsible office. Ezzidio carried the title "The Honorable," and the gravity was not lost on his fellow Africans. Even by the standards of his own meteoric rise from rags to riches, his installation as an officer of the state was obviously a great personal achievement for Ezzidio. It was, by the same token, a triumph of recaptive assimilation into the new society being created in Africa. Seen in that perspective, it sheds light on the initiatives of earlier pioneers like Paul Cuffee and his Friendly Society.

The gravity of the event was not lost on the Colonial Office in London, either, and Ezzidio was the last African to be so elected. The Colonial Office, already opposed to partnership, took a no less dim view of the policy of African representation, lest elected Africans be tempted to think of themselves as answerable to their constituents rather than to the Colonial Office. As a precautionary step, governors themselves were to chose Ezzidio's successors and thus preserve the principle of colonial suzerainty.

Such fears notwithstanding, while he served in the Legislative Council Ezzidio remained an unobtrusive, conscientious member. He consulted dutifully the views and opinions of his constituency and reflected them faithfully in the positions he took on pending legislation. He took seriously his position as representative, seeing it as an honorable covenant with those who sent him to the political chamber. Even the government that was predisposed to mistrust him came to have a high regard for his integrity and fairness. "He was no demagogue seeking public glory in fiery speeches, nor did he misuse his position for personal advantage; often the minutes record only that he was present at a meeting."[27]

Ezzidio was conscious of the role he assumed, referring to himself as "an oracle" of the people, who in turn called him in more earthy terms "the dancing bear," on account of his physical energy and bulk. He was resolved to keep close to his people. What he earned from his business ventures he shared ungrudgingly with others. He kept an open house, welcoming friends and visitors, who returned his respect. Unemployed laborers would gather at his house and sit on the veranda, which accordingly came to be known as an unofficial labor exchange. He gave unstintingly to civic and religious projects, raising money among his English business contacts for the purpose. He devoted time and energy to the Wesleyan mission cause. He ran a Sunday School, was a chapel trustee, and served as preacher and class leader. At the jubilee celebration of the Wesleyan Missionary Society in 1864, he gave the largest single cash contribution to the jubilee fund. He raised money to build a grand Wesley Church to rival the colony's Anglican Cathedral in architectural stature.

Two important themes, already described in previous chapters, have a significant bearing on Ezzidio's life and work. The first is that of the petition as an instrument of settler and recaptive political demands. Ezzidio lent his name to several petitions despite the attempt by colonial officials to discourage the practice. Governors resented the petition's implications of challenge and disloyalty, its assertion that government is a partnership between the natives and their masters, whereas the Colonial Office was inclined to view the petition as a curb on the actions of distant governors seeking to take advantage of their geographical isolation. For administrators, the petition "implied opposition, so that a people grown used to it grew instinctively to regard government as an institution to be opposed. In Sierra Leone, as elsewhere in the Colonies, the government in London neglected the chance of training up a people in friendly partnership with their administrators, shutting their eyes to Burke's picture of the state as 'a partnership in all science; a partnership in all art; a partnership in every virtue, and in all perfection.'"[28]

The business culture Ezzidio and others like him adopted was an extension of the religious doctrine they embraced, and that is our second theme. That doctrine held that no one should be judged on the basis of ethnic or racial origin or on social pedigree. On the contrary, any one could be saved who humbly desired it, God imposing for the purpose no prerequisites of breeding, pedigree, rank, or status. Ezzidio joined the Wesleyan Methodists in 1835 in that spirit and rose successively to become exhorter, class leader, and, in 1842, lay preacher. Charles Marke, also a Nupe,[29] tried to dispel any suggestion of mere religious legitimation of economic success, and reported that Ezzidio exhibited all the marks of genuine conversion, of a heart strangely warmed, with proof of spiritual regeneration being demonstrated in Ezzidio's gifts as preacher and devotional leader. From his own personal acquaintance, Marke testified that Ezzidio commonly withdrew from his shop during business hours for prayer and devotion. "At the family altar, and also at the class and prayer-meetings, his prayer was generally characterized by earnestness, fervency, and reverence . . . his house was open to all."[30]

All this activity proved too onerous for Ezzidio and his local band of stalwarts, and so Ezzidio wrote to London requesting a missionary to come as permanent general superintendent. It was a move fraught with unseen tragic consequences for Ezzidio and, too, for the spirit of ecumenical cooperation and understanding that everywhere fallible seekers after truth promote for mutual safeguard against intolerance.

The missionary who materialized in response to Ezzidio's request was Reverend Benjamin Tregaskis, who arrived in 1864. He has been aptly described as "the King Stork Ezzidio conjured up." Tregaskis was a doughty knight of Nonconformist intolerance, having grown up in England under the shadow of an established church he resented. Nothing of that feeling was softened by the evidence he found in Sierra Leone of Anglicans, Baptists, Catholics, Lutherans, Huntingdonians, Methodists, and Muslims living harmoniously and sharing in one another's life and work. (For example, in the 1840s Muslims began street processions at the end of the Ramadan fast, wending their way past large houses of settlers and recaptives, who gave them presents, and up to Government House to greet the governor.) A devout and devoted Methodist, Ezzidio was nevertheless among the most generous and liberal in encouraging and supporting such ecumenical gestures. As a member of the Legislative Council he supported and introduced on two occasions petitions from the Anglican bishop, while contributing generously to the funds of the Church Missionary Society as an Anglican structure. When in 1861 the CMS started implementing the "three-self" policy of self-propagation, self-rule, and self-support by instituting the Native Pastorate, Ezzidio and other Africans welcomed it as a significant step toward African advancement and the emergence of an African church. They backed it with moral and financial support. The Legislative Council approved the sum of £200 in 1863, raised in 1867 to £500, as an annual grant to the Native Pastorate. Ezzidio joined his colleagues in enthusiastically voting for the grant.

Tregaskis viewed Ezzidio's support for the Native Pastorate as nothing short of treason and accordingly led a personal vendetta against him, alienating his friends from him and halting work that Ezzidio had started on Wesley Church. Tregaskis interceded with London to drop its support for Ezzidio, closing down the avenues for business and social contacts Ezzidio had built up. Tregaskis pursued him with venom everywhere: to England, which Ezzidio visited in 1870 and where Tregaskis had commenced a campaign to have the colonial secretary rescind the actions of the Legislative Council in regard to grants being made to the CMS; to the Aku recaptive community among his former friends and allies; and to the council itself, on which Ezzidio continued to sit as a nominated member. When Ezzidio returned from England in 1870, Tregaskis circulated the malicious rumor that he was dying. When Ezzidio died in October 1872, Tregaskis turned up unprompted at the funeral and was seen openly rejoicing at the graveside.

Tregaskis was adamant that no African leadership should stand between him and absolute control of church affairs. He insisted on this, saying, "I will not have responsibility where I cannot have control."[31] He would surmount great obstacles to turn up at meetings, determined to "mend or end" those who earned his displeasure. By the time he left in 1875, he had succeeded in setting back the cause of ecumenical cooperation and African advancement, having become in the process a symbol of sectarian spite. His brand of Nonconformist rancor was the nemesis that, at the other end of the spectrum, the likes of William Davies tried to flee. Tregaskis would have turned Methodism into a sect had recaptive enterprise not intervened to reassume leadership and to try to stem the disarray following Tregaskis's departure. The very control and authority that he assumed and imposed became a source of weakness in suppressing the emergence of local self-reliance and selfhood, proving that "one of the tragedies of European leadership in Africa is that genuine devotion to the task of training up Africans in self-reliance often [results] in angry resentment when self-reliance is asserted. So Tregaskis, expending all his energies to build up a living Methodist Church in Sierra Leone, stamped implacably on every sign of independent life within it."[32]

Ezzidio was a man of great accomplishments but also of great modesty. Conscious of the scale of his success, he was also all too aware of his own unhopeful origins as a captive bound for the slave plantations of Brazil, and he was not ashamed to recall that. At a meeting of the Anti-Slavery Society in Freetown in 1870 shortly before his death, he testified publicly: "This neck which you see wearing a tie to-day, was invested at one time with a chain."[33] His impact on church and society consisted in the lasting legacy of ecumenical friendship that survived and triumphed over the destructive work of Tregaskis.

It is important, still, to place Ezzidio's life and work on the dynamic frontline of antislavery and antistructure, and to show how, through achievement and adversity, he helped strengthen the foundations of the new society in Africa. In that connection, Christopher Fyfe underlined the unprecedented nature of the society Ezzidio and his compatriots were fashioning in Freetown.

> The recaptives who found in Sierra Leone economic opportunities of a kind they had never known in their tribal homeland, also found a new religion to sustain them. Missionaries of the Church and Wesleyan Missionary Societies, or independent churches—Methodist, Baptist, and Huntingdonian—run by the settled Nova Scotian and Maroon inhabitants, offered them a gospel which took no account of their origins, and addressed them as individuals. Protestant Christianity, with its emphasis on personal conversion and responsibility, appealed to those cut off by their new circumstances from the communal life of tribal custom. Methodist church government (which even the C.M.S. partly adopted in Sierra Leone), where laymen play so large a part, offered the newly-rich trader a chance of social leadership. His talents might be rewarded not only by commercial success but with office as a local preacher, supplementing the work of missionary or pastor, or as a class-leader responsible for the moral welfare of a small group within the congregation. By making use of such laymen the churches spread their influence through the whole community in a way that missionaries working by themselves could never have done.[34]

The American roots of African Christianity continued to receive considerable boost with the continuing influx of new settlers. I have already referred to Daniel Coker. Another was Edward Jones, an African American from Baltimore and an ordained priest of the American Episcopal Church. He came out to Freetown in 1831 and went first to Kent village on the southwestern tip of the Freetown Peninsula. From there he traveled to the Banana Islands, further south. He married the daughter of Nÿlander, the CMS pioneer who arrived in 1806, and was for a time principal of Fourah Bay College. Bishop Edward Beckles commended Jones as perhaps the only colony preacher at whose feet he would gladly sit, such was his moral authority. Thomas Macfoy was another who came out in 1818 with his family from the West Indies. He became superintendent of Wellington village and received a lay preacher's license to assist in church expansion.

On the distaff side Sierra Leone enjoyed the leadership and business success of many prominent settler women. These women owned some of the most substantial property in the town. Sophia Small, for example, was a successful trader who put her profits into real estate. She built a large house valued in the 1790s at £900 sterling. Martha Burthen also went into real estate, which passed to her daughter's family, showing that, unlike in Muslim Africa, here inheritance need not follow the male agnatic line. Yet another was Lettice Demps, who owned substantial real estate, which her grandson was still selling in small lots some half a century later in the 1850s. And then there was Martha Smalley, who similarly owned vast pieces of land. She sent her daughter, Phillis, to England to study, and on her return the daughter opened a school where she taught reading, writing, arithmetic, and needlework for a fee. To help connect him better, the German missionary Nÿlander married her, and she was not the only settler woman to marry a European. A European carpenter married the daughter of Sophia Small, acquiring thereby a large family fortune. Out of the proceeds, he was able to construct a sumptuous house that in 1815 cost about £3,500 sterling. The homes of many of these women served as religious meeting houses, and women were prominent in helping seekers find "liberty."

With Freetown secured and Europe galvanized for the purpose, humanitarians now faced a different sort of question: not whether antislavery had a future, but how soon, with limited resources, the task could be accomplished and new models of community building extended to other parts. The Colonial Office would not encourage overseas territorial acquisition. Europe's national interest, Grey insisted, mandated no such expansionist schemes. The context of the question, we now know, was the tragic failure of the 1841 Niger Expedition, which prematurely embarked on the scheme to move the antislavery cause into Nigeria. The lesson to be learned from that tragedy was that a wider antislavery outreach should be left in local hands. If there was any link between Christianity and colonialism, Grey cautioned, it was that colonialism should follow where mission led and should retrace the admirable pattern of self-support and self-reliance that Christianity pioneered in Sierra Leone.

Rather than rouse the phantom of universal empire, the antislavery out-reach to Nigeria, carried on Crowther's broad shoulders, would prosper if it was allowed to override the default logic of white control. And thereby hangs a tale.

Thus, early-nineteenth-century colonialism, launched by transfusing it with "homoeopathic doses of scientific political economy," as Burton said,[35] was a timorous enterprise, allowing Europe to pursue its course of industrial development without the costs and hazards of acquiring and running distant tropical empires. It is one of the ironies of history that once the cautious, even quiescent, policy of the Colonial Office was replaced with the more aggressive, interventionist mandate of the 1880s and 1890s, the values of indigenous self-support and self-reliance would be overthrown, and Christianity's spiritual interests accordingly severed from its social and material interests. Under that aggressive mandate, commercial Lagos would be set at odds with Christian Abeokuta. In the peaceful, mid-nineteenth-century colonial phase, Governor MacCarthy's neo-Christendom erred only in seeking an outmoded, impractical fit between church and state. But in the later aggressive period, the state appealed to political and economic criteria to justify its actions and demanded from missions compliance and conformity. By that stage, however, Christianity had aroused in Africans hopes of self-reliance and self-support, so that the colonial state and indigenous Christianity be-came fated to get in each other's way. Missions faced a choice in that historical cleavage, and, however they decided, they would affect sig-nificantly Africa's future social and political development.

We must pause here to ponder what long-term damage was likely done to the cause of antislavery and antistructure by the set colonial policy of opposing the decline of chieftaincy rule in tropical Africa. By taking the culture of individual merit, personal achievement, free and open public access to education, and regular and open public assembly for worship and community life and replacing them with the need-blind and gender-deaf cult of human power, colonial administrators aided and abetted chiefs and other traditional rulers in reverting to the old preda-tory morality of feuding and looting. This reversion to the doctrine of the survival of the fittest had every dark incentive to make up lost ground. Yet, however great the damage wrought by the new aggressive style of the colonial state, the situation would have been a lot more bleak without the achievement of antislavery at Sierra Leone.

The roots of that achievement lay, as I have indicated, in the wider, unintended social consequences of the American Revolutionary War, and so in the century preceding classical imperialism. It was thus from the wider effects of the American Revolution that eventually the agents would emerge with the will requisite to the task and provide antislavery and antistructure with a base in Africa. Andrew Walls, who has done so much to call our attention to the subject, has written of how the revival religion of the settlers sealed for recaptives the pivotal role they would play in the religious history of the continent. He writes, "The recaptives, uprooted from their own traditions, became in effect the first mass movement in Christianity in modern Africa. Furthermore, they became, in a matter of a generation, a large and highly mobile missionary force, with an effect right across West Africa and beyond which passed anything Wilberforce could have envisaged."[36]

Young mothers under the whip in a slave caravan. (From *Africa Illustrated: Scenes from Daily Life on the Dark Continent,* photographs secured in Africa by Bishop William Taylor, Dr. Emil Holub, and the Missionary Superintendents [London: Illustrated Africa, 1895].)

Shipping slaves through the surf on the West African coast. (From *Church Missionary Intelligencer*, 7, no. 2 [1856].)

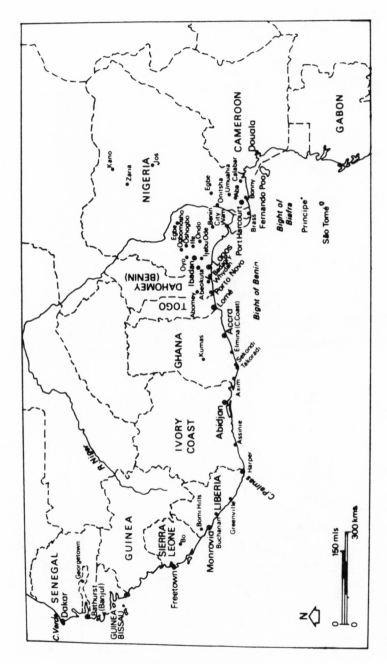

West Africa.

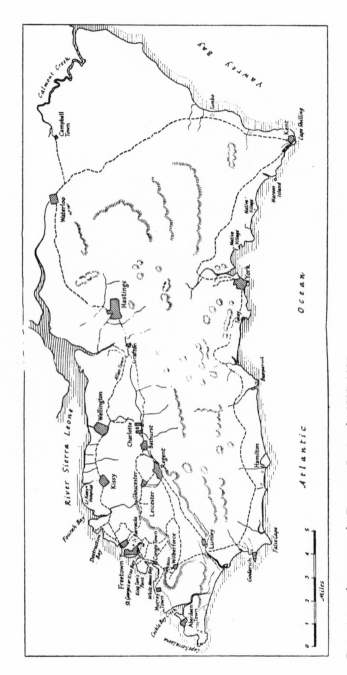

Recaptive settlements on the Freetown Peninsula, 1812–1820.

Samuel Ajayi Crowther, 1888.
(From Jesse Page, *Samuel Crowther: The Slave Boy Who Became Bishop of the Niger* [New York: Fleming H. Revell, 1908].)

Commander Foote and Dr. Irving with the chiefs of Abeokuta, December 1852.
(From *Church Missionary Intelligencer,* 4, no. 6 [June 1853].)

View of Liberia from the sea. (Sketch published as *View of the Colonial Settlement at Cape Montserado* [Washington, D.C.: Way and Gideon, 1825].)

4

The Niger Expedition, Missionary Imperatives, and African Ferment

It was two Hausa Africans (themselves former slaves who had been emancipated in Trinidad) who, showing signs of leadership in the antislavery movement, decided to return to Nigeria. The two men arrived in Freetown in 1837 on their way to Badagry, a slave trading center in the Bight of Benin. While in Freetown they attracted considerable attention among the recaptive population, many of whom became enthusiastic about organizing an outreach to Nigeria. For that purpose, three of the recaptives joined together in 1839 to buy a ship, which they renamed *Queen Victoria;* they furnished it with trade goods, took on a restricted number of passengers, only sixty-seven out of the more than two hundred who applied, and set sail for Badagry.

At this stage the Church Missionary Society was not much in the picture, choosing instead to remain behind the scenes. Yet the 1839 recaptive voyage to Nigeria, by its own measure a highly symbolic venture, would soon draw in the society: after the passengers returned to Freetown they resolved to continue the mission and accordingly petitioned the government and, indirectly, the CMS, to allow them to start a colony at Badagry under the British flag. Alone among Western nations, Britain was distinguished in agreeing to shoulder the heavy cost of abolition and became identified as such with antislavery. It had spent £30 million to underwrite abolition. Thus it requires historical perspective to understand how in this period the British flag was perceived locally as a symbol of antislavery and not as a symbol of the aggressive imperialism of a later age. It was in that spirit that the recaptives said they would be happy to have a European missionary join them as a partner, not as an overlord. The sources reiterate this theme often, suggesting the difficulty in getting the point across.

In the intervening years, between 1839 and 1885, when government and mission were still loath to countenance what they regarded as a reckless scheme of territorial overreach, the recaptives bought ships and traveled up and down the coast, demonstrating that expansion beyond Sierra Leone was a viable and logical development of the antislavery cause. They had the resources to pursue the idea and to build on accumulating evidence of its viability. Growth in the standard of living in Freetown quickened the pace of expansion abroad. As a consequence, the missionary societies of the Anglicans and the Methodists, with the Catholics soon to follow, experienced a revival of interest. Settler and recaptive churches were filled to overflowing, and the missionary societies rebuilt old abandoned chapels and staffed them with recaptive preachers. The school rolls swelled, new schools were opened, and still children had to be turned away. By 1840 over eight thousand children, about a fifth of the population, were at school.

Such advances in the personal circumstances of the settlers and recaptives produced the educated and successful individuals who could plan and direct the outreach to Nigeria and elsewhere. Preachers, pastors, schoolteachers, traders, and clerical personnel composed the ranks of this buoyant cadre of modernizing agents, with their skills supporting their mobile lifestyle. Thus trained, equipped, and resolved, they formed the core of the repatriation movement to Nigeria, ready to establish there the cause of antislavery and antistructure.

Change in the Old Order

Yorubaland, their destination, was no stranger to change, and even before the outfitting of the dramatic Niger Expedition of 1841 there were straws in the wind. The old chieftaincy rule, upheld by slavery, had been in crisis in several respects, as Samuel Johnson (d. 1901), the renowned Yoruba historian who was born in Sierra Leone, amply documented in his *History of the Yorubas*.[1] Oaths were no longer taken in the name of the gods, who were considered too lenient. "May the king's sword destroy me!" was the new oath, with its sharp self-imprecatory edge. The nation, warned Johnson darkly, was ripe for judgment.

The crisis was symbolized by the dramatic story of one *alafin* (chief),

Awole Arogangan, whose insurgent chiefs betrayed him in one of the turmoils in which he was embroiled. The chiefs sent him an empty calabash—for his head. Publicly denigrated, the *alafin* decided to take his own life. He would have the last word, however: He staged a defiant, macabre leave-taking in which he came out to the quadrangle carrying a sacred dish and three arrows, which he shot one each to the north, south, and west, pronouncing a curse with each volley. In the curse the *alafin* prayed that enemies who ventured out to the three points of the arrows would be taken captive. "My curse will carry you to the sea and beyond the seas, and slaves will rule over you, and you their masters will become slaves." With his raised hands he "dashed the earthenware dish on the ground smashing it into pieces."[2] He then took poison and died. With his death were buried the peace and unity of the people. New forces were stirring in the land, to the north first and now to the south, and the center would not hold. The old order was passing,[3] and the ruler's reference to a new order in which slaves, or former slaves, would be rulers would prove prophetic. The only difference was that such an order would mean not the perpetuation of slavery but its destruction.

Samuel Johnson, with the aid of the historical searchlight, cut through the alafin's grim mood of kingly ignominy to discern a new dispensation dawning in the land through the inauguration of the mission in Badagry, and later, in Abeokuta, home of the Egba Yorubas.

> Thus light began to dawn on the Yoruba country from the south, when there was nothing but darkness, idolatry, superstition, blood shedding and slave-hunting all over the rest of the country. There was an old tradition in the country of a prophecy that as ruin and desolation spread from the interior to the coast, so light and restoration will be from the coast interior-wards. This was a tradition of ages. Is not this event [Townsend's mission to Abeokuta] the beginning of its fulfilment?[4]

Johnson made reference to the coming of the Reverend Henry Townsend to Abeokuta in 1843, and a few words of introduction on Townsend and his relations with Crowther are necessary in view of the important role such relations played in the mission to Nigeria. Townsend arrived in Abeokuta on an exploratory visit in 1842. He was only twenty-one, frail looking but keen to run things. He had applied and been turned down for the Niger Expedition of 1841, with Crowther chosen in his place.

Townsend's Abeokuta visit was sponsored by Captain Harry Johnson, a Sierra Leonean trader who gave him free passage on his ship, the *Wilberforce,* together with fifty-nine other emigrants. The party arrived in Abeokuta on 4 January 1843. Townsend met King Sodeke and called him "a powerful king reigning over a numerous people . . . king of the Akus [Lagos Yoruba]."[5] Sodeke received the recaptive party warmly and offered to cooperate with a mission there, giving up a whole quarter of the town for the purpose. Townsend declined to commit the CMS to that extent but was impressed enough with the positive response of Sodeke to return. He wrote a report on that visit and then went to London to prepare himself for ordination. At about the same time Crowther, with the experience of the 1841 Niger Expedition under his belt, was also called to London for instruction at the CMS Training College. He was ordained in 1843 and returned to Abeokuta.

James Fergusson, a Wesleyan Methodist convert, was ahead of Townsend. He visited Badagry in 1841 and subsequently wrote to London asking for a missionary to be sent out. In 1842 the Reverend Thomas Birch Freeman (1809–1890),[6] son of an African father by an English mother, arrived in Badagry from Ghana and reorganized the recaptives there into a congregation. He then struck inland for Abeokuta, where he celebrated the Eucharist, the first to do so, and was warmly received by the Sodeke.

Recaptives and the New Middle Class: Brokers or Collaborators?

Thus, it was African leadership that pushed forward the plan to establish a foothold in Nigeria. One of the guiding spirits was a Yoruba recaptive named Thomas Will. He was among the petitioners asking for government support to carry the antislavery drive to Nigeria. In the words of the petition, he and his people

> feel . . . with much thankful to Almighty God and the Queen of England, who had rescued us from being in a state of slavery, and has brought us to this colony and set us at liberty and thanks be to God of all mercy who has sent his servants to declare unto us poor creatures the way of salvation, which illuminates our understanding so we are brought to know we have a soul to save, and when your humble petitioners look back upon their country people who are now living in

darkness, without the light of the Gospel, so we take upon ourselves to direct this our humble petition to your Excellency.

That the Queen will graciously to sympathize with her humble petitioners to establish a colony to Badagry that the same may be under the Queen's Jurisdiction and beg of her Royal Majesty to send missionary with us and by so doing the slave trade can be abolished, because the dealers can be afeared to go to the said place so that the Gospel of Christ can be preached throughout our land.[7]

Thomas Will died in 1840, leaving behind an estate of £2,000 and prime real estate in Freetown, evidence that the recaptives were growing in wealth and influence. The motives for emigration were also often personal as well as humanitarian. As Crowther described it, many of those who came from Sierra Leone "found their children, others their brothers and sisters, by whom they were entreated not to return to Sierra Leone. One of the traders had brought to Sierra Leone two of his grandchildren from Badagry to receive instruction. Several of them had gone into the interior altogether. Others in this colony have messages sent to them by their parents and relatives whom the traders met in Badagry."[8]

Crowther himself met his elderly mother, Afala, whom he had a son's special joy to see baptized at his own hands and christened as Hannah. She was ninety-seven when she died, a shock of corn fully ripe. At about that time the chiefs also came forward to petition Queen Victoria to open the road to Lagos so they could go there to trade. Crowther received the testimony of the *alake,* the chief of Abeokuta, to the effect that in ten years the community had been transformed and the people changed from the pursuit of war to peace. The roads that had been controlled by armed brigands were now peaceful, and everyone, including women and children, could venture out without fear of being seized and sold. The results of this transformation, the *alake* testified, were plain for all to see. Though he was not himself a Christian, the chief challenged that if Christianity was such a force for good, then he, for one, would wish more of it for his people. Before too long, however, circumstances would change and the chief would be singing a different tune indeed. That happened in 1867 on the Niger between Idda and Lokoja, where Chief Abokko seized Crowther, who was then bishop, and his party and demanded a stiff ransom for their release. True to custom, the chief asked for two hundred slaves as payment, but Crowther vowed he would rather die than pay. Mediation bought crucial time for a British trading vessel, the *Thomas Bagley,* to steam into port and to rescue Crowther, thanks to the timely intervention of the acting British consul, who lost his life in the effort. But in the late 1840s no one foresaw such hostility, and so the chief's resounding expression of confidence in Crowther's personal agency echoed far and wide, and, soon enough, word of it reached Lord Palmerston. Crowther's star was set to rise.

Other recaptives, such as John Langley, the Igbo superintendent of Charlotte village, William Pratt, Benjamin Pratt (no relation), and John Ezzidio, were equally successful and equally committed to expansion. Crowther predicted that, given the enthusiasm for emigration, many, not just Yoruba, but Hausa, Kanuri, Nupe and Igbo as well, would join the stream. His prediction came true, and the mission agencies were stirred to life as a consequence.

Jacob Ajayi has pointed out that the British authorities, including Lord John Russell in London and Governor Doherty in Sierra Leone, wanted to encourage the respectable elements among the recaptives, more particularly those "well-instructed in the arts of civilized life," to emigrate, not to Nigeria, but to the West Indies, on the grounds that the prospects of success for Europe's civilizing mission were greater there. The authorities remained skeptical about Nigeria, considered by them "a land of darkness," but especially about the less "respectable" sorts of recaptives setting out on their own initiative without the authorization of the British government.[9]

Consequently, of the two hundred people who applied, Doherty said he issued passports only to sixty-one, forty-four men and seventeen women, so dubious was he of the whole idea. The mass enthusiasm among the recaptives only strengthened his reservations. He would yield only as support for the plan came from Sir Thomas Fowell Buxton, who contended that "the Bible and the Plough" together would transform Africa from being the Dark Continent to becoming the continent of light and prosperity.[10] Christianity and agriculture, in this reasoning, would make a productive combination, yet the engine that drove emigration was trade, not tillage. The typical emigrant structures were the school and the chapel, not the farmhouse and the toolshed. As the people expressed it to the CMS agent, "Trade we shall, trade our fathers taught us."[11] In a paradoxical way, too, it was the Lagos-based trading interests that opposed the Niger Mission and its antislavery agenda.

Thomas Jefferson Bowen and the Manifest Middle Class

It is true, as Ajayi has argued, that the missionaries wished to see established in Nigeria an African middle class. The pioneer American Baptist missionary Thomas Jefferson Bowen expressed this conviction with uncommon passion and eloquence. Bowen was to write a much acclaimed study of the Yoruba language, *Grammar and Dictionary of the Yoruba Language,* which was published in 1862 by the Smithsonian Institution in its series "Smithsonian Contributions to Knowledge." Bowen was a pragmatist in the old mold, a frontier activist who took America as his example of the story of human progress.

The primary task of mission, Bowen stated, was evangelization, "because the soul is more than the body; but evangelization involves civilization, both as cause and effect, because the body, the intellect, and the affections of man, are so inseparably united, as to act and react upon each other, both for good and for evil." No society of civilization, Bowen challenged, could be cemented and made to thrive without the division of people into higher, lower, and middle classes. Such a social gradation was indispensable to the growth of higher forms of organization. "Take our own country and social state as an example," he urged. "The highest class, which with all its various component parts is a unit, consists of our eminent scientific men, of our great merchants and mechanics (whose ships, engines, etc, are at once the substance and expression of our civilization), of our wealthy citizens, and political leaders and rulers, and in short of all who are truly eminent in any department."[12]

When applied to Africa, this analysis revealed a fundamental lack and disadvantage that missions had to remedy if they hoped to advance the cause. We find in Africa, said Bowen, no class of eminent persons whose attainments might give unity, force, and direction to society, no middle class that could receive impulses of knowledge and wisdom and power from their superiors and transmit them to the common people, which was the function of a progressive destiny. Chiefs were not qualified to perform that mediatory role and so were not entitled to the fruits of agents of social transformation, for their power rested on social stagnation, feeding on itself rather than being a force for progress, knowledge, and dynamic change.

For a middle class to succeed as agents of social change, Bowen contended, it would be necessary for commerce to take root along the lines of planned economic development: lawful produce as the result of the labor of farmers and peasants would be collected and brought by African carriers to the centers of transport and exchange. The income from the trade would be used to purchase European goods for which the requisite local habits and appetite would have been created.

> The general extension of commerce would erect new standards of re-spectability . . . The effects of commerce would be a widening and straightening of streets for the passage of vehicles, and a remodelling of houses to suit the altered circumstances of the people . . . The in-crease of wealth, knowledge, refinement of feeling, and respect for family, which would result from commerce, would operate with other causes to revolutionize the present relations of husband and parents and children.[13]

Undergirding these notions was the new work ethic. The activist im-pulse of new world religion was transposed to West Africa. Industrious-ness, sobriety, the dignity of labor, and personal integrity were stressed as the ingredients of a progressive society. "Manual labor schools or none is my motto," Bowen boasted.[14] Practical education would reform character and instill appropriate lessons of self-support and honest labor. Bowen had unbounded faith in the capacity for improving society and perfect-ing institutions. His philosophy of mission, however, was based on the need for Christianity to strike local roots and to spread from internal stimulus rather than from external direction. The cause would then pros-per "without the instrumentality of foreign missionaries."[15]

The idea of a middle class, advanced here on the basis of trade, was a popular notion with American and European humanitarians and, in-deed, with missions. Yet it would be a mistake to interpret the mission to Nigeria simply in terms of the civilizational motive without regard to the principles of antislavery and antistructure. Bowen hinted at a crucial issue when he noted that chiefs were of limited value in the new scheme of society he wanted to see develop in Africa. Thus, he envisaged that liberated Africans, ex-captives or recaptives, and those likely to be en-slaved would be targeted for improvement and used to lay the founda-tion of a new social organization radically different from the one built on chiefly power and pedigree. Agriculture had its roots in the landed gen-try and manorial privilege. In America and the tropics it smacked, too, of plantation slavery. Trade, by contrast, would produce the new middle class and a meritocracy.

If we view Bowen's ideas in the specific context of antislavery, then their revolutionary social implications become clear. The new middle class he had in mind, embodied, for example, in Crowther's personal history, would be constructed from the ranks of the dispossessed, the marginals, those tribesmen and tribeswomen whose African rulers saw them only as legitimate payment for war, indebtedness, and theft. In effect, the new middle class in these circumstances would be not a seal to canonize the old order but a warrant to change and replace it. His ideas may today sound triumphalist, like imperial or missionary rhetoric, but in the cause of antislavery they implied antistructure. Bowen's language projected a progressive destiny freed of chiefly caste.

With that central piece in place, many of the rest of the pieces of the puzzle begin to fall into a pattern. For example, an Irish missionary who was serving in Calabar east of the Niger Delta was on leave in Newcastle, England, near Darlington, the home of George Stephenson's steam locomotive (built in 1825), where he saw the train that ran between London and Edinburgh. It inspired him to apocryphal visions of world peace. He commented on how with the advance of railway transport border warfare and internecine feuds would disappear. "Old things are passed away, and all things become new," he declared. For a moment, his sense of self-preservation appeared also to have deserted him as he continued: "The baronial and feudal age are gone never to be recalled . . . The lords of the land and the Queen of the realm must come down from their chargers and state carriages and ride in the cars of commerce made by the plebeians for their own use."[16] In spite of its heady rhetoric, and hints of class war, that social radicalism was actually far more plausible for Africa than the apocryphal message of universal harmony.

The new order challenged the institutions and norms of the old order and released new energies for experimentation, individual enterprise, and social and gender mobility. These changes produced new skills to utilize the improved tools and equipment and new forms of association, assembly, and worship that departed radically from the chiefly court, the secret society, the royal entourage, the war council, and the sacred cult. The old gods, with their warrior, Bushido appetite for sanguinary sanctions, were thrown into confusion (as Samuel Johnson observed), their ranks deserted for new opportunities and challenges. As the bewildered Africans confessed, the local gods were dying while the white man's way of worshipping God was spreading and would prevail one day because of the evils and disruption caused by the slave trade. Samuel

Pearse, a Yoruba clergyman, reported in 1863 a conversation with an elderly woman of Badagry who mused ruefully on the strange times people were passing through, times "when the worship of idols being transmitted from one generation to another was in crisis. The horrors of the wars that ensued doomed many [people] to an untimely dissolution and sold them into slavery. In the state of slavery how is it possible they could do such justice to the worship as did their forefathers, and yet the evils came that were never seen nor heard of were the orisas alive?"[17]

Crowther was the ideal "new man" in that transitional order, deeply enough grounded in the old Africa to discern what its authentic values were and yet sufficiently molded by the new forces to be a credible and effective guide. Crowther knew that the old Africa lay in ruins, that precious little of its discredited values could be salvaged. Thus he tried to negotiate between the old customs and the new ideas of civilization so as to buy time to avert a total wrench with the past, though his efforts showed that a decisive drama was afoot. Perhaps that was what David George meant when he told the Baptists in London that the mighty work begun in Africa was unstoppable.

Missionaries obtained a sense of this inexorable drama when they received reports that their arrival in some town or other had been preceded by local prophecies, as Johnson testified. Clearly, effective resistance to the new external forces was being eroded by internal moral fatigue. Even the intensification of the slave trade, or the urgent pleas for domestic slavery as a lesser evil, as a reaction to the growing antislavery campaign was a sign of desperation, not of strength. It was the last gasp of the old system. Soon the recaptives filtered back to their original societies and cultures and began establishing schools and churches, operating their own businesses, writing down their own languages and correspondence, educating their children, worshipping and testifying in churches they built and owned and operated under preachers of their own kith and kin, and establishing structures of equality between men and women and among themselves as Yoruba, Igbo, Nupe, Hausa, Temne, and others. All of that made it clear that the tide had turned and Nigeria, too, would be affected on a scale unprecedented in its diverse, disparate history.

The missionary and imperial rhetoric masked the nature of this change by portraying it as a piece of the engine of Western civilization. The Africans themselves were often misled by the material forms of the change into characterizing it as the extension of European civilization. William de Graft, a native of Cape Coast, Ghana, in charge of Methodist work in Badagry until 1844, spoke of holding a tea party for the children of the mission school on which occasion he served tea, cakes, and bread. The children, he said, were neatly dressed in European clothes. It all appears to conform to the rules of civilization, except that the chiefs who were present took their place alongside the children, exhibiting the kind of social leveling that chiefly honor in other circumstances would not have countenanced. Besides, it says something for antistructure, and for social destigmatization, that de Graft, carrying more than a whiff of stigma as an *emancipado,* should now exercise moral authority over chiefly dignitaries or their peers who had not so long ago put him and his kind in chains. The autonomous, lay-led congregation as the "gathered elect" delegitimized the old slave-based chiefly order. The struggle between the two had long-term consequences for all of society.

All this is not to deny that the new middle class being created would serve the interests of mission and empire and as such advance European civilization in Africa. The evidence points incontrovertibly in that direction. The Reverend Thomas Freeman urged the governor of the Gold Coast, Maclean, to lay claim to Badagry, to hoist the English flag, provide protection for all English subjects, and ensure the safety of Christian mission work. Maclean could rest assured that the mission house in Badagry would become at the same time the fort, the jail, and the temple, probably in that order. Freeman observed with evident satisfaction that the bamboo chapel he built in Badagry at a cost of £300 was a cause for great marvel. "It appeared a thing so novel and extraordinary, that the people were often seen standing in groups at a short distance, gazing at it in astonishment."[18] The Reverend Thomas Dove, head of the Methodist mission in Sierra Leone, said he was expressing the sentiments of recaptive emigrants when he wrote to London that their reason for going to Nigeria was "that the Gospel of God our Saviour may be preached . . . that schools may be established, that Bibles may be sent, that the British flag may be hoisted, and that she rank among the civilized nations of the earth."[19] Lord Clarendon was assured in 1855 by the merchant McGregor Laird, who died in January 1861 while trading on the Niger, that recaptive Africans as civilized natives would return to Africa "carrying English habits and language with them," and that it was best if they were self-supporting.[20]

Yet these recaptives, Creoles, and *emancipados* were not the collaborators of the dialectical school, the *assimilados* who conspired as paid foreign agents to insinuate themselves into the space out of which the chiefly clans had been driven. On the contrary, reprieved and given a second chance, they formed a crucial buffer between an ascendant European order and otherwise uncomprehending hinterland populations. Thus, in his peroration on the fate of the old royal and chiefly heritage in his native society, Samuel Johnson, for example, preserved a distinctly Yoruba national sensibility that animates all his dynastic material, his native sympathies, and his international and cosmopolitan outlook, as well as his depiction of the new emerging class of liberated, modernizing Nigerians. His own example is worth recalling: born in Sierra Leone of recaptive parents, he became an articulate chronicler and interpreter of the history of his people, applauding European interest where it served his people and often enduring European slight for not knowing his place. For all that, had he become a collaborator? Scarcely, though he was no less effective as a cultural mediator between Europe and Africa. He was an example that inspired the first breed of nationalists, whose own modern agenda of *vox populi* reflected the priorities and norms of antislavery and antistructure, to wit, that rulers should come from among the ruled.

Crowther and the Niger Expedition

In 1841, with public support for the scheme, Lord John Russell, then colonial secretary, authorized an expedition to the River Niger in response to the ideas of Sir Thomas Fowell Buxton. Its purpose was to open up the riverain system to lawful commerce and to help put down the slave trade. The expedition was given power to enter into treaty agreements with the chiefs to suppress the slave trade and support commercial enterprise. Factories would be established at trading stations. With government plans set out thus, the Church Missionary Society agreed to equip a missionary party to accompany the expedition, placing James Frederick Schön and Samuel Crowther in charge. It would prove as hazardous an enterprise as it was momentous, because, to begin with, without armed protection the missionary party would be at the complete mercy of the well-armed and better-equipped slave traders who controlled the riverain channels. In addition, the members of the expedition would be exposing themselves to the dreaded malaria fever, at that time understood only in folklore terms as a disease of contaminated vapors, hence its name "mal-aria," "bad air." It was not until 1897, the year of the scientific discovery of the malaria parasite, that those who for centuries had wistfully "questioned the winds and waters" could abandon their mute oracles and scatter.[21] Yet if Crowther carried off the challenge, he would establish the case for decisive African leadership in the anti-slavery campaign.

Three ships were fitted out for the voyage: the *Albert,* the *Wilberforce,* and the *Soudan.* In charge was Captain Trotter. Of the members of the expedition only Schön and Crowther had any missionary experience.

The two kept journals of the expedition, which on 1 July 1841 left Sierra Leone and entered the marshy delta uneventfully in mid-August. Within days, however, they were recording grim news. The chief medical officer reported that by 4 September "[f]ever of a most malignant character broke out in the *Albert,* and almost immediately in the other vessels, and abated not until the whole expedition was paralyzed." The *Soudan* was loaded with 40 of the sick and dying and, like a scapegoat, was turned loose and made to turn around, to be followed two days later for the same reason by the *Wilberforce.* Only the *Albert* forged on ahead, making encouraging progress among the chiefs. By 3 October, however, malaria was carrying off so many on the last ship that Captain Trotter, by then three hundred miles up the Niger, contemplated abandoning the enterprise altogether and admitting defeat. The decision was taken to quit. It was a ragged retreat. No sooner had he turned around than Trotter himself went down with the fever, as did the 3 engineers and then Mr. Willie, the navigator, who died soon after falling ill. Others followed him in rapid succession: 3 officers and a marine died and were buried at sea. Of the 145 Europeans, 130 had contracted malaria and 40 had died.[22]

Many of the survivors, racked with high fever and suffering aches and shivers, were delirious to the point of requiring to be tied down. Some flung themselves into the river, only to be rescued by an alert African attendant. Rio Nun, where the expedition entered the delta, earned the nickname the Gate of the Cemetery. Members of the expedition entering the river did so with the Nunc Dimittis on their lips. Buxton was so distraught by the hapless expedition that he scarcely could bring himself to mention it again. In fact it broke his spirit, and he died three years later, a belated casualty.

In spite of the hazards and difficulties, Crowther, who survived along with Schön, accomplished a surprising amount of work on the Niger. His journal entries show him making detailed observations and reports of his progress on the banks of the Niger. He became most interested in the religious ideas and practices of Africans, and his inborn flair for field research led him to inquire diligently, to listen closely, and to depict as accurately as he could what he observed and heard for himself. In matters of such importance, he was always eager to corroborate, to test, and to confirm, leaving issues of dispute open to opinion. The rush to judgment was never a weakness of his. Thus, although he noted somber aspects of their customs and traditional practices, Crowther was nevertheless enthusiastic about what he learned of the Igbos' religion. He found that the people had concise, clear ideas about God, ethics, and moral conduct. He said he had heard references to such things among the Sierra Leoneans of Igbo background but had refrained from stating them as facts "before I had satisfied myself by inquiring of such as had never had any intercourse with Christians . . . Truly God has not left Himself without witness!"[23] The idea that premodern Africa had anticipated in all relevant respects Christian teaching was stated by Crowther with such natural conviction that it marked him as a native mouthpiece, not just as a foreign agent. His views had none of the collateral safeguards of planned economic development as an investment for mission, because he never believed that salvation needed an economic alibi, unlike the next generation of missionaries, who came under the spell of social evolutionist doctrine.

At any rate, Crowther credited the Igbos with crucial theological advantage. One cannot help comparing him on this point to Olaudah Equiano. Crowther's account in Schön's journal is worth citing here.

The Ibos are in their way a religious people, the word "Tshuku" [Chukwu], God, is continually heard. Tshuku is supposed to do everything. When a few bananas fell out of the hands of one into the water, he comforted himself by saying, "God has done it." Their notions of some of the attributes of the Supreme Being are in many respects correct and their manner of expressing them striking. "God made everything. He made both white and black," is continually on their lips. Some of their parables are descriptive of the perfections of God, when they say, for instance, that God has two eyes and two ears, that the one is in heaven and the other on earth. I suppose the conception that they have of God's omniscience and omnipresence cannot be disputed.

It is their common belief that there is a certain place or town where Tshuku dwells, and where he delivers his oracles and answers inquiries. Any matter of importance is left to his decision, and people travel to the place from every part of the country.

I was informed today that last year Tshuku had given sentence against the slave trade. The person of him is placed on a piece of ground which is immediately and miraculously surrounded by water. Tshuku cannot be seen by any human eye, his voice is heard from the ground. He knows every language on earth, apprehends thieves, and if there is fraud in the heart of the inquiring he is sure to find it out, and woe to such a person, for he will never return. He hears every word that is said against him, but can only revenge himself when persons come near him . . . They sincerely believe all these things, and many others respecting Tshuku, and obey his orders implicitly; and if it should be correct that he has said that they should give up the slave trade, I have no doubt that they will do it at once.[24]

In Onitsha, Crowther took notes on what he and his party observed of the cult of Tshi, a deity with power to preserve people from witchcraft. A goat was sacrificed to the deity, the blood allowed to run into a bowl, and an invocation made over the victim: "I beseech thee, my guide, make me good; thou hast life. I beseech thee to intercede with God the Spirit, tell Him my heart is clean. I beseech thee to deliver me from all bad thoughts in my heart; drive out all witchcrafts; let riches come to me. See your sacrificed goat; see your kola-nuts; see your rum and palm wine."[25] (It is an intriguing thought that the invocation equates witchcraft with "bad thoughts in [the] heart," showing, as Edward Evans-Pritchard observed in his classic study of witchcraft and magic among the Azande, that it is ill will [and who is innocent of that?] that establishes witchcraft, and witchcraft that establishes the existence of the witch, and not the other way round.)[26]

In light of his close investigations into African religions and customs, it could rightly be said of Crowther that he regarded traditional Africa as abounding in the resources capable of being claimed for the antislavery campaign and, thus, as something to be drawn upon to support the case for Christian mission, too. In that regard, Crowther believed that a modernized, progressive version of Chukwu should be drafted into the ranks of antislavery and antistructure, and the advantages of deference to Him diverted into the new paths of emancipation and productive enterprise. Furthermore, Chukwu could be used to justify depersonalizing authority, bypassing the chiefs or traditional titleholders who made and executed laws, and centering authority instead in local affirmations of the values of life, liberty, and productive enterprise. Crowther promoted such an adaptive, moral response.

There would, however, be a certain limitation to such modernization of Chukwu: he would be useful initially as deterrence, in what he forbade and the sanctions attached to prohibition. Being a probationary rite and a negative cult and, furthermore, being the linchpin of the establishment status quo, Chukwu would bind, limit, restrict, and exclude, in a ritual more like a hazing than a communion, with ordeals and sanctions having primacy over redemption, love, and hope. Thus, the more positive doctrine of the providence of Chukwu in the redemption of creation and in investing outcasts and underdogs with the dignity of divine adoption and hope for a second chance would have to wait for the Christian encounter. Yet the seeds of that possibility were sown in soil so well prepared in Chukwu that Crowther was glad to have discovered it. He was confident the two complementary traditions would eventually converge.

I must again stress that Crowther was no mere romantic, intent on idealizing native custom and practice. His natural habit of stringent scrutiny of the evidence he never abandoned to the heady fervor of nativistic pride, and so he plunged into remote hinterland districts, grateful for what he discovered of positive encouragement there, certainly, but resolved also to confront what he judged harmful. On the Niger he found evidence of both. Chukwu belonged to the encouraging side. On the negative side, Crowther once met a crowd shouting and crying as people made their way to the river, "dragging a poor young girl, tied hand and foot, with her face on the ground . . . for they believe in making a sacrifice for their sins by beating out the life of a fellow-creature in this manner. As she is drawn along, the crowd cry, 'Aro ye, Aro, Aro!' i.e., 'Wickedness, wickedness!' and believe that the iniquities of the people are thus atoned for."[27]

A similar spectacle greeted Crowther when a recent Christian convert gave birth to twins and, because of the traditional stigma attached to twin births, fled in terror into the bush at night. When a missionary intervened to try to save the babies, "a furious mob of five hundred men armed to the teeth with guns, cutlasses, spears, clubs and arrows . . . who surrounded the mission compound, demanding that the babies be given up to them."[28] In the melee the children were secreted away and conveyed to safety aboard the ship the *Wanderer,* then anchored in the Niger. The possibility that from such an encounter a creative intercultural process would be ignited, with victim populations thereby empowered, drove Crowther forward.

Only his courage could match the daunting challenge he faced. He reported that on a pastoral visit to Obitsi in the Niger Delta, after taking the service there, he received an invitation to visit the chief of Atta,

> to which I consented to go. After the accustomed etiquette of offering the kola nuts and palm wine as marks of friendship and kind reception, the subject was broached, namely, their wish to be correctly informed whether what the Onitsha converts had told them in their preaching was correct, that, when any of their chiefs or persons of rank die, they should keep the body for many days, during which time they keep up firing guns, drumming, and dancing until they obtain a slave for human sacrifice to be buried with the dead. The Christians never did such things, but quietly bury their dead as soon as possible. I confirmed the teaching of the converts as being quite correct, that at no death of a Christian in any part of the world would a human being be killed to be buried with the dead, how honourable soever the dead might have been in his lifetime, because this act is a great abomination in the sight of God; neither would the relations of the dead make that an occasion for drumming, dancing, and firing of guns for days, which I endeavoured to explain to them as utterly useless to the dead as marks of honour; that if the dead be a Christian, as soon as his soul leaves the body he is carried by angels into heaven, where he will enjoy everlasting happiness with Christ, who has washed the soul clean with his own most precious blood.[29]

With incredible stamina and fortitude, Crowther would stand in the midst of the death and defiance of slave markets and propound antislavery. He described how on one occasion (but not the only one) he found himself, as it were, in the lion's den. Sure that his readers would understand the feelings welling up inside him as he stood in the middle of a slave market, where he would likely have intimations of his own capture and sale, he confessed that his customary discretion abandoned him. Holding forth in the Hausa language,

> from a sense of duty I expressed my feelings to all who were present under the shed. I informed them, that the chief design of our Expedition was to put an end to the trade in human flesh and blood; and expatiated on the sinfulness of the practice, it being against the laws of God and the laws of the most enlightened kingdoms of the world, and productive of innumerable evils among themselves. Conscious of the justness of the cause I was expounding, I could do it with perfect calmness of mind, and free from apprehension of the displeasure of those against whose interest I was speaking.[30]

The slave vendor at the meeting told Crowther he could not fault his reasoning, but as long as the local king did not revoke the law on the slave trade, he as a merchant had no choice but to carry on with it. Crowther replied that he would do what it took to lay the ax to the root of the slave trade.

Crowther's moral commitment to antislavery, sharpened by the events of his own personal history, sprang nevertheless from what I described in Chapter 2 as the general cause. Africans were no exception to the rule of righteousness, a rule opposed to any compromise with slavery and its supporting structures. Crowther would not thus denounce or applaud indigenous institutions and authorities merely for their being African. Rather, he demanded of them an unyielding, stringent compliance with the credo that slavery "is a great abomination in the sight of God." Pledging his total commitment to the cause, he wrote, "For Zion's sake will I not hold my peace, and for Jerusalem's sake will I not rest, until the righteousness thereof go forth as brightness, and the salvation thereof as a lamp that burneth."[31] He would not spare tainted institutions and customs or exempt them from the purifying pains of critical historical scrutiny.

The importance of making advances on that front urgently, and preferably with indigenous cooperation, was crucial to Crowther, and it did a lot to modify his views on civilization, if we may revert to that issue once more. Emmanuel Ayandele, the Nigerian historian and himself a lay Baptist leader after the legacy of Thomas Bowen, has entered a stern, if not wholly unjustified, judgment on Crowther's attitude to African culture:

Bishop Crowther was more accommodating to European civilization than people like James Johnson and Mojola Agbebi, and saw no conflict in Nigeria's interest in the penetration of the country by it, but rather hoped that the country would derive cultural, social and above all, religious advantages from it. Always wearing English clothes, he refused to allow the vernacular to be taught in the Niger Mission. As late as 1890 he emphasized that the medium of teaching throughout the Mission would be English. He ridiculed as "quixotic" the attempt by some European missionaries who sought to convert people by identifying themselves with their culture in dress, in food and in lodging. Unlike James Johnson he had no intention of studying African institutions and religion with the hope of understanding them and grafting Christianity on [sic] their healthy parts. Rather, he had the worst epithets for these institutions and [for] the Delta peoples. He pronounced irrationally on polygamy and thus misled the Lambeth Conference of 1888 on the real position of polygamy in African society.[32]

That is a serious charge against Crowther, even though it preserves essentially an important dimension of the complex story of the man. The evidence supports that view but also supports a more lenient view than that. Ayandele himself goes on to say how such a view was not the whole story, nor, in the final analysis, was it the most lasting of Crowther's legacy.

First, Crowther clashed with the CMS policy of transferring leadership of the Niger Mission to European missionaries. Second, Crowther was not a crusader against polygamy, nor did he ever establish the monogamous rule as a prerequisite for Christian baptism. Thus in fifty years of missionary work in the Niger Delta he presided at not a single monogamous marriage, yielding on this issue to indigenous exigencies.[33] Third and most significant, Crowther's pioneering linguistic and translation work in African languages, in particular his recognized contribution to Yoruba as a national language, formulated terms that became a permanent frame of reference for Christian Africans and others. His own testimony on this matter is worth recalling. We have an account of his experience at a Christian religious service in January 1844 in Freetown, where Yoruba was used as the language of liturgy for the first time.

A large number of Africans crowded thither to hear the words of prayer and praise for the first time in their own tongue in an English church. "Although it was my own native language," says the Rev. S. Crowther, "with which I am well acquainted, yet on this occasion it appeared as if I were a babe, just learning to utter my mother-tongue. The work in which I was engaged, the place where I stood, and the congregation before me, were altogether so new and strange, that the whole proceeding seemed to myself like a dream . . . At the conclusion of the blessing, the whole church rang with *ke oh sheh*—so be it, so let it be!"[34]

Although he did not say so at the time, and although he thought strictly within the constraints of continued British colonial rule, it is nevertheless evident that Crowther was in fact laying the foundation for Christianity as an African religion. Using African languages in Scripture, prayer, worship, and study, and promoting the African cultural context, he sought to transform and promote the religion. As John Peel has argued, even Crowther's adoption of Hannah as the baptismal name of his mother was inspired by regard for an old African narrative. In the Bible Hannah is the mother of Samuel, the name also of Crowther himself, after his missionary sponsor. But in the light of the christening of his mother, Samuel became reaffiliated to Hannah by the double cord of birth and baptismal rite. Consequently, Ajayi

was no longer just *any* Samuel, a Samuel named for an obscure London vicar or the bearer of a name without intrinsic meaning, but Samuel, son of Hannah. He thus fashioned a new narrative for himself . . . The story is told in 1 Samuel 1:2, and a strikingly Yoruba story it is, too . . . Crowther's reconnection with his past, in the person of his mother, through the medium of a narrative that grounded his own religious commitment thus served to relaunch him on his life's career.[35]

At a minimum, this example suggests a recasting of new and foreign materials in line with Africa's awakened aspirations and new possibilities. Even on that limited ground, Crowther was not, then, as *deraciné* and *outré* as it might first appear.

In any case, his African bona fides being impeccable as they stand, it is difficult to pull him down as a mere dupe of the colonial establishment. There is, undeniably, a great deal of ambivalence in Crowther's cultural attitudes, but he loved his people and his culture too much to connive in sequestering it—few could accuse him of that.

Yet liberal historiography has not been kind to Crowther or, for that matter, to the Church Missionary Society. Crowther has been attacked for being a foreign mouthpiece. Geoffrey Moorhouse, for instance, has described Crowther's journal as "the diary of a fellow who has acquired opinions of his own and the confidence to pronounce them with some authority; basically they are echoes of attitudes which Crowther must have heard expressed many times in the CMS headquarters in London and elsewhere in his widening experience."[36] Moorhouse takes particular issue with Crowther's implicit faith in the alliance of mission and colonialism. Thus when news of the Indian Mutiny of 1857 reached West Africa, Crowther used the occasion to launch a spirited defense of the pacifying and civilizing value of missionary work, saying that if Western critics had not stood in the way of missions converting the Sepoys of India, then the cataclysmic events of the mutiny might have been averted. At least, he hoped, the event might open the eyes of many to the merit of allowing native converts to mingle with the community as an example of enlightened, orderly conduct. According to Moorhouse, by this stage of his career, Crowther was becoming steadily "less the pure African and more the hybrid Afro-European in outlook."[37] This is undeserved and would stand only if we grant its unstated premise, to wit, that Africans could not succeed except in their native quarantine.

As it was, Crowther's opinions on the Indian Mutiny carried no weight whatsoever and should be given little historical significance. Instead, we should note his own labors to establish a new, radical anthropology for Christianity, which reveal that the work of missions in rolling back frontiers of cruelty and breaking down structures of oppression and injustice was relevant in mitigating the cleavages induced by imperial rule and prone to erupt in events like the Indian Mutiny. In any case, even Moorhouse is willing to moderate his strictures against Crowther, saying finally Crowther "never entirely loses his personal and native gentleness and shrewdness."[38] Nevertheless, Crowther seems to suffer the fate of Olaudah for showing native enterprise.

As with Olaudah, we should persist with Crowther and see how he looked at the question of encouraging African agency and preserving the native perspective. We may do that by examining Crowther's views about creating a middle class in Africa to institute reforms in religion, politics, society, and economics. As mentioned above, Lord John Russell and Governor Doherty were inclined to see West Indian blacks as better suited than an indigenous recaptive population to bridging the gap between Europe and Africa. Their attitude implies that alienating Africans from their culture was the most desirable way of going about the civilizing mission. In their view receptive Africans were at a disadvantage from their very limited exposure to European values.

By contrast, West Indian blacks, long uprooted from Africa, would be less likely to harbor any lingering nostalgia for African traditions and thus less likely to lapse into Africa's unredeemed past. As such, they were more likely to provide the civilized, intermediary threshold that Africans could cross without stumbling. When we put the issue in those terms, we reveal the implicit thesis that African culture, prone to proliferate in its natural setting, was best kept in the background, where a transplant European civilization could smother it without costly contest or resistance.

Crowther had some opinions of his own on that civilized plan. He was not moved by the argument that West Indians (in his paraphrase) would "in many respects be better qualified than the Liberated Africans at Sierra Leone: they have seen more of European habits; are better acquainted with agricultural labours; and have a much greater taste for European comforts, if that be considered an acquisition." In fact, he countered, the very reasoning the officials used to commend the West Indians, the reasoning, that is to say, of their alleged proximity to European culture and, correspondingly, their alienation from African culture, was a weakness, not an advantage. The one salient requirement that the West Indian argument had not satisfied was the commitment to antislavery, for which a black skin was no automatic qualification. In the case of the West Indians, he contended, we should remember that some of them could, in theory, "carry a recollection of the [slave] driver's lashes with them; and many more [may harbor] a disposition to inflict them on others," and thus by their conduct oppose the cause of antislavery and antistructure.[39] For that reason, receptive Africans represented the best hope, and the last chance, of securing the future of the cause in Africa. Their closeness to their people, their natural connections to the culture, and the fact that they had never been socialized in Europe or in European establishments qualified the receptives for their pivotal role as agents of social change.

Such was his natural civility that Crowther said he would offer his apology if his words caused any offense to the people of the West Indies, but if there be any fault in what he had to say, it should be attributed to his knowledge of what happened in the settlement of Liberia, where the cause of antislavery received a setback by the inflexible policy of introducing all free blacks, many of whom promoted the slave trade (see next chapter).[40]

The Niger Mission Resumed

The Church Missionary Society was so impressed with Crowther's achievement in the otherwise disastrous 1841 expedition, that it decided to resume further exploration with his help and leadership. Accordingly, he and Townsend were sent to Abeokuta in 1846, with Townsend based at Ake and Crowther at Igbein. Success soon followed the establishment of the mission in Abeokuta, and in 1848 the first baptisms were performed.

The missionary presence in Abeokuta helped strengthen the Egbas in their confrontation with Dahomey, Abeokuta's unreliable neighbor, whose king invaded the territory in 1864 and was accordingly repulsed. Townsend became a promoter of Abeokuta as the headquarters of the CMS in Nigeria, replacing the Niger Mission for that purpose. His report urging such a shift of strategy was submitted to the CMS in London, which in turn placed a summary version of its key recommendations before Lord Palmerston, the foreign minister. Palmerston dispatched Captain John Beecroft in 1850 to Abeokuta on a diplomatic mission that also took him to Dahomey. As it happened, Beecroft found the king of Dahomey in no mood to conclude an antislavery treaty with Britain, because he was preparing an attack on Abeokuta, which occurred later in 1851, as did an attack from Lagos.

Crowther's value in bringing pressure to bear on the British government to intervene in Nigeria was apparent to the CMS, and so in 1851 Crowther was summoned to London to appear before the British public urging intervention in Nigeria: before the lords of the Admiralty; before Palmerston; at the University of Cambridge; and before Queen Victoria and Prince Albert, where he was escorted by Lord Wriosthesley Russell, the brother of the prime minister. The subject of these meetings was Lagos and the need for British action to subdue it and annex it to Abeokuta's cause. Palmerston wrote Crowther to thank him for his mediation on the matter. A blockade was immediately ordered on Dahomey and an ultimatum sent to Lagos to reinstate King Akitoye.

But Britain still hesitated to take military action against Lagos. It was finally moved to act through a clumsy mix of blunder and bluster. Beecroft decided on a show of force to intimidate King Kosoko, thinking that was all it required to achieve his purpose, but he was unexpectedly repulsed. Implicated in that repulse was the prestige of Britain, which could no longer allow the status quo to continue in Lagos without compromising itself in the eyes of local chiefs. In December 1851 Britain launched an attack on Lagos, drove Kosoko out, and installed the amenable Akitoye, by now, though, too compromised to be effective. A treaty renouncing the slave trade was signed by Akitoye and the chiefs of Abeokuta in 1852. The takeover of Lagos suited the interests of the British traders based there. It also allowed Abeokuta to be strengthened as the headquarters of mission work. Consequently, the two centers became rivals and were often at cross-purposes, indicating that commerce and civilization might not work to the benefit of Christianity, as conventional wisdom would have it. The alliance with commerce more often hindered than helped missionary work, and vice versa. Lagos epitomized the conflict.[41] Opposed to missions, the traders there saw Crowther as their natural foe and plotted his demise. For his part, Crowther fought valiantly to ensure that commerce was domesticated by antislavery rather than the other way around.

Crowther, meanwhile, was persuaded of the wisdom of proceeding on the Niger in such a way as to advance the general African cause, with due care and caution. In 1857 Onitsha and Igbebe stations were opened, but, following armed conflict, Igbebe was moved in 1866 to Lokoja for better protection. Notwithstanding that development, the pace of establishing new stations continued to pick up in the 1860s, especially in the delta, which had been neglected in the dash to move up stream into neighboring Hausa country.

Crowther was occupied establishing such pioneer mission stations in the Niger Delta, organizing their local administration and support. In 1861 he established a station at Akassa, at the entrance to the River Nun, and three years later he was invited by the local ruler, King William Pepple of Bonny, to open a station at Idah. Pepple's son and successor, George, was educated in England and was a committed Christian. In the same year Bonny was occupied as a mission base. In 1868 Crowther expanded into Brass and Tuwon, and the following year, into Nembe. A mass conversion of the Brass people occurred between 1876 and 1879. On the same east side of the Niger the Kalabari and Okrika kingdoms were penetrated, the Kalabari in 1874, and Okrika in 1879. Domestic slavery flourished in these states. The evangelical doctrine that was so suited to fomenting antislavery also elevated preaching into a primary office, as I noted in Chapter 2. In frontier Africa, however, Crowther made the teaching of the word more important than the preaching of it. In that work local cooperation and sympathetic understanding were indispensable: missions simply could not do without them.

Crowther encountered militant alternatives to his gradualist policy. There was, first, the policy of those we may call cultural prescriptivists, who believed that a ready-made, one-size-fits-all imported template should be imposed on Africans, if need be at the unobtrusive hands of civilized West Indians. Another was the evangelical pietism that, with its gnostic tendencies, eschewed having any truck with worldly arrangements, including indigenous cultures, and trusted instead in the preaching of the word of God to effect the wholesome moral and social transformation necessary for salvation.

The answer Crowther gave to the cultural prescriptivists, the answer, that is, of the need for receptivity to African culture, was similar to the answer he gave to the evangelical pietists. Christianity, he said, did not come into the world to undertake to destroy national cultures. Even where it sought to correct false and oppressive ideas and structures, Christianity must still do so "with due caution and with all meekness of wisdom."[42] The system of mutual aid that might be found in African society should not be condemned or despised but appreciated for the example it offered Christians entering the culture for the first time. Even those aspects of traditional culture that might strike the foreigner as puerile amusements lacking the ideas of the spiritual and the eternal, such amusements as stories, fables, proverbs, and songs, said Crowther, were actually a storehouse of knowledge and original thinking.

Similarly, local religious terms and ceremonies should be carefully observed, because even where such things were improperly made use of, that "does not depreciate their real value, but renders them more valid when we adopt them in expressing Scriptural terms in their right senses and places from which they have been misapplied for want of better knowledge."[43] Crowther had not developed an African Christology— that would have been too much to ask for—but his theological method, based on the new anthropology of indigenous languages, local religions, and social custom, grasped the sources required for such a Christology.

The political implications of this policy of indigenous appropriation were obvious to Crowther's critics. Not only had he abandoned pure evangelical doctrine (one critic followed Crowther around closely and found that when he preached that he made no mention of sin and the atoning sacrifice of Christ), but he was now contending that African culture must set the terms for Christianity. When Crowther made the address just quoted, in 1869 at Lokoja as a public charge to the clergy under his jurisdiction, he was under a Townsend-inspired investigation from the CMS for compromising its missionary warrants. It shows how much Crowther's thinking was modeled on his African experience. Reflecting on the methods and goals of the enterprise in which he was engaged, he said he and his agents must act "as rough quarry men do who hew out blocks of marbles from the quarries, which are conveyed to the workshop to be shaped and finished into perfect figures by the hands of the skilful artists. In like manner, native teachers can do, having the facility of the language in their favour, to induce their heathen countrymen to come within reach of the means of Grace and hear the word of God. What is lacking in good training and sound Evangelical teaching" would be supplied by others more qualified.[44]

Crowther intervened once, in a situation of extreme tension when the priests of the traditional religious rites, the *babalawos,* of Abeokuta banded together in 1848 to resist Christian incursions. A group of catechumens was being prepared for baptism on the day of the Oro festival, and Crowther feared that the converts' withdrawal from the traditional rites would have been taken as a slight. (Oro is the society of collective male ancestors, taboo to women.) He saw the political nature of the ceremonies, a four-night festival, and so counseled Christian restraint to avoid causing needless offense and exposing Christians to greater harm and ill-will than would be justified by the gains to be derived from defiance. In one dramatic story, Crowther entered an Ogboni shrine in Imo township near Abeokuta to find the remains of a human sacrifice, only to be accosted by two men who challenged his right to enter the sacred grounds. (The Ogboni is a political secret society organized in lodges. A reformed Ogboni Fraternity was founded in 1914 to appeal to Christians.) The *Sagbúà,* the township chief, ordered an official inquiry into Crowther's conduct but acquitted him on the grounds "that Crowther had intended no harm by his actions, and that he had been in fact motivated by anxiety for human welfare."[45] The nature of the work he was doing made it inevitable that Crowther would antagonize the guardians of established structure. Yet Crowther's qualities of interfaith statesmanship were nevertheless appreciated even by those whose interests he challenged.

Crowther pursued this idea of conciliation and gradualism with dogged resolve, despite being dragged through a process of ecclesiastical inquiry, in fact through a humiliating public censure. What was at stake was not only Crowther's episcopal authority and honor, for self-preservation had never been his preoccupation, but also the trust of his African agents and their faithful growing flock. He had been accused by the Parent Committee of the Church Missionary Society in London for not taking tough, punitive sanctions against those of his African assistants who had been charged with offenses. Where discipline was called for Crowther offered solicitude. Crowther responded that he preferred trying first admonition, private counseling, temporary suspension, reprimand, and relocation before resorting to final expulsion.

Summoned to England at the same time as the 1888 Lambeth Conference to explain himself, Crowther made representation before the Parent Committee to the same effect, repeating his general view with the aid of an arresting figure. He said a freshly made fire was bound to make a lot of smoke at first, but that if the cook at that early stage decided to pull out all the logs that smoked, the food would never be cooked. Instead, an experienced cook would look for a fan to blow the fire and wait patiently. He continued: "We are all weak and imperfect agents, faulty in one way or another, which need be strengthened, supported, reproved and corrected, when not beyond amendment."[46] Those sentiments would be used against him as proof of indecisiveness and weak leadership. Yet they showed rare maturity and wisdom.

Antislavery and Its New Friends

Just about this time there erupted in mission circles a major intellectual argument that had considerable impact on the moral credibility of antislavery and antistructure. American Presbyterians had opened a mission in Calabar east of the Niger Delta. In 1849 the United Presbyterian Church severed ties with the Presbyterian churches in the United States that tolerated slavery.[47] In 1853 the Presbyterian missionaries in Calabar made a modification of their own to this policy, urging that slave owners not be barred from receiving baptism on the casuistic grounds that the slaves of local slave owners should be considered domestic servants rather than slaves. Such a concession, the missionaries argued, would remove an important obstacle to the growth of the church and at the same time allow the church to introduce gradual reforms in the system. Hugh Goldie used his linguistic knowledge of Efik to argue that the word for slave, *Ofu*, was better translated as servant or tributary; thus sweetened, the term was evidence of there being little difference "between the condition of the master and the slave."[48] But somewhat inconsistently, Goldie argued that Calabar society did not recognize manumission and that those slaves emancipated and brought to the mission stations continued to be regarded by the Efiks as slaves, suggesting the futility of antislavery. Anthropological realism supplied the easier argument needed to budge more difficult theological scruples.

The Presbyterians in America, mired in denominational issues, fell for this argument and for the inverted logic which held that while it was wrong in American Christianity to approve slavery, such was not the case in Calabar, where Christianity had not been firmly enough established to impose Christian rules on the society. Only when Christianity was a significant presence, the missionaries argued, could antislavery become a compelling cause.

Crowther (wonder of wonders!) was also carried by this argument. It appealed to his gradualist, noninterventionist instincts even though it conflicted with the specific terms of his vocation to suppress slavery and the trade that supported it. In writing to the Church Missionary Society, he put as innocent a spin on domestic slavery as he could. "The slaves and masters in this country," he insisted, "live together as a family; they eat out of the same bowl, use the same dress in common and in many instances are intimate companions, so much so that, entering a family circle, a slave can scarcely be distinguished from a free man unless one is told."[49] After making the mandatory theological feints, CMS General Secretary Venn concurred.[50] Both had overlooked the denominational self-interest of the proslavery apologetic and its unreconstructed Protestant view of the social order.

The real effects of such a change of policy took time to show, but one clear implication was the recruitment of chiefs to become important links in the chain of command established for local administration. This change gave rise to the system of warrant chiefs, who stood on one side with the traders and colonial officers. Opposite them were the recaptives, their missionary allies, and the new social forces spawned by the emerging middle class of Bowen's prescription. Warrant chiefs ostensibly conformed to the principle of African leadership, but stripped now of any antislavery scruple. The real question for Crowther, then, was whether he would allow his form of gradualism to merge with that of the humanitarians who wished to civilize Africa in stages by planned economic development and who were accordingly willing to drop the demand for antislavery and the sanctions of evangelical doctrine. Even a charitable answer to that question would test the long-term leadership value of Crowther to the cause of antislavery and antistructure, and challenge his significance for the "Ethiopianism" (the political activism of religious inspiration) of James Johnson and Mojola Agbebi. If Crowther's gradualist allies abandoned him, as they ultimately did, would he be able credibly to turn to the antislavery—and, by that stage, anticolonial—movement? Crowther's dilemma was symptomatic, too, of the transition to the more interventionist policy of the classical empire regarding indigenous customs and institutions. That policy for the most part cultivated chiefs as native authorities and, as a corollary, condoned slavery.

The Native Pastorate and Its Nemesis

In 1851 Henry Venn decided to push ahead with the plan to promote the Africanization of the clergy to create a Native Pastorate. He instructed that two more Africans should be ordained in Abeokuta as soon as the bishop arrived there from Sierra Leone. The two Africans were T. B. Macaulay, trained, like Townsend himself, at the Islington institution, and Theophilus King. Townsend opposed this native policy, saying Africans lacked the stability of character to become anything except schoolmasters and catechists. The placid logical flow of words of objection became a torrent when Townsend learned that the Church Missionary Society was proposing to elevate Abeokuta into an episcopal see and to appoint Crowther to it. Townsend drafted a petition to oppose this plan, obtaining signatories for the purpose. The petition argued that even if Crowther was fit and qualified, his being black tainted him: he would never have the respect and influence worthy of his high office. Native teachers have been received and respected by the chiefs and ordinary people, Townsend maintained, but the ordained office belonged only to the white man. The natives accepted Crowther as a priest only by treating him "as the white man's inferior . . . This state of things is not the result of the white men's teaching but has existed for ages past. The superiority of the white over the black man, the negro has been forward to acknowledge. The correctness of this belief no white man can deny," Townsend concluded triumphantly.[51] In other words, seigneurial tenure was the divine right of whites, and blacks knew that truth, notwithstanding their character defect.

The architect of the CMS mission in Abeokuta, Townsend stepped in to attack the new conception of society in which a recaptive African like Crowther was being given a second chance as leader of the African mission. He said as long as Africa remained what it had always been, no native without a traditional title, rank, or pedigree could command respect and acceptance outside the protective custody of the mission stations, except, that is, as a subordinate agent and servant of the white man. He implicitly rejected the idea of mission as giving former slaves and ex-captives a second chance. Africa had no precedent for it. According to Townsend, there was such endemic jealousy in the culture, such tribal malice and ethnic intolerance, that Crowther's ethnicity would be called into question and damage whatever credibility he had. He implied that the CMS should conspire to conceal Crowther's true identity from his own people, or else reduce him to being a native informant, useful but inferior. Undeterred, Townsend decided the lottery was worth a jackpot, and so he bargained his theological stock. "There is one other view," he said, "that we must not lose sight of, viz., that as the negro feels a great respect for a white man, that God kindly gives a great talent to the white in trust to be used for the negro's good. Shall we shift the responsibility? Can we do it without sin?"[52]

Venn sinned and had Macaulay and King ordained in 1854, to be followed in 1857 by three more ordinations of Africans. In Sierra Leone he proceeded to institute the Native Pastorate and to give it control of the churches in the colony. The work was expanding, more qualified hands were needed and available, and so they were appointed. The Native Pastorate thus moved forward inexorably. Townsend objected. Wherever he could he placed obstacles in the way. He wrote defiantly against giving Africans any idea that they could transcend their inferiority. As Jacob Ajayi so well put it, Townsend felt he had proved the superiority of one race over the other by arguing to keep the worst of the one over the best of the other. The Parent Committee of the CMS felt compelled to admonish Townsend that the tone and manner of his letters were unworthy of his vocation. Townsend's only advantage, and a critical one at that, was the appeal of his racial views among all the white missionaries at the time, as the CMS found out when it asked directly which of them would be willing to serve under Crowther. It was a disconcerting discovery. Some arguments Townsend won, not from theological veracity but from sentiments of white superiority or by threatening local discord. His tactics were those of direct action, not of theological proofs or moral suasion.

We may ask, had the CMS done right by Townsend? Much, indeed, could be said for him given his role in the Yoruba mission.[53] As the driving force behind the Abeokuta mission he was entitled at least to a share of the responsibility for directing CMS work in Nigeria. Venn's policy of native agency, Townsend would be right to feel, unjustly deprived him of the power to which in other circumstances he would have acceded quite naturally. Yet power, whether ecclesiastical or political, is not a natural right but a responsibility exercised with the agreement and support of those concerned. Therefore, Townsend's sense of entitlement gave the impression he would take autocratic power with the same sense of natural right. That troubled Venn, and, accordingly, he wrote to Crowther commending him for keeping the peace, promoting harmony and reconciliation, and showing real wisdom and humility amid all the bickering, ugliness of spirit, and struggle for power.[54]

Whereas Townsend tried to make an invidious distinction between the Yoruba mission and the Niger Mission, giving equal weight to each, Venn ruled otherwise, making the Yoruba mission an extension of the Niger Mission and vesting authority for both in Crowther—at least initially. Venn asserted this view several times, presumably because Crowther was mindful of not stepping on Townsend's toes. In fact, Crowther responded to Venn by saying the time was near when he should retire from the Niger Mission altogether and be allowed to pursue his linguistic work and the translation projects that had suffered neglect on account of the heavy demands of administering stations on the Niger. When the time was right, Crowther pleaded, "I should like to spend the remainder of my days among my own people, pursuing my translations as my bequest to the nation."[55] Venn would not hear of it. He thought Crowther would make an excellent bishop to run the Niger Mission and thus to complete the process whereby indigenous leadership would assume full responsibility for the cause. Crowther was sincere when he asked to be relieved of the work, but Venn preempted him by speaking equally sincerely of the mission's continuing need for Crowther. In this context, however, the office of missionary bishop that Venn suggested was odd, for it repudiated native leadership. If you establish a missionary or colonial bishop, then you must abandon a native episcopacy except as a suffragan office. Yet Venn repeated that he was committed to the strategy of there emerging "a native Church." He would have sensed by now the painful contradictions.

Martin Delany: Anatomy of a Cause

Then, unexpectedly and fatefully, the American factor intervened to pack the fuse, to Townsend's apparent advantage. Dr. Martin Delany (1802–1888), who had organized a colonization movement among African Americans in the United States and Canada, and Robert Campbell, a Jamaican printer, arrived in Abeokuta under the aegis of the African Aid Society, created by cotton manufacturers in England with the aim of assisting African Americans to return to Africa. Delany had been active in journalism in Philadelphia and in Rochester, New York, campaigning actively between 1836 and 1849 for antislavery. He was for a time associated with Frederick Douglass, the famous black antislavery activist, though Douglass was opposed to black emigration.

The passage of the U.S. Fugitive Slave Act of 1850 proved a turning point, however. Until then Delany believed that African Americans stood a chance of improving their situation in the United States, provided they applied themselves. Consequently, he saw emigration to Africa as a distraction from domestic reform. The act changed all that, for it made clear to him personally, he said, that African Americans were locked in what he called "a prejudice of caste."[56] To fortify himself accordingly, he entered Harvard Medical School in the autumn of 1850, sponsored, along with two other African Americans, by the Massachusetts Colonization Society. But in the winter of 1851 he and his companions were sent down from Harvard following a racially motivated petition for their dismissal. That experience disillusioned and embittered him. In April 1852 he wrote a book about the experience called *The Condition, Elevation, Emigration, and Destiny of the Colored People of the United States, Politically*

Considered. In it he argued for emigration as the solution to the U.S. black question. It was an early form of the Back-to-Africa movement promoted by Marcus Garvey in the 1920s and 1930s.

In 1858 he launched a grandiose scheme called the Niger Valley Exploring Party, inspired by the stories of David Livingstone and Thomas Bowen. It was a scheme that would take the notion of African leadership a bold step forward. At about the same time a Yoruba movement among African Americans in New York City was campaigning for emigration to Yoruba country and Lagos. The cause was taken up by the *Christian Intelligencer,* a publication of the Dutch Reformed Church. Delany began a recruitment drive in which he succeeded in obtaining many volunteers, finally embarking for West Africa with forty-four passengers and arriving at Cape Palmas, Liberia, in July 1859.

There Delany met Edward Blyden, who wound up singing Delany's praises, saying Delany would be the "Moses to lead the exodus of his people from the house of bondage to land flowing with milk and honey. He seems to have many qualifications for the task. Let him be encouraged and supported," Blyden urged.[57] But Liberia depressed Delany. Besides, he rejected any religious role for himself, a decision that handicapped him unduly, given the prominent role religion played in African American life. The fact that even Blyden could conceive of him only in religious terms shows what a distance Delany himself would had to have traveled to attain his objectives.

In any case, undaunted, Delany pressed on to Lagos, about which he wrote effusively, "This is the great outlet of the rich valley of the Niger by land, and the only point of the ocean upon which the intelligent and advanced Yorubas are settled." Lagos, he boasted, "must not only become the outlet and point at which all this commodity must centre, but the great metropolis of this quarter of the world."[58] He was confident, he said, that Lagos "is destined to be the great black metropolis of the world."[59] From Lagos he journeyed to Abeokuta, where, at last, his path crossed that of Crowther and Townsend. Delany promoted a scheme, with support of the African Aid Society in Britain, for growing cotton in Nigeria, saying the country and the people were suited for it, which was far from the truth. Cotton originated in Persia and was ill suited to the tropical climate of Nigeria. Furthermore, it was the shop and the school, not the plough or the shed, that brought recaptives the wealth and influence they sought.

Delany described the advancements he saw as part of the new society being created in Africa, a society developing as a successful alternative to the oppressive and obstructive chiefly establishment.

> I have not as yet visited a missionary station in any part of Africa, where there were not some, and frequently many natives, both adult and children, who could speak, read, and write English, as well as read their own language; as all of them, whether Episcopalian, Wesleyan [Methodist], Baptist, or Presbyterian, in the Yoruba country, have Crowther's editions of religious and secular books in the schools and churches, and all have native agents, interpreters, teachers (assistants) and catechists or readers in the mission. These facts prove great progress . . . Both male and female missionaries, all seemed much devoted to their work, and anxiously desirous of doing more. Indeed, the very fact of there being as many native missionaries as there are now to be found holding responsible positions, as elders, deacons, preachers, and priests, among whom there are many finely educated, and several of them authors of works, not only in their own but the English language, as Revs. [Samuel Ajayi] Crowther, [Theophilus] King, [John Christopher] Taylor, and Samuel Crowther [junior], Esq., surgeon, all show that there is an advancement for these people beyond the point to which missionary duty can carry them.[60]

Delany's observations show that he understood the significance of developing indigenous leadership to advance the gains of antislavery, and the role of missions in that, which was the heart of Crowther's work. Yet, without realizing it, Delany had also wandered into a sticky patch. He was religiously too tone-deaf to pick up vital signals in Lagos or elsewhere about what he was getting himself into. The white missionaries complained that Delany and Campbell had not discussed with them their settlement plans, which involved a treaty reputedly signed on 27 December 1859 for a settlement of blacks "on land of their own purchase," which even Crowther belatedly felt was ill-advised.[61] An 1861 revised version of the treaty put matters differently, saying, "The king and chiefs on their part, agree to grant land and assign unto the said Commissioners on behalf of the African race in America, the right and privileges of settling in common with the Egba people, on any part of the territory belonging to Abbeokutta [sic], not otherwise occupied."[62] Samuel, the eldest son of Crowther, who attached his signature to the treaty as a witness, with his father attesting it, said the wording was amended still further to refer only to "the right and privilege of farming in common with the Egba people and of building their houses and residing in the town of Abeokuta, intermingling with the population."[63] The numerous changes being made to Delany and Campbell's treaty reflected the bitterness of the controversy surrounding it.

The veteran Sir Richard Burton, who was visiting Abeokuta in 1861, described the treaty as an infringement on the authority of the *alake* and his associate chiefs. He said the treaty would create an *imperium in imperio,* "bringing into the country a wholly irresponsible race . . . Moreover, though signed by eight names, of whom half had died before the end of 1861, it was never submitted to the greater chiefs and to the Ogboni lodges, or Upper and Lower Houses of the land, and it degrades the people because it places their freedom in the hands of a king and a few chiefs."[64]

At the root of Burton's criticism of the treaty was his hostility to the American nature of it, something that offended his notion of Britain's unique imperial mandate, which he thought sensible African rulers shared or jolly well ought to. He said while the *alake* and chiefs were ready to admit settlers subject to the British authorities at Lagos and amenable to English law, they were not disposed to extend the same treatment to "irresponsible adventurers" from America. The idea of such resettlement, Burton alleged, could be traced to an earlier proposal Abraham Lincoln had put forward. Lincoln's scheme had "proposed shunting off his spare contrabands into the Republics of Central America, who, as might be expected, gratefully declined the boon, declaring, like the Abeokutans, that they are ready to receive emigrants of every colour, but not those who appear as an independent power."[65] With characteristic pugnaciousness, Burton scorned the treaty, saying it was "sublime in its impudence."[66]

Townsend, whom Burton met and emboldened with his support, turned on the Americans. He echoed Burton, criticizing Delany and Campbell's scheme as a subversive move calculated to injure the interests of the mission, and wrote to Venn in those terms. The association of the two Crowthers with it, he insinuated, proved a certain malice on their part. The settlement scheme would in fact form an irresponsible state-within-a-state, as Burton said, and would thereby threaten the safety and security of the Egba state. Townsend alluded to Delany's secular agenda,[67] saying Delany and his allies were proposing to taint the Christian colony with a wayward heathenism that prostituted the name of Christianity.

The Crowthers, being Oyo Yoruba but not Egba, had dug themselves into a big hole, and Townsend was determined to have them figuratively buried in it. He indicated to the *alake* of Abeokuta that with Delany and Campbell the Crowthers had connived to cheat them out of their land and inheritance. Many of the chiefs and local elders were angry, too, "and were seized with violent indignation," in Burton's words, that they had never been consulted. The *alake* appropriately reneged on the treaty, saying he would now listen only to the British authorities and the missionaries. Townsend had provoked major discontent, and such was the fury that Samuel had to flee for his life, leaving Abeokuta in February 1861. The Foreign Office asked the African Aid Society to leave Nigeria and look elsewhere.

The episode was an ignominious personal rout for Crowther and a blow to his goals for assuming a leadership role in the grander mission of which Abeokuta was a key part. It was, at the same time, a public triumph for Townsend. Yet the episode also left Abeokuta deeply divided between Townsend, on the one hand, and the emigrants, on the other, who reacted in the strongest possible terms to Townsend's assault on Crowther. Townsend and Samuel Crowther Jr. were recalled to London in an attempt to effect a reconciliation. In the meantime Britain abandoned its Abeokuta policy and annexed Lagos, much to Venn's disappointment and to Townsend's alarm. With his power base at Abeokuta, Townsend knew that the rise of Lagos would eclipse him and shift the ground from under him, unless he flowed with the tide and attached himself to Lagos. It would also divide Christianity's material interests from its spiritual interests. Townsend returned to Abeokuta in March 1862 and tried gallantly with conciliatory overtures to Lagos to prevent a rival authority from being set up there, but to no avail. And so the flames he fanned to bring down the Crowthers in Abeokuta ended up scorching him, too, such being the undiscriminating logic of historical reversals.

Perhaps without realizing the full political implications for mission of the annexation of Lagos, or what separatist twist annexation would give to Townsend's ambitions, Venn went ahead and authorized the consecration of Crowther as bishop in June 1864. What exactly he was bishop of was never made clear, perhaps because the CMS was torn between the pressure of the traders and its own missionary concerns. In the meantime Townsend was stirring himself to restore the authority of the white man, confiding in a missionary friend in London about the lamentable loss of white prestige. In January 1864 he announced that the impending plans to consecrate Crowther were misguided and potentially divisive, an opinion expressed in a way calculated to carry a whiff of threat. He said so to Venn, too, even after the fact. Crowther, Townsend uttered with one part of his mouth, was too partisan and obnoxious, too deeply marked with the captive's chain, to be esteemed with respect in native society or to be acceptable to the chiefs and people. But, with the other part of his mouth, Townsend avowed he was unwilling to place himself under the episcopal rule of Crowther because Crowther "is too much a native."[68] Townsend instead advocated appointing a white missionary or a colonial bishop with jurisdiction over white religious personnel, in other words stripping Crowther of his leadership role and relegating him to the African hinterland. Venn rejected that approach as totally unacceptable to the British government. Townsend was left with two alternatives: secession from the Crowther-led wing of the CMS, or a modification of that move with the promotion (and incitement) of Lagos as a rival personal base.

Crowther's episcopacy was compromised by the kind of ideological opposition Townsend mounted and by the halfhearted definition the CMS gave to the diocesan boundaries in question. In one regard and as Townsend intended, the CMS ruled that Crowther would not have jurisdiction over Abeokuta, Ibadan, or Lagos, the areas with white missionary concentration. Instead, his diocese would include stations of the Yoruba mission outside the European sphere. This anomalous arrangement was made even more so with Crowther being headquartered in Lagos. Townsend derided him as an absentee bishop, intending to drive him from Lagos, which, in any case, was hostile to Crowther for its own commercial reasons.

Debacle

The Church Missionary Society in London adopted the mood of opponents of the Native Pastorate policy as formulated by Henry Venn for the Niger Mission, a policy that had as its central premise African leadership. In particular the Lagos-based traders saw the mission as an obstacle to their control of the riverain channel, and so they campaigned for its removal or, failing that, its drastic curtailing. The occasion to intervene presented itself when Crowther obtained possession of a steamer named the *Henry Venn*, donated by his admirers in England. Crowther decided to place the ship in the hands of an African merchant, with the idea of trading on the Niger and contributing its profits to mission work. But the new society secretary, T. J. Hutchinson, countermanded Crowther on the matter and gave control of the ship to J. H. Ashcroft, a layman, and one James Kirk. Hutchinson went further by asking Ashcroft and Kirk to assume authority for all the African agents of the Niger Mission, in effect demoting Bishop Crowther without his knowledge or consent.

A Commission of Inquiry was then set up under J. B. Wood. The inquiry was a direct response to complaints by European traders that the African assistants of Crowther were venturing out into commercial work and neglecting spiritual concerns. Innocently, Crowther asked his assistants to cooperate fully with Wood, who arrived to begin investigations. It did not take long for Wood to produce his report. It was a hatchet job, highly damaging to Crowther and the mission and libelous to the extent that it was secreted out to London without Crowther or any of his assistants getting a glimpse of it. Wood requested that Crowther never see it. Crowther learned of the contents of the report only when bits and pieces drifted back to Nigeria, spread there by Lagos-based traders and visitors keen to be rid of the religious nuisance Crowther was deemed to be.

The charges and allegations in the report had a serious impact on CMS morale in London, leading to widespread and open doubts about the wisdom of continuing with the African apostolate. It was in this highly wrought context that Wood finalized his report and filed it under classified cover. The CMS decided to mount a full-scale ecclesiastical trial of Crowther's people.

The commission sat in Onitsha, in August 1890. Its secretary was the Reverend F. N. Eden, a young Cambridge graduate in his early thirties. Crowther, then aged over eighty, was chairman, though in that position he was constantly overruled by Eden. Crowther felt troubled by the all too apparent anomaly of a junior priest exercising veto power in his episcopal jurisdiction. This anomaly can be explained only by the growing demand in the CMS to remove Crowther and replace him with a European.

Crowther long understood in no uncertain terms the nature of what was afoot. It was, he argued, the conflict between the old Native Pastorate policy of putting Africans in charge and the new missionary policy of transferring authority to Europeans. Crowther wrote in November 1868 with uncanny prescience and characteristic acuity that it was "like the meeting of two tides till one entirely submerges into the other when there would be an easy and regular flow in one direction."[69]

It was time to choose that direction. Twelve of the fifteen Africans in the Niger Mission were summarily dismissed at the commission's hearings, largely as the result of Eden's sole decision. It was all Crowther could do to contain himself as he watched powerlessly. For the sake of the record, he challenged the secretary of the commission to say whether he "alone is empowered to dismiss and suspend and do everything in the Mission . . . Will you write down, say, please, Bishop Crowther expresses surprise at the statement of the Secretary that he has power as the representative of the C.M.S. to suspend any clergyman from his duty."[70] Eden responded by reprimanding Crowther for defending the censured pastors, charging him with conduct unworthy of his sacred office. Crowther was dismissed from the commission. He died on 31 December 1891.

Reaction and Resistance

During the years of turmoil, beginning with the Commission of Inquiry set up in 1880 and continuing into 1891, Africans had watched with dismay as the Church Missionary Society, pressured by the Niger Company, allowed the props to be pulled from underneath the Niger Mission. The Nigerian Baptists, spiritual heirs to Bowen, were among the first to react. The path was cleared for them by the temporary withdrawal of Southern Baptist missionaries during the American Civil War, so that by the time the missionaries were able to resume work in the 1870s, local Baptists had assumed control of the mission. Although there was at that stage no breakaway movement among the Baptists, the scene was ready for one, lacking only a *casus belli*. That was supplied when African leaders in the Baptist Church, at first encouraged by evidence of the support the CMS was giving to the idea of a Native Pastorate, grew dismayed at the treatment of Crowther and his assistants. The local Baptists experienced a reawakened mistrust of missionary direction. As one African leader declared, the Africans did not lose sight of the irony that the American Civil War, which achieved the liberation of slaves in America, had also advanced the cause of self-reliance and self-support among the African churches. Baptist evangelical teaching in any case does not have a strong ecclesiology, emphasizing instead congregational autonomy and local independence. Accordingly, in March 1888 a group of them split off to form the Native Baptist Church, taking with them all the great African pioneers of Baptist work in Nigeria. The Baptist secession "ushered in a new era of Christianity among the Yoruba. A spell had been broken,"[71] and secession now had an encouraging precedent and could, therefore, be adopted with assured impact.

The Southern Baptists tried to answer the African secessionists with a demonstration of superior financial resources by undertaking prestige projects that would show Africans where real power lay. As a consequence, the Americans built the Baptist Academy in Lagos in 1883. They also built a large church in the center of Lagos. In response, the Africans charged that the missionaries were contravening the very rules and procedures they themselves had laid down for running and maintaining congregations and stated that Africans would not be cowed into submission by the display of financial and material wealth. Furthermore, they would not be stampeded into a barracoon, a reference to the new church the Baptist missionaries had just completed. Such missionary measures inflamed secessionist passions.

In December 1890 Dr. Edward Blyden arrived in Lagos from Freetown, calling for the establishment of a quasi-political religious organization, which he called the West African Church. It was established in March 1891 but modeled too closely after the secular program of someone like Delany to stand much chance of carrying even the disaffected elements within the mission churches. The reason was that African cultural roots resonated more easily with Christianity's spiritual message than with the progressive secularism of the West. Notwithstanding that fact, the creation of the West African Church proved that a great intellectual ferment had been stirred among Africans.

The telling response to Crowther's displacement came in August 1891, when a resolution was adopted as the foundation statement of the United Native African Church (UNAC). The statement affirmed

> that Africa is to be evangelized and that foreign agencies at work at the present moment taking into consideration climatic and other influences cannot grasp the situation; resolved that a purely Native African Church be founded for the evangelization and amelioration of our race, to be governed by Africans.[72]

Eventually the Africans' response led to their establishing in 1892 an independent Niger Delta Pastorate (NDP), staffing it themselves and launching a major fund-raising drive to underwrite it. Five of those dismissed by Eden joined it as leaders, keeping alive the flame Venn lit with his plan for native Christian leadership. Repercussions were felt across West Africa and beyond.

Like all pathfinders, however, both the NDP and the UNAC were laying only a modest trail, the limited trail, that is, of qualified administrative independence of denominational missions. So close to the turmoil of the Niger Mission, the NDP and the UNAC saw matters only in the narrow frame of the machinery of denominational control, which they wanted to put into African hands in order to deal with the immediate grievances produced by the Crowther debacle. The NDP and the UNAC conserved the Anglican forms of worship and liturgy, retained the staid dignity of the hymns of Isaac Watts, and kept as close to Thomas Cranmer as was credible in the richly textured vernacular. Thus, in translation the supple Yoruba and Igbo absorbed with little awkwardness the angles, points, flowing cadence, liquid lines, and nasal sounds of the devout English masters.

The larger and much bolder question of freeing evangelical doctrine from denominationalism, and of the indigenous theological adaptation that Crowther had done so much to pioneer with his linguistic and ethnographic work, was left to others to pursue. This became the supreme domain of African independent churches, those charismatic and Pentecostal revival movements that rocked the landscape with their music, dance, healing, and prophetic pronouncements, much in the manner of settler and recaptive preaching, testimony, and prayer. These churches, powered by mass popular response, scrambled the structured symmetry of the book of offices and infused their own warmhearted spirit into it. Their bold style clashed with the sedate manner of their more restrained counterparts in the NDP and the UNAC. But their story, with its striking American connections and parallels, comes into its own only in the second decade of the twentieth century (and is thus beyond the scope of this book).

The Niger Mission needs to be seen in historical context rather than as a page in the annals of patriotic struggle. The mission illuminates a deeper antislavery logic than one that portrays the debacle as mere cannon fodder for patriotic fury. Andrew Walls describes the general historical background and context of that debacle, observing that

> European thought about Africa had changed . . . the Western powers
> were now in Africa to govern. Missionary thought about Africa had

changed since the days of Henry Venn; there were plenty of keen, young Englishmen to extend the mission and order the church; a self-governing church had now seemed to matter much less. And evangelical religion had changed since Crowther's conversion; it had become more individualistic and more otherworldly. A young English missionary was distressed that the old bishop who preached so splendidly on the blood of Christ could urge on a chief the advantages of having a school and make no reference to the future life.[73]

Yet by committing itself to the pivotal challenge of antislavery, the Niger Mission awakened forces that could not be suppressed. It was in the name of that antislavery cause that Crowther as a recaptive was commissioned as a strategic leader, a cause for which it was deemed right and proper to defy opposition in London and assume the risk of entering Nigeria. In the final analysis, however, the Niger Mission threatened to subvert the very end it existed to promote.

Yet the mission, having committed itself to recaptive leadership as being decisive for African credibility, formulating its goals and methods principally to promote Crowther's personal authority and influence, could not with impunity abandon that policy and retreat. Consequently, its debacle was more than just a sad anecdote of missionary high-handedness, without relevance to the historical antislavery movement. In conception and design the mission was intended, as Bowen said, to promote the forces of progressive destiny, to advance the cause of moral reform, social reconstruction, productive enterprise, and mutual support, with local agents assuming personal responsibility for the cause. Its mandate was to put an end to the slave trade and to teach victim populations to avenge themselves justly on their exploiters, both African and European, by becoming free and useful. In the words of Wadström, the success of antislavery required not just the intervention of Europe but a decisive moral change in the self-understanding of slave and captive populations themselves, so that they would "feel the nobility of their origin, and shew them of what great things they are capable." From that moral consciousness Africans would be empowered "no longer to suffer themselves to be dragged, or to conspire to drag others, from their simple, but improvable and beloved societies—which will teach them to avenge themselves on the blind and sordid men who purchase them, only by becoming more useful to them as freemen, than ever they have been, or can be."[74] Wadström's "nobility," on which slavery trampled, was what evangelical religion seized on to propound antislavery and to institute in Africa a social revolution against oppressive slave structures. Antislavery and antistructure were thus two sides of the same coin.

In that context, Crowther's leadership was a suitable symbol of the new beginning and new dispensation. In that context, too, the Niger Mission can be seen to fit into a much broader antislavery perspective. The place of the Church Missionary Society as an evangelical, ecumenical, and international movement within that broader historical perspective merits a special word. A new world order came into being in Africa, not by military might but by belief in the power of redeemed and sanctified persons who as slaves, captives, and other downtrodden members of society the chiefly structures exploited and repressed, and yet whose freedom, dignity, and enterprise evangelical religion championed as its own.

Thus, the small trickle started in 1837 by two Hausa ex-slaves coming from Trinidad to Freetown and finally to Badagry grew into the checkered movement that opened up Nigeria to antislavery and much else besides. A major change took place in Nigeria on account of it. Jacob Ajayi reflects on this broader historical perspective and argues that the importance of the recaptive emigrants in Nigerian history was out of all proportion to their number. The missionary movement they led kept them a cohesive, self-motivated group and focused them on a few strategic centers. Had they been scattered, each left to pursue his or her own personal interest and inclination, their impact would have been diluted and their legacy weakened. As it was, traders, catechists, evangelists, and schoolmasters found themselves bound together by the same purpose and united in the same enterprise. It was they who brought the cause to Nigeria and they who remained indispensable to its future success.[75] In spite of painful missionary reversal and colonial suppression, the recaptives' achievement was considerable, for Nigeria as well as for the tradition of evangelical social activism. The denominations that entered the field were deeply affected by the stress on social justice that had been the hallmark of recaptive Christianity, and when colonial rule intervened between Christianity and its social agenda,[76] African Christianity turned to protest and resistance to free itself from "Europeandom" and to maintain its evangelical social roots. It was a just and fitting outcome for antislavery and antistructure.[77]

5

American Colonization and the Founding of Liberia

We saw in Chapter 1 how Thomas Jefferson appealed to the classics on the matter of slavery, warning Americans about embarking on emancipation without considering the wider issue of racial mixing. He argued that while the Romans could deal with the problem of slavery with the simple step of emancipation, Americans needed to take a further step. When the Romans freed the slave, they allowed him or her to mix with the rest of society without the risk of racial unrest. Americans, by contrast, could not follow that example, for an interracial society for them was out of the question. Consequently, antislavery must be qualified by racial separation through deportation. Racial difference, which justified black slavery, would not disappear with emancipation but be exacerbated by it. Intolerance, discrimination, and prejudice had an objective foundation in genetic type and could not be dismissed by a simple wave of the magistrate's magic wand. Slavery and race thus made a fateful combination in the new world.

The clamorous ideals of northern abolitionists, which would later crystallize in William Lloyd Garrison's manifesto of 1831 calling for total and immediate emancipation,[1] and the swelling silent forebodings of southern slaveholders warned of the dangers of ill-conceived and precipitate action on the matter lest the teeming and restive slave populations, with energy and grievance on their side, erupt in violence and destruction. As blacks could never become the equals of whites, emancipation would only enlarge their ranks as the enemies of whites. Americans had to contemplate with dry eyes the issues at stake. The recognized evil of slavery could not be remedied with the unrecognized peril of white-black racial strife. Slavery had been sustained within the reasonable bounds of a stable, workable society, but emancipation would uncap sudden and unforeseen forces too menacing to be reconcilable with a well-ordered society, with a society that was not, admittedly, perfectly just, but was not, at the same time, perfectly iniquitous. The slaves who had been socialized to forsake their appetite for freedom would, under emancipation, acquire the violent temper to rise and smash the bonds of their inferiority. Emancipation would make a utopian moral grievance the license for unparalleled social mischief. It would incite wickedness more damaging than the injustice of the slavery it would remedy. While it was clear that slavery would end, Americans had to control how that happened.

With the path of successful assimilation into white society foreclosed by racial difference, slavery had to end by conceding the ground to racial separation. Thus, to return to the opening point of this chapter, Jefferson concluded that while emancipation must be granted to the slave, "When freed, [the slave] is to be removed beyond the reach of mixture."[2] But how, when, or where, he did not say. While Jefferson was short on the political heavy lifting required to bring about the change he wished to see, he was long on his philosophical justifications, as we saw earlier. "Nothing," he asserted, "is more certainly written in the book of fate, than that these people are to be free; nor is it less certain that the two races, equally free, cannot live in the same government. Nature, habit, opinion have drawn indelible lines of distinction between them. It is still in our power to direct the process of emancipation and deportation, peaceably, and in such slow degree, as that the evil will wear off insensibly, and their place be, *pari passu*, filled up by free white laborers."[3]

Colonization Sentiments

These sentiments were the intellectual background to the founding of the American Colonization Society. In 1790 Ferdinando Fairfax, sharing Jefferson's view that a biracial society in America was impossible, proposed that Congress acquire a colony in Africa and send free blacks there. The existence of such a colony would itself induce white slave owners to manumit their slaves without fear of being overwhelmed by what Jefferson called "a revolution in the wheel of fortune." According to Fairfax, an African colony would be in the native climate for blacks and would be far enough away to forestall violence and hostility between the races. Furthermore, American blacks could carry Christianity with them to civilize Africa's primitive tribesmen, thus solving a domestic social menace with moral benefit abroad. Eventually, American traders and merchants would be able to obtain profits in a tropical colony ruled by America, profits that would more than compensate for the cost and investment of establishing a settlement there.

St. George Tucker, professor of law at the College of William and Mary, was an outspoken critic of slavery, but he was also an advocate of racial separation, saying in 1796 that black slaves after emancipation should not be allowed to remain in the United States, where they would become "the caterpillars of the earth, and the tigers of the human race." But Tucker disagreed with Jefferson about the role of the federal government in sponsoring such a free colony in Africa. It simply was not feasible, with expenses and difficulties too great to overcome. Instead, Tucker preferred that the estimated 300,000 slaves in question emigrate voluntarily and in small enough numbers to avoid the problems of sudden mass deportation with its risks of death by famine, disease, and other accumulated miseries. He concurred with the views of James Sullivan, governor of Massachusetts, who contemplated the mass deportation of blacks as something fraught with gloomy prospects, adding, "We have in history but one picture of a similar enterprise, and there we see it was necessary not only to open the sea by a miracle, for them to pass, but more necessary to close it again, in order to prevent their return."[4] Not given to trust in miracles, Tucker was instead inclined to look toward the Louisiana Purchase of 1803 and the vastly improved territorial possibilities it offered the new republic. Perhaps blacks could be resettled in a small corner in lower Louisiana, where the climate was more agreeable to the African constitution. If such a colony succeeded it would perforce make a favorable impression on the slave states and lead them to relax the laws against manumission, knowing freed slaves would flock there. Whatever the case, Tucker was persuaded that while slavery must be abolished, freed slaves must be removed rather than allowed to live cheek by jowl with whites in America.[5]

A Quaker voice was added to the debate when John Parrish, a Quaker from Philadelphia, argued in favor of Jefferson's plan of emancipation and deportation, recommending that Congress set aside a portion of the western wilderness for establishing black homesteads and attracting to them free Negroes. White slave owners, otherwise determined to hold on to their slaves for fear that slaves so freed would stop at nothing to exact retribution, would be persuaded to manumit their slaves as long as removal was a prerequisite. Parrish reasoned that, divested of what he called "this dreadful evil," America could then enjoy "that sabbath which is prepared for all those who do justly, love mercy, and walk humbly with their God,"[6] citing the reference from the prophet Micah (6:8).

In 1801–1802 the Virginia House of Delegates debated the creation of a penal colony for rebellious slaves and free Negro criminals. The debate was fueled by the abortive Gabriel slave insurrection near Richmond in 1800, prompting worried legislators to run the penal colony idea by the governor, James Monroe, who considered it a more humane alternative to capital punishment, the other option. But the Virginia House took no action, and the proposal was allowed to lapse.

As noted in Chapter 1, Samuel Hopkins of Rhode Island and Ezra Stiles of Connecticut were also involved in a scheme to repatriate trained blacks as missionaries to Africa. Hopkins, a New England New Light divine and a disciple of Jonathan Edwards (the New England founder of the Great Awakening), wished to prove his doctrine of dynamic evangelical Calvinism and its missionary principle of carrying the gospel to the unredeemed of the world. (In 1773, when Hopkins was promoting his missionary plan, the idea of mission was still undeveloped in modern Protestantism. At the time there was not a single missionary in Africa. Hopkins's minority theological position thus shows how the intellectual fringes of the religious establishment would provide the impetus for effecting the major missionary transformation of mainline Protestantism in the late eighteenth and early nineteenth centuries.)

Commercial Motives: Purse and Principle

The outbreak of the American Revolution interrupted the plans of Hopkins and Stiles. But after the Revolution Hopkins merged the remnants of his missionary plan with the much larger colonization plan of the wealthy English Quaker William Thornton, who was visiting America at the time and charming his way through high society in New York City. Thornton's widely noted lavish sartorial habits—involving powdered wigs, silver buckles, and other bits of showy finery—earned him the unflattering epithet "wet Quaker." His gregariousness sat poorly with the dour image and studied modesty of old-fashioned Quakers. In political background Thornton was a humanitarian, a pragmatic human rights activist who balanced his commitment to antislavery with preservation of his investments. His was a case of the welfare of general humanity being first and best served by self-interest.

The opportunity to demonstrate such a humanitarian commitment presented itself in 1785, when Thornton unexpectedly inherited a large number of slaves in the West Indies. Thornton's plan was to dispose of his slaves and be rid of a moral burden but to do so profitably. Consequently, he considered establishing a colony of such slaves either in the West Indies or in Africa, where the slaves would labor and from their accumulated earnings pay for their freedom. The West Indian authorities discouraged the plan for fear that a free colony would incite adjacent slave populations to insurrection.

With the West Indian option ruled out, Thornton was left with the West African alternative, in which connection he met Hopkins.[7] Hopkins's idea of a religiously based free colony of blacks appealed to what remained of Thornton's Quaker conviction. Such a colony would provide examples of the value of industry, morality, and good behavior. A shrewd businessman, Thornton set out to appeal to prevailing American ideas of emancipation and deportation, calculating that America would make a difference to the success of such a settlement scheme in West Africa and, therefore, to his own considerable investment in it. He thus played on the dual Jeffersonian theme of emancipation and deportation, avowing he was convinced that emancipation was desirable but aware that free blacks had no permanent place in American society—"there could be no sincere union between blacks and whites," he asserted. Thornton toured in New York, Boston, Providence, and Newport, preaching the virtues of African colonization with himself as benevolent benefactor. Of such free blacks he said, "I think by proper laws they may be made a good and happy people. The minds of many Africans," he persisted, "are ripe, and their understanding clear." They would flourish in a colony where "their own laws are alone to be regarded . . . and where a man that Nature cloathed [sic] with a white skin, shall not, merely on that account, have the right of wielding a rod of iron."[8]

Thornton's pragmatic commercial sense guided his idea of antislavery. Wealth and profit were allies of right and virtue. A free colony of blacks in West Africa could be made profitable by honest industry and use its wealth to drive the slave traders out of business. Wealth creation was the remedy for injustice, inequality, and inhumanity, and the source of all desirable virtues. Human rights would flourish or wither by that rule alone, but so also would the peace and tranquillity of American society. An industrious and prosperous black colony in Africa, appropriately Christianized and hitched to the free enterprise locomotive, would repay the investment in black ransom and repatriation, undercut the slave trade, create an abundant and alternative source of tropical goods for Western enterprise, and reconcile blacks to ungrudging coexistence with white members of what had been the master race. "By proper encouragement and perseverance, a most valuable country would soon become the seat of commerce, of arts and the manufactures, of plenty, of peace, and happiness," Thornton claimed.[9]

The Americans were not persuaded, and the Massachusetts legislature declined to vote money for a colonization scheme not based in America. France, which Thornton also approached, turned down the project, too. For their part, British philanthropists thought the plan rash and undeveloped, and, with a veiled rebuke, advised Thornton to think of more prudent ways to manage his inheritance rather than being consumed in visionary schemes. One close associate said Thornton's imagination had produced a moral perfection of government that was just as impracticable.

The Humanitarian Motive and the Evangelical Impulse

Historians have demonstrated the connection between, on the one hand, the rise of benevolent societies and the evangelical awakening and, on the other, the antislavery movement. In the examples of Samuel Hopkins and Ezra Stiles, for instance, we see this evangelical connection at work. Yet, as the nineteenth-century American evangelist Charles Finney pointed out, revival religion was not so much a miracle, not so much an antinomian retreat into self-exile, as an example of applied religion, as the robust employment of means, methods, and tools designed for maximum tangible result. Thus, revival religion only partly looked to spirit-filled awakenings and zealous charismatic outpourings. It was characterized not by the flamboyant possessions and tear-drenched, emotion-gripped testimonies of faith and deliverance but rather by mass mobilization and the growth and proliferation of voluntary associations, such as Bible and Sunday schools, missionary commit-tees, lay leaders, and women's groups, all of them spin-offs of large, community-style congregations thriving on detailed planning, voluntary giving, and organized fund-raising. In few other places can we observe a more authentic expression of American national culture than in the ethos of the evangelical movement, a movement that would part company with an unreconstructed Protestantism and its repudiation of missionary evangelism as something too Roman Catholic.[10] We have by virtue of the evangelical movement such institutions as the American Bible Society, which by the 1830s could claim 645 auxiliaries, the American Sunday School Union, the American Tract Society, the American Peace Society, the American Temperance Union, the American Board of Commissioners for Foreign Missions, the American Education Society, the Marine Bible Society, the American Home Missionary Society, the American Seamen's Friend Society, and the American Society for Meliorating the Condition of the Jews.

Revivalism in its popular appeal was necessarily too sporadic an event, too much at the mercy of mass emotion, to assure consistency and conti-nuity. While it was a useful jump-start, revivalism was not a reliable engine for the long haul. Its explosive charge was soon spent, unless, that is, it was absorbed into the quieter and more sustainable rhythm of planning, organization, statistical results, educational support, lay and youth agency and enterprise, intergenerational transmission, material provision, and set priorities and direction.

This organizational impulse fed on fuel supplied by evangelical relig-ion and found a natural outlet in the contemporary antislavery and colo-nization movements. Accordingly, in examining the effects, both direct and collateral, of evangelical revivalism, the historian must analyze the several strands of the evangelical theme in an attempt to clarify the economic forces, political background, social context, and cultural influ-ences and presuppositions, and must resist the right-wing polemical rehearsal of compressed facts and figures of conversion. Yet, at the same time, the historian must also guard against the equally polemical left-wing tendency toward abstract analysis of thick religious themes and skepticism about motives overturning the concrete facts of religious life. In appealing for a reappraisal of evangelical revivalism, I suggest we come to grips with religion in its dynamic social and public expression rather than domesticating it as a false private residue. The connections, for example, with antislavery and American colonization indicate a much wider field of engagement for evangelical religion than the spread-eagle pietistic rhetoric of American organization as guarantee for the world's spiritual conquest, in the language of Rufus Anderson (1796–1880).

I have argued here that evangelical religion, particularly the African and African American version of it, promoted a concrete and socially responsible view of religion, contrary to the popular charge of antinomian sectarianism or dogmatic essentialism. Hopkins, for example, said evangelical religion was allied to what he called the good cause, defined as the public good or general welfare. He argued that the good cause would prosper from the disinterested benevolence of the committed and faithful. Those experiencing real spiritual regeneration, he contended, were those "pleased with the public interest, the greatest good and happiness of the whole." The roots of benevolence lay in religion, with evangelical doctrine securing a populist, lay basis for it, thereby transposing it into something eminently public and social in its usefulness. Hopkins was sure that in a society where disinterested benevolence held sway, the social evils of poverty, slavery, intemperance, infidelity, war, and crime would be eradicated, or at least would be repudiated as moral offenses. He also believed that doctrinal disputes were socially harmful as well as religiously damaging, and accordingly would be eradicated with religion as a public ethic.[11] William Wilberforce repeated the sentiment when he observed that benevolence is the rooting out of our natural selfishness.[12] As a Puritan divine expressed it in an earlier century, from the unity of true affections there springs forth a community of charitable actions.[13]

In other words, in evangelical religion people carried a high sense of public social duty, to be discharged with respect to improving conditions in society and fighting against the evils that barred the way to perfection. This melioristic doctrine of public benevolence, freed of state control and of ideological denominationalism, was the intellectual ancestor of the "social gospel" movement of a later age, and it produced an identical view of an activist public morality. Religion and the public good were complementary. Social deeds were to promote the general welfare, and for that reason "the principle of association," as Tocqueville called it, was needed to produce a social movement and a civil society with a public ethic.

It was natural, given its heightened sense of social duty, that the new evangelical movement would take notice of the communities of blacks proliferating in the cities and towns of the northeast, and that was what happened. The Reverend Robert Finley of Basking Ridge, New Jersey, whom I introduced in Chapter 2, observed the growing number of blacks in his neighborhood who lacked education and the tools for leading socially useful lives. Finley was speaking of the phenomenon of the multiplication of free blacks in America. Both John Jay, the first chief justice of the U.S. Supreme Court, and Alexander Hamilton, the first U.S. secretary of the treasury, for example, had noted the growing society of free blacks in New York City and sought to do something about it. In 1785 they organized the African Free Schools, run by the New York Manumission Society. One future distinguished pupil of the school was Alexander Crummell (about whom more later). In 1790 there had been less than 60,000 such blacks, but by 1820 the numbers had skyrocketed to 250,000. Finley felt colonization in Africa was the only solution and would accomplish three objectives all at once: (1) it would rid America of a social and moral problem; (2) it would allow Africa to receive partially civilized and Christianized blacks; and (3) the blacks themselves would therewith achieve freedom and opportunity. To sell the colonization idea, Finley and his associates employed the language of poetic hyperbole, saying that in such a Christian colony in Africa "sable hands will strike the lyre and weave the silken web."[14]

Samuel John Mills was appointed the agent to raise money for colonization under an organization called the African Education Society, which was created to train potential black emigrants. Mills was thirty-three and a professional traveling agent for numerous benevolent societies with a national reputation as a successful fund-raiser. He was also well known in revival circles, where he set hearts on fire. He was one of the three initiators in the founding of the American Board of Commissioners for Foreign Missions, the founder of the Marine Bible Society, and the cofounder, with Elias Boudinot, of the American Bible Society.

Mills was an activist of the classical school, a fixer of problems, a can-do optimist with energy to spare. He had given thought to the problem of settling freed slaves in their own community, perhaps in a colony in Ohio, in Indiana, in Illinois, beyond the Mississippi, or even along the African coast: his mind ranged far and wide. No scheme was too far-fetched; he would perish in one such. He had heard of Paul Cuffee and (as noted in Chapter 2) had gone to meet him to seek his advice. In consultation with Finley, Mills advanced the goals of colonization by traveling throughout the mid-Atlantic states canvassing for support for the combined program of African education and colonization. The joining of African education and colonization bolstered the campaign, as the practical-minded Finley intended. Mills would soon emerge as the agent to take colonization to Africa.

Meanwhile, Finley unveiled his plan for a colonization scheme in West Africa at a public meeting in Princeton in November 1816, before townspeople, professors, and students. Modeled on Freetown, Sierra Leone, his colonization scheme required the support of a federal grant, with Congress and the president taking responsibility for finding a suitable site in Africa.

Finley felt that the inherent capacity of slaves for self-improvement was being thwarted by the circumstances of slavery and race prejudice, and that a free colony in Africa would allow their inborn leadership capabilities to emerge and flourish. He was a believer in social progress and human equality and, therefore, in the imperative of antislavery, which would free up the reserves of benevolence and nature. In Africa, Finley boasted, American blacks would experience a resurgence of virtue and improvement. "Their contracted minds will then expand and their natures rise," he affirmed. A sense of place and power would "create the feeling that they are men."[15] And, as so many people before him had said, colonization would also allay southern fears about the destabilizing effects of general emancipation.

But another motive for the colonization plan was the view that it would spread civilization and Christianity in Africa; as a missionary enterprise colonization would establish "a seat of liberal learning in Africa from which the rays of knowledge might dart across those benighted regions." Africa was a sorrowing mother who would soon "forget her sorrows . . . and . . . bless the hands of her benefactors" for restoring her kidnapped children to her. The encouraging example of Sierra Leone warranted a similar attempt elsewhere because, in Finley's view, Sierra Leone was a providentially inspired experiment, "designed by God to obviate every difficulty, to silence objections, and point out the way in which every obstacle may be removed."[16]

It was important, Finley insisted, that the whole nation take responsibility for his colonization scheme in as much as the whole nation was implicated in the evil of slavery. Thus it would be fitting for the nation's public representatives to show pluck and make "atoning sacrifice" for the public sin of slavery, and to correct "injuries done to humanity by our ancestors."[17]

Colonization without Empire: America's Spiritual Kingdom

The issue of America as a democratic nation being opposed as such to colonialism was a particularly prickly one, but Finley gave little evidence of being deterred by that thought. Several European nations already had established colonies in Africa, but in their case, Finley charged, they did so for the selfish purpose of bringing strength, fame, and honor to themselves. American colonization, he pleaded, would be different in being the exception to the law of the vanity of empire building. For America was destined to fulfill the exalted responsibilities of a spiritual empire, to forge an empire of ideals and redeem with the light of liberty and truth, not to run a political empire and rule with the corrupt sword of power and domination. America would be a light to other nations, the symbol of every blessing, civil and religious, leading by ideals and moral example rather than by force and subterfuge.[18] By entering upon its divinely appointed course of world deliverance, America would join the stream in which the current was pulling the other nations of the world, toward reform of their corrupt societies and extirpation of gloomy superstitions. America was different from these other nations, not simply materially or militarily, but morally and spiritually. America had to transcend the prerogatives of privilege and caste and hasten the dawn of liberty, equality, and opportunity for all.[19] It was Africa's turn to be drawn into the transforming net of American benevolence, and America could meet that challenge by agreeing to return to a much aggrieved Africa its absent sons and daughters as tokens of restoration. "Happy America," Finley intoned, "if she shall endeavor not only to rival other nations in arts and arms, but to equal and exceed them in the great cause of humanity."[20]

When Finley journeyed to Washington, D.C., to promote his African colonization scheme, he strategically targeted people with clout and influence: Henry Clay, John Calhoun, Daniel Webster, General Lafayette, and, of course, President Madison himself, a fellow Princetonian. His most useful personal ally was Elias Boudinot Caldwell, Clerk of the Supreme Court and a powerful figure in high Washington society.

Caldwell had also attended Princeton and was deeply influenced by the evangelical atmosphere of the time. A first-rate organizer, he used his considerable knowledge and influence to bring together a group of high-profile people in Washington to push the plan for colonization. Finally, in December 1816, the fateful meeting took place, with Henry Clay, then Speaker of the House of Representatives and nicknamed the Compromiser because of his role as architect of Missouri's admission to the Union, presiding.

In moving the plan for colonization, Clay repeated the old arguments of emancipation accompanied by repatriation, saying freed blacks in America lived in an untenable limbo between legal freedom and the "unconquerable prejudices" that prevented their assimilation.[21] But he added, in a departure from Finley, that colonization should be carefully separated from the issue of slavery as such: colonization was for free blacks, not for slaves, lest slave owners be unnecessarily antagonized. He said the successful establishment of a free colony in Sierra Leone showed colonization to be beneficial.

Other voices in the meeting added their weight to the wisdom and benefits of colonization, and all concurred with the Jeffersonian rule of race separation as the necessary corollary of emancipation. It was, for example, pointed out that those who believed that education would advance the condition of blacks in America were mistaken, because education would imbue free blacks with a "higher relish" for privileges that were denied them on account not simply of slavery but of race. In fact it was cruel to give free blacks the advantages of education, and with that the principle of opportunity, and then deny them the practical means to exploit those advantages. One of the members of the meeting echoed Clay when he said that colonization would offer a route by which free blacks could be taken away, and with them a source of insecurity for slave owners who feared that free blacks fomented trouble among slaves by running errands, circulating rumors, aiding and abetting runaway slaves, and acting as "depositories of stolen goods."

The free black, given thus to slave tampering, was a "bugbear" for manumission, whereas colonization would facilitate manumission. In an opinion rendered some years later, Clay returned to the issue of colonization and manumission. "What is the true nature of the evil of the existence of a portion of the African race in our population?" he asked. "It is not that there are *some*, but that there are so *many* among us of a different caste, of a different physical, if not moral constitution, who never could amalgamate with the great body of our population." In these circumstances, colonization might be the project to answer the danger the free African presented, a project "by which, in a material degree, the dangerous element in the general mass, can be diminished or rendered stationary."[22] Primarily for tactical reasons Clay was careful not to make that part of the argument about colonization helping to undercut slavery. He saw no point in taking on the powerful slave interests in the South.

Colonization before Antislavery: Mission of Inquiry

With the subject of colonization thus delineated, the goals defined, the reasons set out, and the plans laid, the meeting reassembled in late December 1816 in a hall of the House of Representatives and framed a constitution for the American Society for Colonizing the Free People of Color in the United States. A campaign was launched in the press to circulate news of this American Colonization Society and the eminent names associated with it. It received endorsements from benevolent and philanthropic societies as well as groups opposed to allowing free blacks to live in the United States. The Virginia House of Delegates gave the colonization plan its formal endorsement, instructing Virginia's senators and congressmen to work for federal adoption of the scheme. Alerted to moves among free blacks in Philadelphia to oppose colonization, Finley hurried there to quell the murmurings and to reassure and reconcile black leaders, but he met with mixed results. Many in the black community would not back colonization for fear it would undercut efforts toward reform at home. The Quakers, too, remained skeptical of the motives of colonization, moved by the same fear of undermining antislavery efforts in America. Unfortunately for the organizers of colonization, Congress was similarly skeptical, urging instead that Americans collaborate with the British in Sierra Leone rather than seek to duplicate that effort.

At that point, the members of the Colonization Society began to amass factual information and field accounts to press their argument for moving ahead with the project. The American embassy in London was asked to obtain information from the African Institution. Letters were sent to William Wilberforce and Thomas Clarkson requesting concrete information about life and conditions on the West African coast. Samuel Mills decided in the meantime personally to embark on a "mission of inquiry" in England and West Africa, gathering information from the records and officials of the African Institution in London and visiting field sites in Africa in a publicity blitz that would "help to keep the subject alive in the public mind,"[23] before a final push in Congress. His mission of inquiry would gather unimpeachable information with which to move a still skeptical Congress and the nation. Auxiliaries of the Colonization Society were set up in Philadelphia, New York, and Baltimore. Their establishment epitomized the benevolent spirit as well as the networking, fund-raising, organizational, and communication skills that strengthened with the revivalist impact.

Francis Key, the chief agent in Baltimore, who worked with Mills to found the auxiliary there, spoke in flowery language of what the auxiliary groups in particular and the colonization movement in general would accomplish. He referred to "spires of temples glittering in the sun . . . harbors shaded by the snowy wings of departing and returning commerce . . . the hum of industry resounding in the streets," and how Africa would point to the star-spangled banner in profoundest gratitude for the blessings of civilization.[24] When the Baltimore auxiliary was set up, Robert Goodloe Harper, a former senator and a Federalist heavyweight, took charge, transforming the auxiliary into a colonization powerhouse in Maryland and beyond.

It was at this point that Mills decided the time was right to embark in earnest on his mission of inquiry, and for that purpose he recruited as companion another Connecticut native, Ebenezer Burgess. In November 1817, after overcoming last-minute snags, the two set sail for Africa via London. After an eventful voyage that nearly cost them their lives, they arrived travel-soiled in London and made contact with the officers of the African Institution, including William Wilberforce and the duke of Gloucester. On 2 February 1818 they left for Freetown, which they reached on 12 March.

Freetown made an immediate impression on the impressionable Mills and Burgess. They met John Kizell, president of the Friendly Society, which Paul Cuffee had founded. Kizell had been a slave and lived in South Carolina until the American Revolution, when he was evacuated with the British to Nova Scotia and eventually to Freetown. He became Mills's interpreter, a personal association of much less value than Mills expected.

Kizell warned Mills and Burgess of the risks of dealing with untrust-worthy chiefs who remained implacably suspicious of intrusions into their slave-based domains by Europeans. The party visited the Banana Islands and met the chief, Thomas Caulker, a British ally, who endorsed Mills's colonization plan. Thomas then sent them to the Plantain Islands to secure similar approval from his nephew, the British-educated George Caulker. Their aim was to go to Sherbro Island to establish a colony, but George Caulker warned Mills that the chiefs there were notoriously un-predictable and would think to place obstacles in the path of such a settlement. Chiefs were natural foes of antislavery, and so, after shaking hands with them, you counted your fingers. ʿ

Forewarned but not forearmed, Mills and Burgess pressed on to Sher-bro Island, due just south of Freetown. They would recall George Caulker's warning when they found the chiefs there to be tricky custom-ers, a genuine force to reckon with in general but tantalizing partners in the extreme on approach. At the village of Bendou they met Kings So-mano and Safah in a "palaver house" (from the Portuguese *palavra*), the "house" being a conical-shaped thatched structure twenty feet in diame-ter. Safah arrived attired "in a silver-laced coat, three-corner hat, and long mantle that dropped to his bare feet. Somano wore a gown, panta-loons, hat, and shoes."[25] Mills and Burgess stepped forward to shake hands with each of the forty or fifty natives who stared at the strangers, and then, still following custom, they offered presents to the chiefs: trade cloth or "bafta," a keg of powder, bars of tobacco, and finally the pièce de résistance, the mandatory bottle of rum. Mills took consolation from his vision of Americans putting a stop to this vice and weaning the natives from bad habits as soon as they took over. The natives had other ideas.

Chiefly honor demanded a bottle of rum each for the two men, So-mano and Safah. The offer of only one bottle they considered *infra dig,* and, thus slighted, they insisted that the Americans rectify the shortcom-ing before they could begin the palaver. In the course of the discussions Mills and Burgess explained the purpose of their mission, saying that wise and good men in America wanted to bring a colony of free blacks to settle on Sherbro, and that such a colony would bring material benefits and a better life to the people. Would the chiefs agree to cede land for the purpose?

The chiefs replied that they feared an American colony would grow strong and make war on the natives. More haggling and further delays ensued before Safah and Somano admitted that in fact they had no power to give away land without the final authority of King Sherbro, the paramount chief of the island.

Frustrated by being drawn into a fruitless round of negotiation designed only to part them from their goods, Mills and Burgess occupied themselves with prayer meetings and hymns as they waited to meet King Sherbro. As they made their way through the villages of the island, the bemused Africans watched in curious incomprehension while the Americans staged a two-person devotional spectacle of direct access to the Supreme Ruler. They looked a forsaken, improbable pair.

Finally, the Americans met King Sherbro, a barefoot potentate carrying a fly wisk as his royal symbol of office. The uncomprehending Americans, barely catching their breath, were dragged flat-footedly through yet another round of elaborate greetings and presentation of customary gifts. Then the king suspended court and summoned more chiefs to the meeting. The chiefs were slow in turning up, delayed by a traditional funeral, by the vagaries of travel, by demands for more gifts, and, finally, by a request that the president of the American Colonization Society, Bushrod Washington, send a letter personally addressed to King Sherbro, before the chiefs would be willing to give land. The native rulers had no intention of selling land, but they were happy to receive free bottles of rum while the Americans learned the truth for themselves. Such, then, were the ways of chiefly protocol, effective in extracting gifts and favors as well as resisting unwanted requests.

While they were left suspended in this state of deferred decision, the Americans were told by the king's favorite son and chamberlain that the granting of land was not after all a chiefly prerogative but a matter exclusively for the citizens of Sherbro as a whole. When Mills then asked for a general convention of such citizens, he was told that it could not be done as it was planting time and people were too busy on their farms. Disconsolate, Mills and Burgess left, taking with them their keen sense of unrequited benevolence. Back in Freetown they unburdened themselves of the details of their abortive mission of inquiry. Despite their experience they remained unchastened and still enamored of establishing a free colony in Sherbro. Governor MacCarthy, noted for his establishment view of things, could not help warning the Americans that a private colonization society had no hope of succeeding in establishing a free colony in Africa without government assistance. The slave trade was much too powerful a force for a private endeavor to take on. The Americans thanked him for his unsolicited advice and left for England on the brig *Success*, an apt symbol of their own judgment on their mission. Mills wrote defiantly: "I am every day more convinced of the practicability and expediency of establishing American colonies on the coast."[26] Mills jotted down in his report a strong recommendation to build a free colony on Sherbro Island, with a Paul Cuffee–like figure appointed as governor. The United States should provide naval protection and a gunboat to enforce antislavery. "If the people are troublesome," he wrote, "fire a big gun out in the bay, and they will all fly to the bush, and not an individual (will) be found."[27]

Sadly, Mills did not survive the voyage back. The dry cough that first started on the outbound voyage erupted into the ominous symptoms of consumption, and he died. As his companions prepared his body for burial at sea, Burgess was left with the somber prospect of appearing unaccompanied before the American Colonization Society, armed with only the report Mills had drawn up.

African Resettlement: Fact and Fiction

In presenting his report, Burgess painted a gloomy and dishonestly exaggerated picture of the devastating effects of the slave trade on village communities, social relations, and economic life in Africa, all in an effort to manipulate public opinion in America. "In village after village," he alleged, "the slave trade had drastically reduced the population. Once prosperous communities were decaying. The grass grew wild, and banana, orange, lime, and plantain trees were unattended. Lonely natives howled about the sacred trees of the dead. Many had forgotten how to raise cotton, indigo, and sugar cane . . . The governor of Sierra Leone asserted that two-thirds of the active slavers were American."[28] Henry Clay was handed a copy of the doctored report together with supporting documentation, with the request to move a resolution for government action. The report would result in the disaster it courted.

To prepare the way, Congress passed a measure transferring responsibility for disposing of rescued blacks from the states to the federal government, with President Monroe deputed to assume charge of the matter. Included in the measure was provision for America to send a naval squadron to Africa to resettle recaptive Africans, much in the manner of what was being done in Sierra Leone. Congress approved $100,000 for that work. On 4 March 1819 Congress passed into law the Slave Trade Act, with the assistance of Charles Fenton Mercer, a congressman from Virginia called the American Wilberforce on account of his decisive legislative role.

The act did not specifically authorize colonization, but that did not register among the officers of the Colonization Society. They urged President Monroe to take a liberal interpretation of the measure and sanction the purchase of territory in Africa to establish a free colony. Monroe shared the sentiments of the officers but as president felt the idea needed to pass more stringent constitutional tests. So he took the idea to his cabinet, where John Quincy Adams opposed it as unconstitutional. The Slave Trade Act, Adams insisted, contained no provisions for the purchase of land in Africa for any purpose, and, furthermore, there was nothing in the Constitution that supported the "establishment of a colonial system subordinate to and dependent upon that of the United States."[29] The argument that had been put forward, namely, that the Louisiana Purchase and the settlement at the mouth of the Columbia River fully established a valid constitutional precedent for such an interpretation of the Slave Trade Act was specious, he felt. Colonization advocates had created a kind of Indian cosmogony, "mounting the world upon an elephant and the elephant on a tortoise, with nothing for the tortoise to stand upon."[30] The cabinet concurred. It was a shattering defeat for Burgess and his cohorts, though they would never give up completely.

In investing so much in a federally sponsored scheme for African colonization, the Colonization Society was now reduced to John Quincy Adams's figure of a tortoise with nothing to stand upon but with still a lofty goal to reach. The effort was subsequently shifted to find another basis on which to pursue the colonization scheme.

One has to appreciate that the colonization movement stirred widespread interest throughout the nation, becoming what Adams called "a trap for popularity," having grown and spread from the organizational skill that had built it up in the first place. The colonization movement had availed itself of the most sophisticated techniques of mass propaganda, of a web of interlocking local agents fanning out and cohering in one active, coordinating site, with an uncanny ability to pick on the right subject for maximum public effect. As it was contemplating its next move, an incident occurred that was a godsend. Newspapers in the South reported the story of the impending sale of thirty or forty Africans seized from a Spanish slave ship. The slaves were taken by the federal authorities and surrendered to the state of Georgia in accordance with the terms of the 1808 Slave Trade Act. The governor ordered their sale, an order challenged by members of the Colonization Society on the basis of the 1819 Slave Trade Act, which gave the federal authorities power to act in such situations. President Monroe was urged to intervene and to have the Africans resettled in Africa. But his attorney general, William Wirt, instructed to study the case to see what role there might be for the federal government, answered, with Adams's strong encouragement, that the 1808 act could not legally be applied retroactively.

William Crawford, the secretary of the treasury and a political foe of John Quincy Adams, acted in the interests of the Colonization Society. He decided not to contest Monroe's attorney general on his narrow interpretation of the law but to shift the ground entirely. Under Georgia law the rescued Africans were to be sold unless a party like the Colonization Society intervened to claim them by paying all expenses incurred on their behalf. Crawford urged the Colonization Society to stop the sale of the Africans at an auction set for 3 May. The effort, hastily put together as it was, faltered, though the publicity surrounding the issue raised the society's national profile even more.

In the fall of 1819 Francis Scott Key called on President Monroe to abandon his self-imposed rigid adherence to the terms of the Slave Trade Act of 1819. He recommended Monroe agree to a plan to appoint an agent, send a warship to the African coast, and transport free blacks as colonists. Monroe gave signs he was willing to yield provided the Colonization Society would take responsibility for buying land, only for Wirt to resist him. The members of the society and their friends and sympathizers, in a chorus of outrage, demanded a reversal. Crawford insisted that the power to return rescued Africans was a principal power belonging to the president by intention of Congress. Even Wirt was carried by the force of Crawford's argument. Yes, Wirt said, the president could after all establish an African agency, send carpenters and other skilled workers to set up shelters, protect and support the station, establish a government for the resettled blacks, and dispatch free blacks from the United States if such a course was necessary to the safe and comfortable removal of the rescued Africans. But Wirt, with a flea in his ear, still demurred, saying in the end that perhaps Congress had not intended such wide powers to devolve on the executive and should, therefore, be given time to clarify its wishes.

Offered such wide latitude, the president did not wait but seized the opportunity and announced in his 1819 inaugural message that he would send out two agents with teams of laborers and mechanics to prepare an African station. Samuel Bacon, a young Episcopalian cleric and Harvard graduate, was appointed, with the Colonization Society's approval, as the governments principal agent. John P. Blankson was made his assistant. Together, the two set out to equip an expedition party, of up to three hundred free blacks if necessary, with the government paying for wagons, wheelbarrows, plows, iron work for a sawmill and a grist-mill, two six-pound cannons, one hundred muskets, twelve kegs of powder, a fish seine, and a four-oared barge. The secretary of the navy, Smith Thompson, ordered an American warship, the *Cyane,* to go as convoy with the other ship, the *Elizabeth.* Eventually, on 31 January 1820, only eighty-six people sailed out, one-third of them men. Bacon and Blankson were accompanied by Samuel Crozer, the agent of the colonization scheme. Crozer was to buy land at Sherbro and set up a government for the colonists.

The expedition made landfall at Freetown in early March 1820 and, driven by its compulsive mission, headed immediately to Sherbro, that is, the Sherbro of Mills and Burgess's description, a place of vacant, abundant arable land presided over by poor, weak, friendly tribes eager to welcome their saviors. John Kizell, remembering his meeting with Mills and Burgess, expressed delight at seeing the Americans again, whom he invited to settle on his land, on which he had built several huts for the Americans. But with abundant land ready to be had for the asking, Bacon opted instead to negotiate a better deal with the chiefs, though the Americans would in the meantime settle temporarily at Campelar, Kizell's little village outpost of twenty huts.

Campelar was a miserable place for a dwelling, a low marshy strip shrouded in dense thickets, mango trees, and gurgling fetid streams. Drinking water was a problem, and, though he concealed the truth, even Kizell had to import the precious stuff from the mainland, as well as food. Bacon decided to put in at Campelar, advice to the contrary notwithstanding. Crozer, making a virtue of necessity, set off after the elusive chiefs to talk them into ceding land. As long as the gifts and presents were forthcoming, the chiefs were happy to keep on talking and to put off signing anything. ⌡

In the midst of these protracted, spirit-sapping negotiations the heavy rains started. As the rains progressed, the colonists began running out of food and supplies and getting on one another's nerves. And then the deadly malaria struck. Forty victims groaned in delirium, their heads pounding with the frenzied fever, their bodies quaking with the spasms, their eyes inflamed and joints aching. Several died. Crozer, who had been away on his fruitless negotiations with the chiefs, returned to stricken Campelar to fall ill shortly thereafter. He, too, died subsequently, followed a day later by Townsend, an officer of the *Cyane.* They were both buried the same day. Blankson, also struck down by the fever, rallied briefly and then suddenly declined, never to recover. Bacon defied the odds and scurried around to minister to the sick and dying, but he, too, succumbed to the illness. A British schooner nearby was detailed to take him to Freetown, but as the canoe carrying Bacon got close to the schooner, the ship suddenly and inexplicably weighed anchor and headed out to sea. Bacon's African oarsmen rowed furiously for several hours in the scorching tropical heat to catch up with the fleeing ship, which they miraculously did, and then landed the sick Bacon, at that point delirious from the malaria and exposure to the sun. Bacon was too far advanced and died the following day. Local people looted the settlement at Campelar, with Daniel Coker, appointed agent by Crozer, watching helplessly while John Kizell handed over to the grasping chiefs the remnants of the stores. Coker took the rest of the settlers to Fourah Bay in Freetown for safety.

The disaster was a bitter blow to the Americans, especially to the officers and supporters of colonization, who blamed Mills and Burgess for concealing the truth and manipulating audiences back home. As one of them put it, "It is only to be regretted that those gentlemen [Mills and Burgess] had not spent a longer period in that country, explored the coast more exhaustively, and used the means of acquiring a more exact and certain knowledge of the different subjects on which they were obliged to report."[31]

It is difficult to explain how President Monroe, still reeling from this blow, could decide to equip yet another expedition, but, emboldened beyond retreat, he did. The second expedition was headed by the Reverend Ephraim Bacon, Samuel Bacon's brother, and Jonathan B. Winn, with the Colonization Society sending two representatives, the Reverend Joseph R. Andrus and Christian Wiltberger. With thirty-three emigrants, they set out from Hampton Roads, Virginia, on 23 January 1821. Arriving in Sierra Leone they interviewed Daniel Coker and then visited the villages along the coast south of Freetown. Andrus signed a treaty with the king calling for annual tributes of $300, which the managers of the society rejected as unreasonable. Dr. Eli Ayres of Baltimore was sent out to replace Andrus. When Ayres arrived in November 1821, he found that Andrus and Winn had died of malaria, and that Bacon, crippled by the illness, had fled to the West Indies to escape an otherwise certain death. Only Wiltberger, defying the odds, remained alive. Ayres tried all the means at his disposal, including threats of severe punishment, but he could not get the survivors in Fourah Bay to follow him to a new colony.

The Founding of Liberia: Privatization of Public Responsibility

Having come this far, the Colonization Society was not about to give in, and so it persuaded Monroe to send out Lieutenant Robert Field Stockton, a naval officer and close associate of Finley, to take matters a stage further. Stockton's grandfather had been a signatory of the Declaration of Independence, and the family, established in New Jersey, continued to take an active part in state and national affairs. Taking command of the schooner *Alligator,* Stockton set sail for Africa in 1821, with unlimited power to purchase land for an African colony. He went to Cape Mesurado, which Andrus and Bacon had earlier visited, thinking it a suitable site for a colony, and decided to intercede personally with the reluctant King Peter, who had refused the offer of Andrus and Bacon.

Stockton, accompanied by Ayres, was not loath to try strong-arm tactics if conciliation failed. On 12 December 1821 the two men landed at Cape Mesurado, surrounded by armed and suspicious natives. Ayres explained in his high, cracked voice, and with a directness of manner whose aggressive import was not lost on the Africans, that the Americans wished to come and settle there, to build houses, make farms, set up schools, and do trade with the people. Their meaning clear by now, the Americans summoned King Peter to a palaver. He turned up under duress, "wearing a cotton toga with wide blue and white stripes. An attendant held an umbrella over the royal head."[32] King Peter was told of the benefits the Americans would bring, but the palaver pointedly omitted any reference to Christianity and civilization, since any good-faith negotiation was now out of the question.

King Peter thanked the Americans graciously for their gifts of rum and tobacco but repeated that he was not free to sell them land. To do so would be at the certain cost of his life, and his "women would cry aplenty." But, to avoid slighting his guests, he agreed to meet the Americans the next day and "make a book" for the land, a cryptic phrase the Americans preferred to understand as his agreement to conclude a land deal.

On the appointed day Stockton and Ayres duly turned up at the seashore but King Peter did not; only subordinates appeared, with whom the Americans held futile discussions. The next day, following their own counsel, the Americans returned, expecting to meet King Peter. When the king failed to turn up, the irate Americans sent him word demanding to meet him. The king replied that he had no desire to meet them and would not sell them land.

Infuriated, Stockton took the decision to pursue the tribal monarch, with Ayres in tow. Led by native guides, the Americans plunged into the jungle, wading through mud and water, cutting their way through the dense, swampy undergrowth, and climbing over jungle stumps and limbs for about seven miles, till finally they stood defiant before the astonished king.

Provoked by this peremptory intrusion on his royal seclusion, the king cast aside the stiff dignity of his elevated office and asked bluntly, like an embattled hustler, "What do you want that land for?" Ayres stepped forward to answer, repeating the lines he had given out before, only to find himself surrounded by an angry, noisy crowd who shouted recriminations and flaunted threats. The Americans were accused of kidnapping the son of a neighboring chief, of sowing discord on Sherbro Island, and of destroying the slave trade on the coast. Stockton, of an excitable nature in any case, was by this time puffing with rage. He drew a loaded pistol and cocked it before handing it to Ayres with instructions to fire if necessary. He then took out a second loaded pistol, which he trained at the head of the petrified king. The action cowed king and crowd, whom Stockton proceeded to address calmly about how the Americans were not their enemies but only wanted to bring to the people and the whole country the benefits and blessings of enlightened rule. Having demonstrated his superior power, Stockton adjourned the meeting and told King Peter to turn up the next day to sign a deed of land.

On 15 December 1821 King Peter and five of his subordinate chiefs arrived promptly to cede Cape Mesurado, not, surprisingly, to the American Colonization Society but to Stockton and Ayres personally. The title deed granted rights in perpetuity to those two men by name. There was no reference whatsoever to the American Colonization Society, its agents, or any other publicly accredited body as such. The land, with ill-defined boundaries, was simply handed over lock, stock, and barrel to the legal authority of Stockton and Ayres personally.

The area in question was a strip of land one hundred and thirty miles long and forty miles wide, bounded by the Junk and Mesurado rivers and the ocean. For payment the chiefs received muskets, beads, tobacco, gunpowder, clothing, looking glasses, much other bric-a-brac, and food and rum, together worth less than $300. The chiefs had no idea they were selling their country. Stockton and Ayres signed, but for themselves, not for the Colonization Society. The territory was given the name Liberia, a free if extorted colony, and subsequently the first settlement called Monrovia, after President Monroe.

However ebullient their mood at the successful establishment of Liberia, the officials of the Colonization Society were painfully aware that Liberia was a private settlement scheme, not a federal scheme, and for that reason was not entitled to government financial subsidy or military protection. A security risk by its origin, Liberia was after all the expression of the pessimistic impulses of antislavery and colonization, the impulses, that is, of the caution of antislavery at home and of the precaution of colonization abroad. Northern liberals had offered it as a sop to southern slave interests. As one New England campaigner put it, "The object of this wholesale banishment of the free blacks [to Liberia] is the security of the slave system."[33] To aggravate matters, the laws, policies, regulations, and norms governing Liberia were the acts of a group of private individuals acting in their own capacity, not the directives of a congressional mandate. The managers and agents of colonization discovered soon enough that donations were more generous for removing blacks from the United States than for maintaining them in Africa, and even that generosity was at the mercy of domestic social inclinations. Thus Monroe's personal association with the settlement, however useful as a public relations master stroke, nevertheless represented no official boon for Liberia, alas.

The constitution of the new settlement at Liberia was framed long before the colony ever came into existence.[34] All power was put in the hands of the managers and their agents. The legal tradition was based on American common law, in which slavery was outlawed and alcohol banned. The constitution provided for probating wills, holding jury trials, distributing land, and engaging in legitimate trade with the natives. Whites could not own land, and missionaries required the permission of managers to enter and settle. A colonial agent was appointed with the powers of governor, judge, lawgiver, and military commander. The colonists were regarded as American citizens but were given no bill of rights. American political idealism was promoted as a substitute for the practical challenges involved in establishing an American colony in Africa. Liberia was in that sense left wide open to the constant threat of chiefly reprisal and equally to guaranteed congressional neglect. It had need of neither.

The colony was constrained to live from hand to mouth. Ayres tried to put the establishment on a secure footing, but the odds were against him. The settlers did not have adequate food or equipment, were unfamiliar with the soil and its natural produce, and could not adapt their tastes and habits to take advantage of what was at hand. Ayres vainly sent desperate messages for help, with King Peter in the meantime plotting revenge for his humiliation at the hands of Stockton. The king threatened to sell the settlers into slavery unless he received "cole" (tribute). Miraculously, the U.S. brig *Strong* arrived in August 1822 (in response to an earlier campaign by Andrus and Bacon for support) with a reinforcement of eighteen recaptive Africans and thirty-seven immigrants, led by Jehudi Ashmun of New Haven, Connecticut, a tall, slender, handsome man given to ascetic inclinations. He was converted at age seventeen in one of the Methodist revivals and later studied for the priesthood in the Episcopal Church. Ayres went to the United States on a hastily arranged trip to procure more supplies and more settlers, leaving one of the colonists, Elijah Johnson, in charge of the settlement. Johnson had been with Samuel Bacon on Sherbro Island. Johnson and the rest of the small band of settlers moved to healthier ground, clearing a site that ultimately became Monrovia. The *Oswego* left Baltimore in the autumn of 1822, followed by the *Fidelity*, both with more settlers and supplies.

But 1822 was a fateful year for the fledgling settlement. (It was, coincidentally, the year also of the famous slave plot at Charleston, South Carolina, led by Denmark Vessey, a free black who planned an insurrection against whites. Vessey, having been betrayed, was seized, and, along with thirty-four of the ringleaders, hanged. One effect of the incident was to deepen distrust for emancipation and to increase demands to send free blacks out of the country.) The managers of the settlement faced that year the prospects of bankruptcy. The total revenue was only $800, compared to the $10,000 spent for supplies in the boom years before. Clearly, the Colonization Society could be successful at networking and mobilizing an army of public relations dragomans but was not equipped to set up and maintain a morally perfect government. There was nothing in its revival equipment of faith and discipleship to furnish men and women with the tools necessary for the science of governance, let alone for the business of running a tropical colonial empire—the task once described as "to evangelize the heathen, and build up an empire in Africa."[35] The society made the sunny assumption about the federal government being its ally in antislavery until it bumped up against a remote tropical frontier where to its cost it found that assumption to be sadly misplaced. Its main critic, John Quincy Adams, was closer to reality than many of its friends when he said that colonization was a tortoise standing on no solid ground and carrying a beguiling superstructure of claims and expectations, a sentiment Governor MacCarthy later expressed to Mills and Burgess in more diplomatic language but with the same intransigent result.

While Dr. Ayres was away scrounging for supplies in America, the settlement became embroiled in disputes with the neighboring chiefs. With its origins marked by force and intimidation, the settlement could not avoid being on a war path with the local chieftains. Elijah Johnson spent much of the time preoccupied with providing defense for the settlers and otherwise fending off the antagonistic attention of hostile neighbors. Johnson's companion was Lott Carey, a black Baptist preacher from Virginia in the mold of David George. Ashmun had had a hand in selecting Carey for the voyage to Liberia. Together Carey and Johnson helped move the settlement to the mainland.

Ashmun took over the military security of the settlement, for the chiefs were disinclined to live at peace with a colony that had been forced on them. It was twice attacked by King Peter and his chiefly cohorts, and each time the attack was repulsed. The chiefs were being aided and abetted by Cuban slave traders who had settled in the adjoining Gallinas country. Using the chiefs as timely allies, the slavers were determined to prevent the permanent establishment of a free colony in Liberia for fear of what it would do to the slave trade.

In these conditions the settlers naturally recognized the advantages of long-term reconciliation over the costs of endemic enmity. Ashmun engaged King Boatswain of Boporo, a powerful inland Mandinka ruler,[36] to broker peace. Boatswain turned up in person and handed down word that the Dey tribesmen, his villeins and on whose land the settlement was established, should henceforth relinquish all customary claim to the land and desist from mounting raids against it. It was only after this attempt at reconciliation in April 1822 that the settlement felt secure enough to move to the mainland. But, grasping a weapon with one hand while they labored with the other, as Carey expressed it, the settlers could not exactly let down their guard. Ashmun, for example, would not take the risk and summoned three American warships to patrol the area at the mouth of New Cess River, a place infested with Spanish slave traders whose factories were razed in a series of engagements. But the slavers kept replenishing their numbers until a combined British and Liberian action in 1842 helped put down their repeated challenge.

King Boatswain might have done enough to restrain the Dey people, but such was the complex nature of chiefly rivalry that his word alone was insufficient to quell all local opposition. Who knew where such Western territorial encroachment would end or what threats it carried for indigenous political systems? Accordingly, in early November 1822 an attack was launched against the settlement, which was repelled. A few days later another attack was mounted, but that one ended with a truce being signed following the mediation of Major Laing and Captain Gordon on behalf of the government of Sierra Leone.

As the settlement struggled to cope with external threats and danger, it tried to quell dissension and unrest within its walls. The black settlers suspected the white members of wanting to take complete control and resented the authority the whites exercised over them. Ashmun recognized the problem early but was slow to respond effectively. Eventually he allowed some responsibility to devolve on the African Americans. Elijah Johnson was made commissary of stores, in charge of rations and supplies, or what little was left of these. R. H. Simpson, a fifty-year-old from Virginia who had purchased his freedom, was made commissary of ordnance. Lott Carey was appointed health officer and government inspector.

Ashmun's administration did not succeed in scotching settler disaffection completely—in fact, his gesture hardened attitudes and raised the question of settler cooperation as the basis for a sound and peaceful administration. The settlers rebelled twice, with Lott Carey at their head, and each time they seized food stores and arms. After the second revolt Ashmun abandoned Monrovia, fearing for his own safety.

Sir Harry Johnston, the eminent British scholar and official, famous for his historical and linguistic researches in central and southern Africa, undertook an ambitious study into the history and physical life of Liberia, with the results published in two volumes, richly illustrated and still considered a classic in spite of blemishes. In giving an account of the early troubles under Ashmun, Johnston was inclined to trace the source of those troubles to unresolved issues in antislavery in America:

> several of the colonists took to dissolute or drunken habits, others were lazy, and a good many disliked agricultural work. Ashmun for his firmness and courage was detested by the slave-trading chiefs in the vicinity, who called him the "white American devil" of Cape Mesurado. An intrigue was started within the colony against him, and news of it reached the American Colonization Society. In this body there were some who disapproved of Ashmun's vigorous attacks on the slave trade: it is hard to say from what point of view but several of these philanthropists, though easily moved to tears over the woes of the freed slaves in America, seem to have had very little sympathy for the indigenous natives of Africa, who might or might not be despoiled by American slave traders, under the eyes of the freed slaves whom the Society was repatriating. Their sympathies apparently were restricted to those Negroes who had embraced the Christian faith, wore the white man's clothes, and talked his language.[37]

Carey later recanted his role in the troubles and made a public apology for his conduct as rebel.

In July 1824 the American Colonization Society sent out the Reverend Ralph Randolph Gurley to investigate and report on the affairs of the settlement. Gurley, who wrought mightily with the pen and played havoc with the purse, was a graduate of Yale and a long-time associate of the Colonization Society, where he was noted as an editor and orator with an influence ranging to England and Scotland. "Utterly unlike in their private practices, what Henry Clay was in the Halls of Congress, Gurley was to Colonization, essentially a peacemaker and a lover of the Union."[38]

Gurley stayed for ten days before returning to America to submit his report. The report at first disappointed the managers, who criticized it for being too complicated and intricate for the simplicity of a few settlers. The managers wished instead for a settlement founded on republican simplicity and Christian plainness, where invidious matters of hierarchy, title, and dignity could be avoided altogether—such was the evangelical ignorance of political institution building. The fact was that Liberia was a beleaguered huddle of unwanted blacks who left America, where their race conflicted with their freedom, to find refuge in Africa, where their freedom conflicted with their security. In the end, however, experience on the ground carried the day, and Gurley's recommendations were put into practice after a six-month delay. Under the new arrangement, Ashmun was left in general control of affairs but with significantly reduced powers. And an advisory council was created in which the settlers were given a voice in running their own affairs. The new arrangements led to Lott Carey being appointed vice-agent for Liberia in 1826.

Lott Carey and Liberia

Lott Carey was born on a Virginia slave plantation in about 1780. He converted to Christianity in 1807, the year of the abolition of the slave trade. In 1813 he was able to save enough money to purchase his freedom and that of his two children for $850. Spurning prospects of settling at home in America and earning a comfortable living, Carey took appointment with the Richmond-based African Baptist Missionary Society and embarked on the voyage to Africa determined to preach Christianity to his African brethren. It was as such that he came to take a leading part in the pioneering counsels of the settlement at Liberia.

In a letter he wrote on 13 March 1821 Carey spoke about the constraints Liberia imposed on the kind of religious and social initiative he was keen to seize. He said he was desirous of undertaking a missionary outreach among the inland Mandinka population, where there was regular trade. "If you intend doing anything for Africa," he argued, "you must not wait for the Colonization Society, nor for government; for neither of these are in search of missionary ground, but of colonizing grounds; if it should not sow missionary seeds, you cannot expect a missionary crop. And, moreover, all of us who are connected with the agents, who are under public instructions, must be conformed to their laws whether they militate against missionary operations or not."[39]

Carey was active in the defense of the settlement against external threats and in the fight against disease from within. He organized defense activities while taking responsibility, as health inspector, for looking after the sick and dying. In March 1828 Ashmun himself fell fatally ill and returned to America to die at age thirty-five. He was buried in New Haven, which had a street named for him. Before Ashmun's replacement arrived, Carey assumed supreme charge of the settlement. He spent most of his time with his finger in the dike holding back the flood waiting to swamp the settlement in the menacing form of attacks by the natives, lawlessness by the settlers, and disease, hunger, and starvation. It says something for the desperate times in which they were living that the settlers could under these circumstances speak with one voice about how fortunate they were to be "forming a community of our own, in the land of our forefathers, having the commerce and soil and resources of the country at our disposal we know nothing of that debasing inferiority, with which our very colour stamped us in America . . . It is this moral emancipation—this liberation of the mind from worse than iron fetters, that repays us ten thousand times over, for all that it has cost us, and makes us grateful to God, and our American patrons, for the happy change which has taken place in our situation."[40] If the bitter pill that was Liberia was deemed sweet, as this testimony contends, then one can only imagine the terrible malady for which it was prescribed.

Carey died in 1828 in the course of helping the settlers prepare for an impending attack by organizing an arms cache, when a lighted candle accidentally set the store on fire. Carey and seven others perished in the flames, and all the store was destroyed. Dr. Richard Randall, Ashmun's successor, arrived at the end of 1828, and among his first official acts was founding a colony in 1829, Careysburg, named for Lott Carey. Randall himself was soon after struck down by malaria and died in April 1829.

Carey, ever conscious of the historical difficulties of the Liberia venture, tried gallantly to resolve some of its contradictions. An official not inclined to pander to black sentiments was moved to testify to Carey's courage and example with reference generally to his leadership and specifically to the role he played in the memorable defense of the settlement in 1822:

> In order to relieve . . . the sufferings of his people, Mr. Cary [sic] turned his attention to the diseases of the climate, made himself a good practical physician, and devoted his time almost exclusively to the relief of the destitute, the sick, and the afflicted. His services, as physician of the colony were invaluable, and for a long time, were rendered, without hope of reward, while he made liberal sacrifices of his property to the poor and distressed. But amid his multiple cares and efforts, he never neglected to promote the objects of the African Missionary Society. He sought access to the native tribes, instructed them in the doctrines and duties of the Christian religion, and established a school for the education of their children . . . To found a Christian colony which might prove a blessed asylum . . . was with him an object with which no temporal good could be compared.[41]

Carey's surviving missionary colleagues in America, handed the opportunity to make hagiography, could barely resist, eulogizing their deceased friend as an agent of Divine Providence and the architect of a prosperous and growing church in Africa. The context of grief in which those sentiments were expressed prepares the reader to treat the eulogy with indulgence. Carey appears in missionary testimonials as larger than life. Yet, as these testimonials also made clear, the "unwearied diligence and fidelity with which he discharged the important trust confided to his care—his zeal for the honor of religion, and the purity and piety of his general conduct" placed Carey firmly in the tradition of lay evangelical social activism.[42] He was entitled to the unrestrained praise of his people.

Expansion and Exclusion

With the continuing influx of emigrants, the settlement of Monrovia was set to expand beyond its enclave coastal limits.[43] One of the first of new settlements was Caldwell, named after Elijah Caldwell, the secretary of the Colonization Society. In March 1825 66 emigrants arrived from Norfolk, Virginia, and settled there. Many of them fell ill immediately, and Lott Carey tended the sick. Only 3 died. In January and February 1826 more emigrants arrived from Boston and North Carolina, and they too settled at Caldwell, where an agricultural society was formed the next year. A sister colony was established at New Georgia at about the same time as Caldwell. By late 1826 farming was flourishing at both settlements: Caldwell had 77 farms and New Georgia 33. In 1827 schools were founded under the direction of the Reverend G. McGill, an African American teacher. Six schools enrolled 227 pupils, of whom 45 were the children of local natives. Also, in 1827 a school was opened among the neighboring Vai people, with 35 pupils, including the sons of chiefs and other rulers. Lott Carey's school was in the same vicinity, funded in part by the African Baptist Missionary Society.

In February 1828 Carey also directed the founding of a settlement at Millsburg, named after Mills and Burgess. The land was ceded by four paramount chiefs, Old King Peter, Long King Peter, King Governor, and King James, names that suggest proof of well-established contacts with European traders and officials. In any case, Carey supervised the settlement, paying special attention to house construction and crop cultivation, though he noted soberly that the inhabitants would have to continue receiving rations for some time yet, so uncertain were the prospects.

In 1830 additional schools were established at Caldwell, and by 1834 the settlement was even more prosperous than Monrovia, with a growing labor force. By 1851 it grew so large that it was partitioned into Upper and Lower Caldwell. New Georgia also continued to grow. During 1832 a large number of recaptured Igbos and slaves from the Congo were resettled there. Like Caldwell and the others, the settlement eventually joined the Commonwealth of Liberia, created as a confederal association in 1839.

Other settlements included Edina, where in December 1832 thirty-eight colonists arrived. Located in Bassa country, Edina enjoyed some autonomy, although Monrovia retained suzerainty over its affairs. Another was the settlement established on a large tract of land at Cape Palmas acquired by the Maryland Colonization Society. For a thousand dollars the society purchased a large area from the chiefs of Cape Palmas, Grand Cavalla, and Garraway, and in February 1834 the first batch of settlers arrived. The official name of the colony was Maryland in Liberia, and the new town founded by the settlers was named Harper, after Robert Goodloe Harper, the Federalist who made Maryland a favored child of the American Colonization Society.

Bassa Cove settlement followed in March 1835, pioneered jointly by the New York and Philadelphia Colonization Societies. There was a strong Quaker presence in the Philadelphia Colonization Society, reflected among the first settlers at Bassa Cove. The settlement received a baptism of fire. In June 1835, barely three months after its founding, it was attacked and sacked by the local chiefs, and the survivors fled to Edina for safety. There were strong rumors at the time that the colorful French adventurer Theodore Conneau, making his way to West Africa via Boston, had a hand in instigating the attack and was masterminding events behind the scenes. Peace was soon restored, although the wary settlers did not return for several months afterward.

Marshall settlement, so named after the U.S. chief justice, was begun in 1827 by a group of colonists and recaptured Africans. Some 392 plots were neatly laid out for the settlers to occupy, and a school was erected. Bexley colony was founded in 1838. Situated in Bassa country like Edina, Bexley was founded by Lewis Sheridan, a man of private means. It occupied a six-hundred-acre site on the St. John's River. Also in 1838 the Mississippi Colonization Society founded a settlement at Sinoe, which later became Greenville. Most of the settlers came from the State of Mississippi and were cotton planters.

This pattern of colonies shows how immigration from the United States fed the leisurely momentum of expansion and reinforced the logic of social exclusion and land sequestration. The recaptive African element that prevented Freetown from turning into an exclusive overseas project and instead enabled it to flourish as a commercial center was conspicuously missing in Liberia. Over a period of forty years, for instance, only 5,700 recaptives landed in Liberia, and they were treated as second-class citizens. They lived in segregated communities of their own and struggled to eke out a meager subsistence from tillage. They were not allowed to mix freely or on an equal basis with the Americo-Liberians, whose numbers remained relatively static. In the same 1843 census, the population of all the Liberian colonies, excluding Maryland, was put at 30,000, of which 2,390 were Americo-Liberians, the rest being subject races and a sprinkling of recaptives.

The mulatto social class dominated the government between 1847, the year of Liberia's independence, and 1878. (Liberia's constitution of independence was drawn up by a professor at the Harvard Law School.) Native Africans were not allowed representation in the National Legislature until the end of the nineteenth century, and it was only in 1924, during the presidency of Charles Dunbar King, that cabinet positions became open to them. The growing social cleavage was given formal expression in 1950 when Didwo Tweh, a Kru tribesman, formed an opposition group, the Reformation Party, to challenge the dominance of Americo-Liberians. The warning was largely ignored by the political elite, and so a native African would never become a president of the country through the democratic process. It was as if the fact that Liberia was a place in Africa was merely incidental, so dominant were the attitudes and issues originating in America. As Blyden said, Liberia was a little bit of South Carolina, of Georgia, of Virginia, in sum, of the ostracized, suppressed, depressed elements of those states, which was "tacked on to West Africa—a most incongruous combination, with no reasonable prospect of success."[44] The colony had America in its eyes while it turned its back on Africa; though it was necessarily in Africa, it was preferably not of it.

This state of affairs resulted from the perception of Liberia as a colony created to take away America's black rejects to the remote continent of their origin.[45] It led many to challenge the fairness, as well as the practicableness, of using Liberia in that way. Thus, as we saw earlier, African American groups in Philadelphia, for example, criticized colonization as evasive, causing Finley to hurry there to squelch the agitation. One contemporary nineteenth-century writer, acquainted with the ideological background to colonization, insisted accordingly that the slavery question could not be remitted to Liberia and abandoned there. Slavery was intertwined with America's constitutional integrity, raising the question whether an oath to support the Constitution of the United States was an oath to support slavery. If it was, the writer challenged, then the Constitution would require us to overthrow our own liberties, to declare war against universal humanity, to rebel against God, and to incur the divine displeasure. If the Constitution was for liberty and against slavery, however, then it was "our duty and interest to wield it for the overthrow of slavery and the redemption of our country from the heel of the slave power."[46] Colonization should not, therefore, be a diversion from that central issue but should be a reason to do the necessary political heavy lifting to engage it.

In the hurly-burly of domestic debate and argument, the promise of antislavery and antistructure combining to effect was vitiated in the private vacuum of colonization. The tragic fall of Liberia was planted with the seeds of its creation, a private enterprise required to shoulder the responsibility of a public national problem. The United States recognized the government of Liberia only in 1862, when President Lincoln signed a treaty of friendship with the country. And although in the same year Congress voted sums of money to pay for the colonization of freed blacks to Liberia, the discretionary powers vested in Lincoln allowed the funds to be diverted to colonization projects in Central America instead.

In 1912 Liberia was declared bankrupt and placed under international receivership. The first major assistance extended to Liberia by the U.S. federal government came in 1926, over one hundred years after the establishment of the first colony at Monrovia. That same year the Firestone Rubber Company entered the country—a chronological coincidence suggesting the two acts might not be unconnected. In the end Liberia—as the privatization of Christian and humanitarian social responsibility—broke down, incapable of providing an alternative to the prejudice, discrimination, and civil strife that ultimately tore it apart.

Much of this assessment is not simply derived from the benefit of hindsight. It was the view of contemporary observers as well. In the extensive records of the American Colonization Society itself we find ample evidence of African colonization being seriously criticized for preserving rather than destroying slavery, as was the case in Freetown. Colonization became an alternative for antislavery, and, accordingly, antislavery conflicted with colonization. American slave masters were handed a close-range weapon for long-range self-defense: the masters could now deal their slaves the penalty of foreign removal to remedy the injustice of slavery. That way, the salt of expulsion would be rubbed into the wound of enslavement. One slave master admitted as much, observing, furthermore, how joining emancipation to repatriation was economically punitive. He wrote despairingly:

> I am a slaveholder and have it in contemplation to liberate several of my slaves, *provided* they could be removed to Liberia at a cost I could afford. But mine is the common misfortune of most slaveholders—a nominal wealth only the *shadow* and not the substance, the reality. We may give to Freedom—to Liberia—this delusive property (and I dare say with the majority of masters it would be gain) but here would end the *boon*, for with them could be added no purse, or means of emigration or settlement. There are many, very many, slaveholders, I am sure, who would *cheerfully* relinquish all their slave property to Liberia, could they afford the means of equipment and settlement or temporary maintenance of such manumitted slaves.[47]

One witness expressed the prevailing consensus when he said that emancipation without emigration would utterly ruin the state. In fact, he predicted, emancipation would lead to a general race war, "the extermination of the one race or the other—and if so, I doubt if it would be the African. Hence I must oppose it, everywhere, and by all gentlemanly and Christian means."[48] The Virginia legislature stated as early as 1805 that it was necessary to arrest "the progress of emancipation, by requiring the speedy removal from the State, of all to whom its privileges might be extended."[49] Clay repeated the sentiment, saying one race or the other would dominate. The struggle for race ascendancy would not abate but be exacerbated by emancipation, so that the inevitable social collision "would break out into a civil war that would end in the extermination or subjugation of the one race or the other," Clay warned.[50] The prophetic reference to civil war indicated the grave obstacles that still bedeviled antislavery, as Robert Stockton pointed out. Speaking in 1826 before the American Colonization Society, Stockton warned about the consequences of dilatoriness on abolition. "Let us not," he urged, "presume on the tranquility of today. This may be the calm out of which bursts the tornado; this the smooth and deceptive water, on the edge of the cataract. The time may come, when, in the dispensation of Providence, this giant people, too, may be stretched in death before the scrutiny of posterity."[51]

In a similarly acute and perspicacious way, Alexis de Tocqueville situated the Liberian colonization efforts firmly within the context of America's domestic slave dilemma.[52] The terrible principle of negro slavery, he said, was unwittingly adopted by nations that were now not free to get rid of it. With or without slaves America would remain the permanent home of Africans, and no amount of emigration could empty the country of its black inhabitants, who in the 1830s numbered more than 2.3 million, of whom 2 million were slaves. Measures were taken to postpone or even offset the misfortunes that threatened to keep an oppressed and repressed society of blacks within the Union, but those measures were not enough to remove their cause. Abolition would not satisfy the demands of freedom and equality, just as continued slavery inflamed the passion for those rights.

In that setting Liberia was a temporizing scheme. In theory the black emigrants taken there would introduce American institutions and habits of enlightened government: a representative system of rule, jury trial, black magistrates and clergy, churches and newspapers. Having acquired the enlightenment of civilization and learned through slavery the art of being free, these black emigrants would reverse the vicious two-century-old trend begun when Europe first snatched from Africa the slaves whose descendants were now returning in happier circumstances. Perhaps with their return, Africa would be opened to the arts and sciences of Europe, and that would mark a turning point in the continent's dark fortunes.[53] For that reason, Tocqueville continued, "the founding of Liberia is based on a fine and grand idea." Nevertheless, in practice Tocqueville was apprehensive that Liberia was being made to carry an unreasonable share of the problem of America, and, thus cribbed and confined by that tragic history, the idea behind its founding would prove sterile.

The numbers told the story eloquently enough. In the twelve years of the Colonization Society's activities, some 2,500 blacks were transported there. In the same period about 700,000 blacks were born in the United States. Another study found that of the 11,909 emigrants to Liberia up to 1866, 4,541 were born free, 344 purchased their freedom, and 5,957 were manumitted for the express purpose of emigration.[54] It was not reasonable to expect that Liberia would offer a commodious enough receptacle for America's unwanted burgeoning black population, an implicit criticism, too, of Jefferson's formula of emancipation accompanied by deportation.

Tocqueville published his account in 1835, the second part in 1840,[55] but even at such remove from the events of the American Civil War, he could sense the impending cataclysm. Liberia could not hide that fact or detract from it. Tocqueville wrote somberly: "The Negro race will never again leave the American continent, to which the passions and vices of Europe brought it; it will not disappear from the New World except by ceasing to exist . . . I am obliged to confess that I do not consider the abolition of slavery as a means of delaying the struggle between the two races in the southern states . . . For the masters in the North slavery was a commercial and industrial question; in the South it is a question of life and death."[56]

With regard to the South Tocqueville said there were only two alternatives worth contemplating: one was to free the slave and to mingle with him or her, and the other was to remain isolated from the slave and keep the lid tightly closed on slavery. Any intermediate measures were likely, in his words, "to terminate, and that shortly, in the most horrible of civil wars, and perhaps in the extermination of one or other of the two races."

Such was the view the southern whites took of the question, and they acted in accordance with it. As they were determined not to mingle with the blacks, they refused to emancipate them. It was a catch-22 situation, and Liberia, not to be envied in the best of circumstances, was now impaled on the horns of that historical dilemma.

Thus the checkered course of antislavery in Liberia reflected mainland American inadequacies transplanted to African shores. Reports began to circulate that the settlement in Liberia was not bringing antislavery to Africa and that the American Colonization Society was not advancing the cause of evangelization in Liberia. As late as 1833 or 1834, a Reverend Dr. Spring was complaining at a meeting of the Colonization Society in New York that the society "had *done nothing*" for the religious instructions of the emigrants. The remedy he proposed was the employment of missionaries by the managers, acting as a Civil Government, at the expense of the colony, disregarding the objection urged that it would be (as he admitted it would) a 'union of Church and State.'"[57] Although this suggestion was turned down, the Reverend John B. Pinney did go out as a missionary and became governor of the colony. When he returned he revealed that nothing was being done to evangelize the natives outside the colony. An officer of the American Board of Commissioners for Foreign Missions visited Liberia and reported that the colony area was not a suitable base for organizing missions into the hinterland, and that "remoteness from the settlements was far more desirable."[58]

The criticism of the settlement was not mitigated by its association with the Colonization Society, which remained under constant attack from the leaders of the antislavery movement. For example, in a stinging attack on American colonization, the antislavery champions in Britain published in 1833 a public notice protesting at the claims of the American Colonization Society, claims that, in their view, masked its unwholesome origins. The society, the protesters charged,

> takes its root from a cruel prejudice and alienation in the whites of America against the colored people, slave or free. This being its source, the effects are what might be expected; that it fosters and increases the spirit of caste, already so unhappily predominant that it widens the breach between the races; exposes the colored people to great practical persecution, in order to *force* them to emigrate and, finally, is calculated to swallow up and divert that feeling which America, as a Christian and free country, cannot but entertain, that slavery is alike incompatible

with the law of God and with the well being of man, whether enslaved
or the enslaver.

The signatories included William Wilberforce, Zachary Macaulay, William Evans, M.P., George Stephen, S. Lushington, M.P., Thomas Fowell
Buxton, William Allen, and Daniel O'Connell, M.P.[59] O'Connell, the celebrated Irish nationalist, had also joined an antislavery petition in 1842
from Britain directed to the Irish community in the United States.[60]

One of the most tantalizing links with America came with the arrival
in the colony in January 1836 of Thomas Buchanan of Philadelphia. He
was a cousin of James Buchanan, who later became president of the
United States. As governor of Liberia Thomas Buchanan became an energetic suppressor of chiefly and native uprisings and a fixer of internal
disorder, "affecting amicable treaties with the ruthless and turbulent
tribes around us," and spreading the fame of the colony far and wide, as
one settler testified. Under his firm leadership Liberia acquired considerable prestige in the eyes of local chieftains, which opened the way for
treaties of friendship with inland princes.[61] Yet little federal action followed such personal ties.

The raising and dashing of such hopes did not bode well for Liberia or
for antislavery. Could it, in fact, be that Liberia would encourage and
facilitate the slave trade? Samuel Ajayi Crowther said that was his cursory impression, as we saw in the previous chapter. Is there evidence to
support the charge? The official documents of the Colonization Society,
including its official organ *The African Repository,* admitted that the boast
of suppressing the slave trade in Liberia was unfounded, that the slave
trade was practiced in the colony, that the colonists carried on a regular
and vigorous traffic with slave traders, and that the patterns of commerce
developed in the settlements facilitated rather than hindered the slave
trade. "Rum, gunpowder, and spear-pointed knives, have been among
the regular exports from this country to the colony of Liberia. These
are sold to the natives, and especially to the slave traders, being the
indispensable articles of their traffic, and the causes of the wars that
furnish captives to be sold to them as slaves. The slave trade, instead of
being repressed (as had been pretended) has been stimulated and encouraged."[62] It was a devastating admission and showed that Crowther,
for one, had in fact understated the case.

In 1832 the Board of Managers of the American Colonization Society conducted an extensive review of the affairs of the settlement, and its report made grim reading, indeed. It found that since 1820 twenty-two expeditions had gone out to Liberia. In the first eighteen just under 1,500 persons had been transported. Of these, 230 people had died, mostly from malaria, which represented a mortality rate of 15.5 percent.

Black Ideology

The history of the settlement of Liberia was in effect the history of the search for a black national identity, and the blacks who reflected critically on the matter came up with black national consciousness as the required response to slavery and its attendant racial attitudes. On that narrow, rather tenuous ground, black intellectual leaders supported and defended the Liberia settlement. They were making a virtue out of necessity.

Joseph Brown Russwurm

One of these leaders was Joseph Brown Russwurm. Born in Jamaica to a black mother and a Virginia planter, he went to school in Quebec and then removed to Maine, where his father had gone to live. In 1824 he went to Bowdoin College, where he finished his undergraduate degree in 1826, becoming one of the first two African American graduates in the United States. He contemplated emigration to Haiti but decided against it. Instead he turned to journalism and edited the first black newspaper in the United States, *Freedom's Journal,* based in New York. He used the newspaper to give vent to his strong anticolonization views and launched a public campaign against emigration to Africa. But the scoffer later turned militant advocate, dropping his opposition to colonization on the grounds that "full citizenship in the United States is utterly impossible in the nature of things, and that those who pant for it must cast their eyes elsewhere."[63] He followed his own advice by emigrating in the summer of 1829 to Liberia. A highly practical man, Russwurm was also attracted to Liberia by the prospects of better economic opportunities and the availability, as he believed, of limitless natural abundance. Yet ideological motives were always lurking near the surface of his thoughts. In that light he wrote that in Liberia "the Man of Colour . . . may walk forth in all the majesty of his creation—a new-born creature—a Free

Man!"[64] Except for a brief visit to the United States, where he died in 1851, he spent the rest of his life in his adopted country and was honored by becoming the first black to be made governor of Maryland Colony in 1836.

After arriving in Liberia Russwurm founded the first newspaper in the country in 1830, the *Liberia Herald,* which established itself as a leading newspaper and was in demand at home and abroad. He worked for greater cooperation among the settlements, seeking to link them with Monrovia. He was aware of the exposed position of Maryland Colony, lying on the volatile southern border, which was why he became a natural advocate of the confederalism that was established in 1839.

He lived long enough to see Liberia emerge as an independent republic but not to see the admission of Maryland Colony into the republic. That happened only after the colony came under attack in 1856 from neighboring tribes, an attack that ended its independence when it was forced to join Liberia as a fourth county.

Alexander Crummell

The theme of Liberia and the search for a black national identity found another forceful, if somewhat tardy, spokesman in Alexander Crummell, who was born of free parents in New York in March 1819. His father, Boston Crummell, had achieved his freedom by 1813, whether through purchase or absconding, it is not clear. The young Crummell enrolled in one of the schools of the African Free Schools movement run by the New York Manumission Society. His father was active in national efforts on behalf of black social causes, and his influence helped shape Alexander, who added to his father's political activism leadership in black educational and religious causes.

Religion was one of the few public fields of any standing open to blacks, especially to those who aspired to a leadership role. Enterprising blacks flourished in that field and used it to enunciate black demands for racial justice and equal treatment under the law. Accordingly, Crummell decided to pursue a career in the church and to combine that with political involvement. But he was refused admission to the General Theological Seminary in New York, because of his race, he suspected. Wounded by that rebuff and armed with letters of introduction by John Jay, the grandson of Chief Justice Jay, who considered him his protégé,

Crummell traveled to Boston, where he was sympathetically received by Bishop Alexander Griswold. Shortly after that he came to New Haven, where he was given conditional admission to take classes in theology at Yale. At this time he took part in the New York State Negro Convention, then pushing for black suffrage.

Crummell campaigned with the other members of the convention for the abolition of the $250 property qualification imposed on blacks in 1821 and for opening the electoral rolls to all free blacks. He appealed for the political franchise for blacks on the grounds of the "fundamental sentiments of *our common humanity*," and further asserted: "On the ground of our common humanity do we claim equal and entire rights with the rest of our fellow citizens," saying the letter and spirit of the Declaration of Independence and the Constitution supported his case.[65] He interrupted briefly his political activities with a return to religion when he was called to serve as lay reader for a small black congregation in Providence, Rhode Island. He left Yale in 1841 for that reason. The following year he was ordained as a deacon in St. Paul's Church, Boston, by Bishop Griswold. He took up again the cause of the black franchise in Providence, which became embroiled in bitter political dispute after December 1841, when the state voted to exclude blacks from the vote, culminating in Dorr's War in 1842. Shortly after that Crummell resigned his position as deacon in Providence, so restless had he become and so discouraged with political prospects in Rhode Island.

When he turned up in Philadelphia, his controversial past caught up with him there, too, and he was prevented from setting up a black Episcopal church that might challenge for representation in the Diocesan Convention. He stayed for a while in Philadelphia before coming to New York City as a newly married man and an ordained priest. (He was ordained in 1844 by Bishop Lee of Delaware). He continued to take an active role in political issues, pressing for the extension of the vote to blacks but finding little support for the idea among whites, including self-espousing liberals. His attention began to turn inward, to projects that stressed black self-help. Crummell was disappointed to find that not many blacks at the time supported his educational plans, not even Frederick Douglass, who in fact rejected the separatist implications of Crummell's ideas of reform. It was while he was regrouping in the face of his persistent setbacks in America that Crummell thought of going to England to raise support. His mind thenceforth turned inexorably toward England, the England of Clarkson, Wilberforce, and Venn, and, crucially, toward Cambridge, an illustrious center of evangelicalism and antislavery.

In 1848, the year of revolutions in much of Europe, including the Chartist Movement in its later stages in England, Crummell arrived in Liverpool. Everywhere he went he sought to make common cause with supporters of antislavery. He told a meeting of the British and Foreign Anti-Slavery Society in 1848 that "no man is in full possession of freedom, no matter where he lives, while there exists one slave beneath the lash in any quarter of the globe."[66] His evangelical friends arranged to raise funds to send him to Cambridge and to pay for his wife and two sons to join him from New York. John Jay supported the plan, and Crummell entered Queen's College in Cambridge in the autumn of 1849, to the welcome of Thomas Macaulay, J. A. Froude, and others. His Cambridge years were marked by the tragic death of his eldest son, who choked on a button. His own health temporarily declined, with cramping and heart palpitations. But there were encouraging things to revive his flagging spirits. His wife gave birth to three children, including a daughter born in Cambridge in March 1851 and another daughter born in Ipswich in May 1852.

The prospects of returning to New York to resume his clerical duties were not appealing to Crummell, given his mixed experiences there and given the appeal of unexplored opportunities elsewhere. Therefore, it was not surprising that he decided not to return and to resign from the Church of the Messiah, from which he had taken a leave of absence. The catalyst for his decision was the Fugitive Slave Act of 1850, an act that also influenced Martin Delany's decision to leave the United States.

When Crummell considered what he might do after Cambridge, his thoughts turned reluctantly to Liberia, until then a country he felt to be a distraction from the struggle for racial equality and justice in the United States. As a venture of the American Colonization Society, Liberia stood for the principle of black emigration as the price of emancipation, a price Crummell felt added to the burden of slavery the weight of deportation. Whether or not he was making a virtue out of necessity, however, Crummell now took up the cause of Liberia as an urgent, necessary vocation for the advancement of blacks. He wrote to John Jay in those high-minded terms, taking care to distance himself from the American Colonization Society while applauding the civilizational goals of Liberia. This stance was a trace too disingenuous, as Frederick Douglass would charge him in another connection.

With his finals at Cambridge at long last behind him, Crummell set out for Liberia, by then an independent republic, arriving there with his family in July 1853. He came as an agent of the Protestant Episcopal Church, a mission that opened its first station at Mount Vaughan in Maryland County in 1836. In 1838 John Payne came out from America to head the station as missionary bishop. He was in charge when Crummell arrived. Although Payne's view of the role of African Americans in missionary work was soured by his unsatisfactory association with an African American from Maryland via Providence, E. W. Stokes, with whom he parted on the most unfriendly terms, he was impressed enough with Crummell's ability to vest control of the work in Monrovia in Crummell (to the chagrin of Stokes, who left in a huff). Stokes returned to Liberia in 1854 under license from the Scottish Episcopal Church, setting up a rival church movement to challenge Crummell. Stokes died in 1867, while Crummell was embroiled in other controversies.

It was not long before Crummell found himself in conflict with Payne and the church in Monrovia. Crummell was pressing for a grandiose national church to be built in Monrovia, laying elaborate plans for the purpose and allegedly neglecting his duties to his small congregation, which had been dwindling through defections to Stokes. Crummell reacted to Payne's measures to strengthen the work in Monrovia—measures that included the appointment of a white missionary to Monrovia—as an unjustified attack on his leadership. He resigned rather than take second place to the white who was appointed. His announced reasons for resigning fed the rumor mill of racial malice, causing Payne to reassess the feasibility of Monrovia as the base for the Episcopal mission in Liberia. Racial tensions were creating strains too great to overcome with the mission's exposed position.

Crummell now looked to the recently founded, and still floundering, Liberia College for a position, saying he would accept an appointment for an annual salary of $1,500, though no such position was available. In the end Crummell would eat humble pie and turn to Payne, who offered him a position as head of the Mount Vaughan High School at Cape Palmas, but, although he was at first enthusiastically received, Crummell alienated his colleagues and friends by driving the school to the brink of bankruptcy with his undisciplined management style. Accordingly, he was dismissed.

Next Crummell turned to the American Colonization Society, his erstwhile foe, for recognition. During a visit to the United States in 1861–62, Crummell promoted the cause of the Society, writing a letter, "The Relations and Duties of Free Colored Men in America to Africa," espousing emigration. He toured in New York, Connecticut, New Hampshire, and Massachusetts as a mouthpiece for the Colonization Society, a surprising role considering the known opposition of northern blacks to the Society, a position Crummell had himself encouraged until relatively recently. The thought must have crossed his mind, for he declined to accept an appointment as the society's official agent, though he would later write a series of articles for *The African Repository* (between 1864 and 1865), promoting Liberia for the society. In spite of the hype about Crummell's public lectures promoting Liberia, there was a poor response among blacks. Only fifty-five of them went to Liberia in 1861. Shortly after that the society judged it was not worth sending its ships to Liberia anymore. The Civil War had broken out, fueling African American hostility toward Liberia. Only twenty-three emigrants left for the colony in 1864. Crummell declined to address a meeting of the American Colonization Society when called upon to do so in 1862, proof of hardening attitudes. At about the same time he was appointed a commissioner for emigration by the Liberian government, with plans to supervise the transfer of a community of blacks from Washington, D.C., to Liberia. Little came of that effort, and both Crummell and Blyden, who was also charged with the mission, left feeling despondent.

Crummell returned once more to Liberia to face familiar frustration, disappointment, distress, and even despair. Liberia College, on which he continued to pin high hopes, was still floundering, with controversy still raging about finding an appropriate site for it and about establishing a faculty for the college. Crummell was eventually retained for the college as professor of intellectual and moral philosophy and of English language and literature, but when asked to take up his appointment as a live-in faculty member, he objected on the grounds of that being beneath his office as a professor. When he failed to win over the treasurer of the college, he complained loudly about not being paid enough at a salary of $850. When the trustees of the college opposed his keeping a second job as a priest of the Episcopal Church, in which capacity he was campaigning heavy-handedly for the creation of a national church, complete with book, bell, and candle of its own, he protested about being done an injustice. When the General Convention of the Episcopal Church in the United States cold-shouldered his idea of a national church, Crummell accused them of malice aforethought. He then embarked on cultivating partisan support among blacks to remedy the disadvantages of working under white-made church rules. It seemed not to weigh much with him that in the cause of campaigning for the scheme he was stirring considerable factional strife in the colony. When censured for staying away too long from the college on an extended visit to the United States in 1865 and requested to comply with the requirement to inform the college of any planned absence, Crummell objected and fired back an attack on the president of the college, accusing him of dereliction of responsibility. In response, the college convened a meeting in July 1866 and voted to call for Crummell's resignation. Crummell learned of the news only in October, and, characteristically, he picked up the gauntlet once more, threatening to quit immediately and accusing the college of tyranny, illegality, and wrong. He left the college finally on 30 November, an injured, embittered man, though scarcely any more restrained for that.

Crummell next plunged into the hurly-burly of Liberia's truculent race politics. The lighter-skinned Americo-Liberians practiced the politics of racial exclusion toward their darker-skinned compatriots, whose losing cause Crummell chose to champion, drawn to it like a moth to the flame. He blamed the racial attitudes of the light-skinned Americo-Liberians for the failure to attract blacks from the United States. He joined with Edward Blyden and others in 1867 to promote the candidacy of E. J. Roye for president of the republic. A dark-skinned African American who headed the Negro Party, Roye won the election but touched off a constitutional crisis when he was deposed through a conveniently enacted constitutional amendment that extended the term of the president from two to four years, in effect reinstating Roye's defeated presidential rival, J. J. Roberts. Military intervention was threatened unless Roye stood down. In the ensuing conflict Roye's supporters were defeated by force, with many of his front men arrested and executed. Crummell's son, Sidney, was apprehended and sentenced to a term of two and a half years' imprisonment for his support of Roye.

Crummell himself seems to have escaped unscathed the violence and the following reprisals. Uncowed, however, he denounced Roye's political enemies as reactionaries who opposed progress, civilization, enlightenment, and missions. He characterized them as part of a movement set to undo the work of those who meant well for the colony. The country, he warned, was facing ruin and disaster at the hands of Roye's opponents.

The Roye debacle was followed by other personal setbacks for Crummell. In 1871 Bishop Payne resigned, and Crummell promptly applied to fill the vacancy, fully expecting to get the job. In the end the position went to John Auer, a white missionary in Liberia, who was elected in 1872. Disheartened and forlorn, Crummell brooded on fears for his personal safety in Liberia, recounting rumors of assassination plots. He contemplated fleeing to Sierra Leone for safe asylum but failed to find a situation there. Even his friendship and collaboration with Blyden virtually ended over the Roye episode when Blyden accused Crummell of sacrificing their long-established friendship to professional jealousy and joining Blyden's enemies in traducing him by spreading allegations of Blyden being in flagrante with Roye's wife. Crummell repeated the charge to a third party who passed it on to Venn in London, much to Blyden's distress.[67] Venn ordered a termination of Blyden's service with the Church Missionary Society.

Crummell returned to the United States in May 1872, a man of many troubles. He became active once again in the cause of black cultural and political advancement, tangling with leading figures in the field, figures such as Henry McNeal Turner and Booker T. Washington. He accepted a parish position in New York City and then moved in 1873 to Washington, D.C., as a senior cleric. Controversy followed him there, with parishioners calling for his dismissal. That cloud passed, and Crummell went on to establish his reputation in Washington social circles. He took a leading part in the American Negro Academy, which was devoted to educational, cultural, and political advancement among blacks. In 1897 he visited England in connection with Victoria's Diamond Jubilee. He died in his retirement home in Red Bank, New Jersey, in September 1898.

When one considers the life and work of Crummell one is led to the conclusion that he reflected without transcending the shortcomings of Liberian colonization. He embodied many of the themes that defined the position of blacks in the era of antislavery, while his American background instilled in him the conviction that opportunity and exertion would be all it took to achieve progress for blacks. Similarly, in spite of the favorable impression he had of established religion in England, religion for Crummell was nevertheless stamped with a distinctive American character. Religion was a charter for political change, social equality, and collective improvement.

Crummell's case for the plausibility of emigration to Africa was marked by a high-minded romanticism, to which he added a tinge of American positivism. "Races, like families," he wrote in 1887, "are the ordinances of God, and race feeling, like family feeling, is of divine origin. The extinction of race feeling is just as possible as the extinction of family feeling." Divine Providence, he asserted, employed the advantages of natural endowment, like common feelings, blood, and ancestry, to effect the changes necessary in society. "The black Christian emigrant is indigenous in blood, constitution, and adaptability. Two centuries of absence from the continent of Africa, has not destroyed his physical adaptation to the land of his ancestors. There is a tropical fitness, which inheres in our constitution, whereby we are enabled, when we leave this country, to sit down under an African sun and soon, with comparative ease, feel ourselves at home, and move about in the land as though we had always lived there."[68]

A gifted individual by any measure, as W. E. B. Du Bois testified in his famous impressionistic account of the man,[69] Crummell was nevertheless hamstrung by the contradictory impulses that shaped Liberia's destiny. He seemed beset by a double jeopardy, for he saw that colonization should become not just the private hobby of a group of enlightened individuals but the public policy of the United States, while such a course conflicted with his own nationalist, anticolonial scruples. Liberia, he urged, should for a limited time become a protectorate of a power like the United States and as such be placed under what he called "naval guardianship." With that advantage, Liberia could then commence the real and lasting work of civilization in the interior, applying, he said, the force of restoration and progress that would inculcate the superior values of the advancement of women and the importance of the idea of family and home. Crummell had many faults, as his numerous critics, friend and foe alike, were quick to point out, but it was arguably not his fault that his ideas of what was possible in Liberia sounded speculative and romantic. In the absence of any fundamental change in the character of the colony as a private settlement, any agenda for the settlement was bound to sound wistful and abstract. Without public backing in congressional commitment, Crummell and his fellow activists could not help it if their ideology of black nationalism sounded airy.

Edward Wilmot Blyden

The ideological theme found one of its greatest and most eloquent exponents in the person of Dr. Edward Wilmot Blyden. Born in 1832 in the West Indies, Blyden came to the United States in 1850 to pursue theological training. Finding the American racial climate inhospitable, he left later that year and arrived in Liberia in 1851. Although he was only nineteen, his intellectual brilliance was quickly recognized. When Liberia College was founded in 1861 he was appointed professor of Greek and Latin languages and literature, and an instructor of logic, rhetoric, history, Hebrew, French, mathematics, and natural philosophy. The college was a three-story building, the largest structure in Liberia. It remained closed while Blyden and Alexander Crummell toured the United States to raise support for the students. The impending Civil War interrupted their efforts in that direction and so they returned.

In 1864 the New York Colonization Society endowed a chair for the Fulton Professorship at the college, and Blyden was appointed as the first person to fill it. He left his post to serve as secretary of state for Liberia from 1864 to 1866. His active involvement in Liberian politics came to a head in 1871 when his alliance with Roye, the newly elected president of the country, boomeranged amid the deeply splintered racial politics. A mob of mulatto opponents of Roye not only charged Blyden with adultery with Roye's wife, but also dragged him through the streets of Monrovia, ready to have him publicly lynched. Roye was himself deposed and murdered a few months later. Blyden fled to neighboring Sierra Leone, where he founded a newspaper, *The Negro*.

Blyden had broad influence within the administration of Sierra Leone and was appointed government agent to the interior. In that capacity he made wide-ranging contacts with hinterland Muslim elites and educational centers, making an important trip to Timbo in Futa Jallon in 1872. He had studied Islam and Arabic at the Syrian Protestant College in Beirut in 1866. In his attitude toward Muslim Africa he incorporated vestiges of the noble savage idea; he often wrote of the brilliance of indigenous Muslim learning untainted by Western civilization and thus of its being well suited to promoting the native genius of blacks far better than Western missionary schools. For Blyden Muslim Africa bore strains of a native Arcady where still "sable hands will strike the lyre and weave the silken web," as Finley freely fantasized. Blyden became head of the Muslim Board of Education, in which capacity he promoted Islam and Muslims in both church and state. He was instrumental in securing the appointment of Harun al-Rashid, a local African Muslim, as a teacher of Arabic at the recently founded CMS college, Fourah Bay College, and in promoting that of Muhammad Sanusi as government Arabic Writer. Blyden advocated the idea of founding a West African university on whose curriculum Islam and Muslims would be given a central role. Several governors followed his advice and encouragement in promulgating policies to advance Islam and Muslim interests, though the West African university never materialized.

Blyden returned to Liberia in 1874 to be appointed to the Court of St. James in London as ambassador from 1877 to 1878, and then briefly in 1892. He also served as president of Liberia College from 1880 to 1884. In 1885 he ran unsuccessfully for president of the republic. The next year he went back to Sierra Leone, from where he continued to exert deep influence on all of West Africa and on other places farther afield. When he died on 7 February 1912, two years after an aneurysm operation in Liverpool, England, Muslims prominently participated in his funeral in Freetown, where his body was taken.

Much of Blyden's intellectual influence was crystallized in his magnum opus, *Christianity, Islam, and the Negro Race,* published in London in 1887. The book, a collection of his essays, became an instant classic and allowed Blyden's ideas to have the impact they deserved. It marked a turning point in the Western and missionary assessment of the religious and theological challenge of Islam and, accordingly, provoked a sustained debate and discussion in Britain, West Africa, the United States, and the Middle East. A correspondent in the *Times* (London), for example, said Blyden's book "may yet prove the greatest contribution of the age on the gigantic subject of Christian missions."[70] And Robertson Smith of Harrow testified, "I regard . . . *Christianity, Islam and the Negro Race* . . . as one of the most remarkable books I have ever met."[71]

A formal debate on the issues the book raised was held in the halls of Fourah Bay College, West Africa, in 1888, with the proceedings published in the local papers.[72] And in the United States the reviews were fulsome, with the *A.M.E. Church Review* endorsing the book, saying it was "not only the most learned production that ever emanated from a black man, but one of the most learned in the English language . . . The work will be an authority in the higher literary circles for ages to come."[73]

Favorable reviews, comparable in judgment if not in feeling, appeared in Beirut, Constantinople, and Damascus. There was widespread disbelief that a black writer, without much formal education, could have produced a work of such high literary and academic caliber. This consternation showed race to be a major factor of intercultural understanding and, along with the theme of a black writer exploding the myth of race inferiority, explains the tone of many reviews of the book.

In terms of the particular details the book treated, there was much unevenness. But Blyden was a master stylist, and the inadequacies of scholarship he could mask with supreme rhetorical power. His achievement, therefore, lay in the didactic, collective impact of his writing rather than in the analytic task of sifting new evidence or in higher source criticism. As his disciple J. E. Casely Hayford of Ghana put it in 1905, the merit of Blyden's exertions consisted in the general work he had done for the race as a whole, rather than in any specific, detailed advancement of knowledge of Africa.[74]

Blyden's ideology was a turbulent, inconsistent amalgam of colonization, civilization, and indigenization, with a Pan-African element thrown in to ratchet up the whole scheme to an abstract nationalist plane. Colonization, Blyden argued, afforded blacks in America and the West Indies the opportunity to escape the oppression and denigration of slavery and race prejudice, while civilization through education furnished the tools to demonstrate black equality with whites. Blyden struck up a personal friendship with William Gladstone, several times prime minister of Britain and at that time chancellor of the exchequer. Blyden wrote to Gladstone about Liberia, saying that Liberia would extend civilization to other parts of Africa and that, to carry out this work, "we need men of enlightened minds, of enlarged views, of high-toned character." Blyden's own personal ambition to improve his education, he said, "arises from the interest I feel in the Negro race, and my great anxiety is to labour with increased efficiency to promote and accelerate that progress."[75] In 1864 Blyden and Alexander Crummell together founded the Athenaeum Club in Monrovia, where young people could meet and engage in lectures, debates, and discussions as a way of contributing to the improvement of cultural life in the town.

By the time he met Martin Delany in 1859, Blyden was sold on Liberia as a civilizing instrument in Africa, and he exchanged some views with Delany on that score (as pointed out in the previous chapter). On the issue still of civilization, Blyden was, inconsistently, not loath to advocate European imperialism and its secular corollaries, preferably the mild and benign British forms, as a vehicle to forge Sierra Leone and Liberia into a united administration. He was hopeful Britain could bring wider benefits to Liberia and alleviate the sense of insecurity fed by its relative international isolation. Consequently, Blyden was suspected of being part of a political plot in 1909 to mastermind a British takeover of Liberia. In 1906 a British bank conducted negotiations for a loan to Liberia of £100,000 to rescue the country from certain bankruptcy, thus feeding suspicions of British designs on the territory.

Blyden insisted that he opposed that loan because if the president of Liberia was able to carry out the schemes for which the loan was obtained, "he would have sent foxes with firebrands attached to their tails throughout the standing corn of the Republic and produced a general conflagration." Had Liberia succeeded in its plans, he explained, indigenous Africans would have shared the ignominious fate of North American Indians "and a caste system would have been established as oppressive as anything in the Southern States. It has been mercifully arranged by a wise and benevolent Providence in the true interests of Africa," Blyden noted with relief, "that we should have no millions at our disposal, for we should have endeavoured to realise the dreams and visions we brought from the house of bondage."[76] Thus even a prosperous Liberia, unchecked by the ethics of antislavery, bode ill for the rest of Africa.

Indigenization, the third piece of Blyden's ideology, restored black pride by retrieving and developing native talent and wisdom against Western-inspired detractions—anticipating the philosophy of *négritude* promoted by Aimé Césaire and Léopold Sedar Senghor in the 1950s and 1960s. Blyden, however, divided the world into West and non-West, and lumped Islam with Africa on one side against the West on the other, rather than seeing Islam as equally implicated in black Africa's subjugation.

In his understanding of indigenization, Blyden completely misunderstood the role chiefs would play in the new society being fashioned in Africa: it is not clear whether his misunderstanding arose from his ignorance of chieftaincy rule, from the nature of the new society, or from both. No matter. In his reflections on the subject, Blyden urged that chiefs be included in Crowther's Native Pastorate and that the path of inclusion be smoothed for them in a manner reminiscent of the role Constantine and subsequent European sovereigns played in Christendom.[77] Blyden could not conceive a future for Christianity in Africa without chiefs—and how wrong he was.

Blyden's philosophy of Negro pride, to return once more to that, took primary account of Europe's encounter with the black race. He saw that Europeans were the superiors of Africans because of the former's technological prowess, and it was that technology, too, that enabled them to feel themselves the moral superiors of Africans for having abandoned the slave trade. Power invested the powerful with a double prerogative. Western technology conferred the capacity to conquer and suppress, while the West's moral superiority as demonstrated in the enlightened project of abolition gave the right to dominate spiritually and intellectually. America shared in this superiority, though, as Finley contended, its affinity was greater with the spiritual and intellectual dimensions of that superiority than with the political or military.

Blyden tried to respond to this challenge. He said Europe's acquisitive and unsolicitous vehicle of domination came crashing through Africa like the "heavy and crushing indifference of the car of Juggernaut." The conductors of that ponderous vehicle, he lamented, were immune to the feelings of the people they crushed and trampled on. That indifference extended to a complete disregard of the sensibilities that might be lacerated, and a lack of any attempt to cultivate what he called "the well-spring of a nobler life within."[78] African populations thus became the victims of an unsympathetic apparatus of political and commercial machinery. Writing in 1900, Blyden reflected on the fact that there were three important facets of the cultural and historical reality of West Africa: first, that large numbers of its people had been taken into slave exile "for discipline and training under a more advanced race"; second, that they were suppressed and kept separate from the master race; and, third, that a number of them, having been exposed to a more advanced way of life, in the course of time returned to Africa as agents of civilization. These views are similar to the proposal by Lord John Russell in London and

Governor Doherty of Sierra Leone (to let West Indians civilize Africa) (see Chapter 4).

That diagnosis, calculated to inspire, also reveals Blyden's ideological complexity in demanding the imposition of Western colonial rule to help instill order and progress into Africa's affairs. As a neo–Social Darwinist, Blyden believed that struggle and effort refined and elevated the black just as repetition and imitation cheapened and stunted him or her. The only hope was the cultivation of *difference* as defined by Herbert Spencer. Blyden contended that since "evolution is the law of life, we can have neither real permanent life nor vigorous or continuous growth [in the separation from indigenous African life and institutions]."[79] Still, Africans had to acknowledge the importance of Western culture and to study the classics and mathematics in Liberia College to "gain nourishment from them without taking in any race poison."[80] Thus did the ideologue and the realist collide in Blyden freely, creating an intellectual ferment that taxed even his eclectic brilliance. Between Liberia and Sierra Leone, for example, Blyden tried to find a home but ended up restless in one or the other. Even his funeral in Freetown in 1912 raised questions about the relationship between Muslims and Christians.

One comes away from a study such as this one with the marked impression that Liberia, having been wrung out of southern resistance to emancipation, suffered from the northern liberal tendency to equate the colony's exotic remoteness with its proximity to effortless native virtue, the place where, as Finley expressed it, "their contracted minds will expand and their natures rise." Much as the colony was weaned on American ideas of freedom, representative government, the rights of the individual, the rule of law, religious toleration, the dignity of family life and of labor, and respect for international trade and obligations, it was nevertheless abandoned as a distant tropical enclave, without access to congressional support and accountability and to public interest. In theory Liberia should have been a positive launching pad for the combined power of antislavery, evangelical doctrine, and public commitment. In practice, however, the settlement found itself being drawn into America's unresolved dilemma about antislavery and emancipation only to be cast aside from public indifference.

Thus did James C. Minor, emancipated in 1826 in Virginia, and emigrating subsequently to Liberia in 1829, hint at Liberia's isolation, saying the settlement existed to fulfill Jefferson's recommendation: "Let an ocean divide the white man from the man of color."[81] Minor mused ruefully about Liberia's needs being overlooked in America. "I would offer a petition [for help]," he reflected, "but am doubtful whether or not it would be received or noticed." Like Liberia itself, Minor was reduced to living hand to mouth, with little prospect of help from the public purse. Liberians would consequently remain an insecure group of "alien residents," on a free reservation, forced to live by their wits. The group's missionary prospects dimmed as it made enemies of its neighbors.

Nevertheless, the settlers were made to understand that they were in Liberia to make the flame of life, liberty, and the pursuit of human dignity burn bright in Africa, to lift up their eyes to the hills and proclaim antislavery to a still enslaved continent. Lacking the public means or facility to act in that capacity, they were reduced to costly fence mending with their hostile and slave-enriched neighbors, whose dark example they were tempted many times to follow in self-preservation. Against such odds, the settlers continued to speak in their declaration of independence in 1847 of how they came to Liberia "to nourish in our hearts the flame of honourable ambition; to cherish and indulge those aspirations which a beneficent Creator had implanted in every human heart, and to evince to all who despise, ridicule, and oppress our race that we possess with them a common nature; are with them susceptible of equal refinement, and capable of equal advancement in all that adorns and dignifies man."[82] America had profoundly marked their consciousness, but America would not avail them in their need.

Connected thus to America by bonds of history, language, and values, Liberia was still cut adrift, becoming a castaway colony on the shores of West Africa. America had without justification forsaken it, and the local chiefs, with justification, targeted it for retaliation, all of which left Liberia reeling between an obsession with its survival and contrived confidence in its sense of chosenness. Missions entering the settlement found themselves ambushed by Liberia's unresolved race and slave questions. After all, deportation, however mild and voluntary, still carried odious enough hints of nonacceptance, quarantine, and inequality to make it a positive, expansive inducement for reconciliation. The black settlers nursed a sense of resentment for that reason, their presence in Liberia proof of America having rejected them. And it was by no means a settled and foregone conclusion that Liberia was the best place from which to fight that sense of rejection and achieve reconciliation.

It makes plaintive reading to return to the address composed by the settlers and directed to the attention of the Free Coloured People of the United States, written after the settlement was declared official on 2 April 1825. The address spoke in idealistic terms of the settlers being the proprietors of the soil

> we live on; and possess the rights of freeholders our suffrages, and what is of more importance our *sentiments,* and our *opinions,* have their due weight in the government we live under. Our laws are altogether our own; they grow out of our circumstances; are framed for our exclusive benefit; and administered either by officers of our own appointment, or such as possess our confidence . . . The time and mode of worshipping God as prescribed in his word, and dictated by our conscience, we are not only free to follow, but are protected in following.[83]

The sentiment is preserved on the seal of the nation: "The love of liberty brought us here." It is a perfect illustration of how America succeeded in imbuing even the least of these brethren with the potent idea that they carried in them not only a little divine something but a little government, too.

Ultimately, however, such lofty ideals were then made to discharge in isolation, insecurity, confinement, and contested identity. The missionary and antislavery impulses in Liberia faltered from the failure to combine the two effectively. Unlike Sierra Leone, Liberia simply counted for far too little in the strategic logic of the public engagement with the worldwide antislavery movement and in the ideological logic of a burgeoning population of recaptive Africans assuming ultimate charge. Instead, the settlement was hoist with its own petard, tied as it was to the remote ambivalent goodwill of southern slave owners whose insecurity on the slave question in practice, as Tocqueville observed, undercut Liberia's reason for being. Missionary plans developed for Liberia in large measure suffered from those severe historical constraints and as such failed in Liberia, with little repeatable value for anywhere or anyone else. It was a good thing the CMS and Britain had between them secured Sierra Leone and, later, Nigeria for the cause.

Conclusion

Liberia was proof that the antislavery movement needed to break loose of purely pragmatic economic and social considerations to succeed with its goal of achieving permanent results in Africa. Even though the antislavery cause made use of pragmatic ideas and strategies, its moral roots went back to what David Brion Davis called "a turning point in the evolution of [human] moral perception," defined as a major religious transformation that changes people's ideas of sin and spiritual freedom and offers outcasts and the downtrodden a new season of opportunity. The transformation consisted of evangelical faith in instantaneous conversion and demonstrative sanctification, according to Davis.[1] But those moral roots needed public political backing.

In the founding of the Sierra Leone colony, antislavery as the culmination of evangelical social activism became a public cause in the sense of commitment to establishing a new society based on public morality, freedom, human dignity, integrity, the rule of law, and justice. In Liberia, by contrast, antislavery was compromised by being privatized and prescribed as individual inducement for southern emancipation. Weighed down as such with the bells and whistles of antebellum America, antislavery languished in Liberia. It was only as part of Abraham Lincoln's antislavery campaign when he was president of the United States that Liberia gained recognition; but no help came from the federal government, which shows how the colony was dubiously tied to unresolved questions in American slavery.

238

Antislavery

This book, as should be clear by now, is not a history of slavery and the slave trade, but a study of antislavery as a social movement of ex-slaves, ex-captives, and their friends and allies in religion, politics, and society. Several themes converge on antislavery, themes such as slave agitation and self-understanding, the use of the petition, the role and function of black preaching, evangelical social activism, the undoing of Christendom and other establishment structures, overcoming chiefly opposition, the moral transformation of African society, recaptives and the values of antistructure, mission as an antislavery movement, the ambivalent role of traders and commercial agents, the anachronism of late-nineteenth-century colonial hegemony in the face of free settlements, and the securing of thriving indigenous strongholds for antislavery and antistructure.

I have argued that the organizing of the antislavery effort in Europe and North America required a complementary effort in Africa to assure success. Accordingly, the assembling of antislavery views in the West needed appropriate local receptors in Africa to be credible. The central question was, given Africa's historical involvement in slavery, how might the antislavery strategy be developed there? Powerful indigenous political and economic structures prevailed, having successfully exploited the slave trade and become identified with it.

The logical answer was to take former slaves, former captives, and the target victim populations and commission them to assume responsibility for the cause. An important transition could then be made from antislavery as a foreign cause to antislavery as an African initiative in order to remove the objection to it as an intrusion by outsiders. Much uncertainty and numerous mistakes attended the effort, but everyone concerned felt it was right to look in that direction.

That indigenous direction is crucial to my view of the intellectual and social history of antislavery. For example, while it would be natural in a standard history of slavery and the slave trade to indicate the nature and scope of Africa's involvement, I am more interested in how Africa came to be involved in antislavery. If Africa and the West were together implicated in the evil of slavery, however one spreads the blame in that business, they were also thoroughly interconnected in antislavery, in ways with equally enduring effects on the societies and peoples of the continent. As Blyden noted, Africa's relation to the rest of the world had always been strange and peculiar. Africans had not mingled with other people except to serve them,[2] or worse. Antislavery would change that strange and peculiar relationship.

Antistructure

If we were to ask the question, what kind of society would best promote antislavery in Africa? we would have to answer, for reasons already adumbrated, that it would be one not based on the top-dog norms of chiefly lineage and groveling fealty. The old Christendom structures of Europe had favored chiefly society, and the fealty and deference it bred, for the transmission of religion, and that habit survived in the West long after territorial Christendom had broken down. Consequently, kings, chiefs, and ruling castes in Africa were targeted for conversion and alliance. Only the logic of antislavery challenged that habit, reluctantly perhaps, but ultimately inevitably. Thus, even the American Colonization Society, committed already to the new ethic, nevertheless found itself slipping back into old habits and looking to the chiefly lineage to advance the cause in Africa. An officer of the society produced a prince— abdicating, unarmed, and leading a band of civilized ex-slaves—to free and colonize Africa. The officer declared: "The finger of God seems to point to great results arising from the return of the Prince ['Abd al-Rahmán of the ruling house of Futa Jallon]. His life appears like a romance, and the incidents would be incredible if the evidence was not so undeniable. We see in these events," he persisted, "that God's ways are not our ways, nor His thoughts as our thoughts . . . Methinks I see him like a Patriarch crossing the Atlantic, over which he was taken a slave 40 years since, with his flock around him, and happy in the luxury of doing good."[3]

Even such nostalgia had to be tempered with the new realities, identified for now not as antislavery and antistructure but as American interest in lawful trade and in a prosperous society. Yet the officer in question did understand, reluctantly perhaps but necessarily, that kings and chiefs played too prominent a role in slavery to be enamored of antislavery. On the contrary, they were much too invested in the means of slave production to become anything but dialectical class enemies of the antislavery movement. No amount of commercial pressure or imperial ambition could hide that truth, though colonial administrators, emboldened by traders, tried means obvious and devious to mask the fact. So 'Abd al-Rahmán in Africa would regain, not the crown but, under antislavery, far nobler aspirations and "dwell there as the humble dwell."[4]

Just as the old Christendom structures had broken down in Western Europe, and just as that Christendom heritage in New England high society had been bypassed by the antislavery movement, just so had African traditional political structures and social institutions come under direct challenge from the new antislavery forces that were entering the continent. As observed in Chapter 4, Samuel Johnson in his *History of the Yorubas* (1891) referred to prophecies and predictions by local diviners and seers as straws in the wind, portending change in the old order, with the old kingdoms in a state of incipient civil strife. Only the gifted, if not favored, of the traditional rulers could divine the shape of the coming new world order, yet even they would find antislavery as the ruling conviction of that new order inhospitable to chiefly pretensions. The chiefs would find few friends in antislavery and antistructure.

If kings, chiefs, and other local rulers could play no meaningful role in the new society of antislavery, or at least no role that did not conflict with the prerogatives of chiefly power, then it was important for antislavery to fill the vacuum with alternative notions of power and legitimacy. That new society would become in effect what Michael Walzer has called "a substitute establishment, 'in which things were compassed, which legally were never conceived.'"[5] That alternative society, consisting of the wholesome examples of liberated Africans, women, men, and children, I have called antistructure. Its connections with American forms of political republicanism and religious voluntarism are, in the familiar language, self-evident. They require little justification at this point.

The American Factor

From the previous chapter it is clear that the Liberian settlers were inspired by American political ideals, having been weaned on American ideas of freedom and institutions of representative government, of the rights of the individual, the rule of law, religious toleration, the dignity of family life and of labor, and of respect for international trade and obligations. In the settler's view Liberia was anointed to make the flame of life, liberty, and the pursuit of human dignity burn bright in Africa, to proclaim to those in high places the imperative of antislavery. As the American Colonization Society stated exultantly, "The settlement at Liberia has remarkably enjoyed the protection and favour of the Almighty. In times of danger, of trial, and of want, its members have found refuge and resources in God. Their afflictions have served to deepen their pious sentiments, and to direct their thoughts more constantly to the realities and glories of an immortal state. Awakened in such seasons to a conviction of their entire dependence upon the invisible and eternal Being, they have, under the chastisements of his hand, learnt righteousness."[6] In other words, the colonists had learned the hard lessons of rugged individualism. There can be no mistaking how profoundly America had colored the settlers' whole outlook on life.

When we consider, for example, the address written by the settlers and directed to the attention of the Free Coloured People of the United States, we find there the expression of this American political idealism. It was repeated in countless effusions, including these lines written by an enthusiastic settler:

> Liberia! let thy sun go forth
> With freedom's banner waving high;
> Let piety exalt thy worth,
> And deck their memory when they die,
> That all the earth may join to raise
> A Christian harmony of praise.[7]

It is an irony of history that this American view of state, society, and the individual as the framework for antislavery should hold so much promise in Sierra Leone and Nigeria while it remained moribund in Liberia, but that was what happened. Without the ethics of antislavery, Liberia's creation represented a potentially destructive force in Africa, a salutary reminder of what power and money would do to Africa in the era after independence.

By contrast, with Crowther's leadership in the Niger Mission, the promise of the twin cause of antislavery and antistructure set the stage for the Africanization of Christianity. In conception and design the mission was intended to promote the forces of progressive destiny, as Bowen expressed it, that is, to advance the cause of moral reform, social reconstruction, productive enterprise, and mutual support, with local agents assuming personal responsibility for the cause. The mission opposed the slave trade and taught victim populations, in the words of Wadström, to "feel the nobility of their origin, and shew them of what great things they are capable." The sentiment was expressed by Thomas Will, a recaptive himself, who declared that he and his kind found in antislavery a cause "which illuminates our understanding so we are brought to know we have a soul to save."[8] The idea of "a soul to save" represents the moral consciousness that the antislavery movement required for the transformation of society in Africa. The recaptive communities became the bearers of that moral consciousness. Backed by public commitment, they became uncommon partners in the struggle for qualitative social change.

Crowther, the CMS, and Evangelical Religion

In that context, Crowther's leadership was a suitable symbol of the new forces and the new direction. In that context, too, the Niger Mission can be seen to fit into a much broader strategy of developing African leadership. I have highlighted the role of the CMS as an evangelical, ecumenical, and international movement within that broader leadership strategy. I have also stressed that a new world order came into being in Africa not by military might but with belief in the power of redeemed and sanctified persons. As a result of this dramatic change in Nigeria, encouraged and supported by Britain and the CMS, antislavery and antistructure secured a stronghold in a strategic part of Africa.

Colonialism, Christendom, and the Impact of Antistructure

The example of Sierra Leone (especially the portion covered in Chapter 3) shows how colonial officers were cautious about not overstepping the territorial limits of empire. At that stage colonialism, like mission, was identified with antislavery, not with creating political and economic tropical dependencies. Yet Governor MacCarthy's bold plans for government assumed the continuity of Christendom territorial norms, while the CMS, nurtured in the evangelical tradition of freeing the Church of England from subservience to the state, promoted antistructure. The CMS's creation of the unprecedented Native Pastorate in Freetown and Nigeria, for example, showed it to be committed to that strategy, drawing after it a reluctant Colonial Office, which was then averse to any overseas territorial expansionism since Britain's national interest mandated no such expansionist schemes. The tragic 1841 Niger Expedition had only strengthened the Colonial Office's aversion. But the lesson to be learned from that tragedy was that a wider antislavery outreach should be a matter for local agents. Missionary work had pioneered in Sierra Leone admirable experiments in self-support and self-reliance, and it was best to allow that development to proceed on its natural course rather than to allow it to rouse the phantom of universal empire by reckless territorial adventurism. If the flag followed the Bible, as at this stage it tended to, there was reason for it.

This cautious colonial approach would be overthrown in a later generation. Under that aggressive mandate, commercial interests based in Lagos would see themselves as at odds with missionary interests based in Abeokuta. Whereas in the earlier colonial phase MacCarthy could nurse his neo-Christendom illusions by seeking an outmoded, impractical fit between church and state, in the aggressive period of the late nineteenth century the colonial state moved to shunt missions out of the way or else to demand their compliance and conformity. Yet, as Martin Delany noted, by that stage Christianity had aroused in Africans hopes of self-reliance and self-support,[9] so that the colonial state and indigenous Christianity became opposing forces. Consequently, administrators felt driven to attempt to suppress leaders of the African Christian Independency. In a different way, a comparable conflict developed between Lagos as a commercial metropolis and Abeokuta as a haven of Christianity, recalling the view of John Higgenson, the Salem Puritan, that trade and religion made odd bedfellows, that New England was conceived as "a plantation of religion and not a plantation of trade."[10] Antislavery had made a successful, pivotal alliance with Christianity,[11] as with MacCarthy's surviving Christendom attitudes, but had been less successful in securing the commitment of traders. As such, missions moved with great awkwardness into the historical cleavage of trade and religion, and of colonialism and African Christian Independency, for, however they decided, Christianity as antislavery had become also an African cause, administrators and traders notwithstanding. Early signs of such cleavage appeared in Freetown, where the Independent Methodist Church, for example, launched a petition drive in 1796 against the governor, Zachary Macaulay (see Chapter 3).

I asked in Chapter 3 what long-term damage was likely done to the cause of antislavery and antistructure by the set colonial policy of seeking chiefly collaboration, and what effect that policy had on the culture of individual merit, personal achievement, free and open public access to education, and open and regular public assembly for worship and community life. Traditional chiefly power could be modernized and "civilized," but with the limitation that in origin chiefly power was stuck in the need-blind and gender-deaf cult of human power, with a tendency to revert to the old predatory morality of the feud and the loot, tempered only by calculations of self-interest. The achievement at Sierra Leone helped to mitigate the consequences of the restoration of chiefly power, an achievement bolstered by recaptive influx into the settlement.

The historical context of recaptive mobilization was the abolition of the slave trade in 1807, when multitudes of Africans were skimmed off the slave ships that were bound for the new world and brought to Freetown, where they were set free and exposed to the influence of the original Nova Scotian community. A stream of immigrants from hinterland Africa flowed into the settlement and created a lively confluence of cultures and languages. They embraced the view of Christianity as the religion of ex-slaves, ex-captives, and similar unfortunate elements of society. It was a view that allowed them to live in a society where no stigma attached to them on account of their circumstances. It created a dynamic community of individual expectation, opportunity, and responsibility.

The new society thus created in Sierra Leone involved a radical shift from looking to princes and rulers and the nobility, the fittest of the fit, to focusing on ex-slaves and ex-captives, reclaimed, trained, and equipped for leading useful, industrious, and exemplary lives. It was the kind of social restoration that opened the way for people at the bottom of the social heap. That change shaped much of Africa's modern history, and for a proper appreciation of it we have to abandon the structures of corporate Christendom and turn to the voluntary association of the new world.

Christianity for this new society was transformed. The religion was cleared of the mists of ruling genealogies to become instead the cause of slaves, or their descendants, slaves whose capture and sale the chiefs had supported and thrived from. As it turned out, these former slaves eventually came back as bearers of the Gospel, their branded bodies the most credible vindication of their mission, whose central premise was that all human beings were entitled to a second chance and none deserved to be made slave because no human being was created such by God. These former slaves and ex-captives would be the most authoritative champions of the cause. The people whom John Adams once called "the most obscure and inconsiderable that could have been found on the continent" would under antislavery become the agents of a new social order in Africa. Their story as African Americans has been permanently inscribed into the annals of the American Revolution. However, the equally important aftermath of that story in the taking of the antislavery strategy to Africa deserves equal attention.

New World Lessons

With the successful relocation of the antislavery movement to Africa, the slave trade and slavery were dealt a body blow. By the same token, an Africa-based antislavery movement gave validity to the cause of abolition in Europe and the new world. Antislavery as such became a universal movement of human rights,[12] and the structures of gain, domination, and advantage that lived off it were challenged in the wake of the new social radicalism. Humanitarians like Samuel Hopkins and Ezra Stiles of New England, for example, had hoped for something like that, had hoped that mission as a second chance for former slaves would be established in Africa, though they could scarcely have imagined the full implications of that change. And without such a shift of strategy, antislavery would have lacked a crucial element and remained fatally flawed. Africa on the supply side of slavery would have continued to stimulate demand in Europe until the two sides linked up again in a chain of mutual reinforcement.

The fundamental point about antislavery was that slaves, too, were endowed by the Creator with certain inalienable rights, including those of life and liberty or, as James Penington, a former slave, said, those of justice, truth, and honor.[13] Human dignity could not be exchanged for slavery nor yield to what was merely expedient and pragmatic; but it could, indeed, be reclaimed from the travesty of slavery and prejudice. Neither social custom nor racial argument would be allowed to jettison that central theocentric view of human personhood. I have tried to show in preceding chapters that such a theocentric view was embedded in the principles of the American Revolution and enshrined in the constitution of the new republic, as William Goodell strongly argued,[14] and as Joseph

Gaer and Ben Siegel also suggested.[15] Americans anointed freedom with the power of popular sanction because "peoplehood" had for them something of a covenantal status, not just a class or contractual meaning.[16] Caste prerogative or market calculation was not the basis on which they justified the Revolution or framed the constitution, as Charles Beard[17] and Merrill Jensen[18] have independently argued. Rather, the Revolution was justified with reference to those self-evident fundamental rights on which natural law and divine truth concurred.[19] The words "inalienable" and "self-evident" drew their cogency from that double reinforcement of natural law and religion.

A great historical irony was that while Americans embarked with confidence and at great risk on a bold experiment in launching freedom and democracy at home, the exporting of this legacy to other parts of the world was less successful, in part because any such foreign venture was judged too redolent of imperial aggression and too incompatible with democratic liberalism to be acceptable, and in part because Americans were too distrustful of government to be inclined to entrust their own with a foreign mandate, as John Quincy Adams insisted.

In these circumstances, America fared less well in repeating its achievement for other societies. Liberia as America's first overseas imperial opportunity demonstrated this irony of idealism over range. Britain, by contrast, was long practiced in the art of empire and remained unapologetic for it.[20] As such it was equipped to run an empire and to champion there the cause of freedom and democracy, whatever the inadequacies at home. Britain was thus able to preside over the flowering of those liberal social and political institutions whose seeds at long range it had passed on to British North America and which now also in remote Africa it could again safeguard as the framework for antislavery and antistructure. We have here a novel situation in that freedom from slavery and the slave trade thrived under British imperial overlordship, while this same overlordship was the cause of the Anglo-American conflict in the Revolution. At the same time, it was the American aversion to colonialism as the enemy of freedom that prevented Congress from assuming public responsibility for African antislavery.

As a general conclusion we may reflect on the contradictions resulting from the long-range implementation of homegrown principles, whether these be progressive American or conservative European. It is not credible for the historian in any case to proceed in a straight line from principles or ideals to experience and back again, because historical development is far from regular, but instead spins with contrary and surprising consequences. This tendency becomes particularly clear when we compare the case of American democratic progressivism failing to advance antislavery in Africa with the contrasting case of the British imperial tradition providing the congenial setting for free colonies. Although Americans conceded slavery to be contrary to liberty, the foundation of their democracy, they equivocated when antislavery required public responsibility for colonization. The British, who led the antislavery movement and, for the purpose, presided over the establishment of free coastal settlements, took advantage of those settlements to create colonial dependencies in Africa. As part of this complex historical development antislavery as a strategy for developing native leadership carried into its African phase the intrusive impulse of colonial rule but carried also colonialism's nemesis of antistructure in the aspirations of a resurgent class of recaptives. It shows something of the deeper significance of the antislavery campaign that the movement should produce the new African mobile classes whose proven ability would in time question colonial subjugation, a result that would indirectly vindicate, too, the ideals, if not the exporting, of American independence.

We may entertain a final thought here concerning the ultimate significance of the movements of antislavery and antistructure for a postcolonial and post–cold war Africa and ask what relevant influences and effects likely persisted from these movements into the present phase of African history. Were the new political and military elites of postcolonial Africa who connived in despoiling the continent and traumatizing its peoples a reversion to the era of the "courtyard chiefs" who colluded with the captains of the slave trade? As slaves made bad slave masters, according to Crowther, did colonized Africans make bad patriots? What movements in contemporary Africa represented a second chance for the continent's victim populations? What would the ranks of allies, friends, and supporters of the black poor, of the bound and gagged, look like today? Which men and women were the Samuel Hopkinses, the Benjamin Rushes, the John Jays, the Anthony Benezets, the Clarksons, the Wilberforces, and the Henry Venns of the day? Did our concentration on the creation of *new states* in postcolonial Africa divert us from the seminal demand for the ethical imperatives of justice and accountability?

Could the insights of antistructure have prepared us better for setbacks for the rule of law and justice in the new societies of postcolonial Africa? To what extent, if any, did the mass popular appeal of Christianity in postcolonial Africa represent a genuinely grass-roots mobilization of discontent, protest, and resistance, with the churches in effect having to lead a virtual movement of antistructure in solidarity with the new dispossessed, the marginalized, the oppressed, and the excluded?

On one reading of it, the struggle of the antiapartheid movement, the revolt of peasants, and the spontaneous proliferation of charismatic and Pentecostal groups both within the churches and outside the churches belong with Christianity's underdog ethic of good news for the poor, liberation for captives, hope for the hopeless, and recovery of sight for the blind (Luke 4:18), an ethic that in an earlier age empowered the likes of David George, Paul Cuffee, and Samuel Ajayi Crowther. Perhaps, in that case, popular, even insurgent, Christianity represented continuity with the politics of antistructure, with the radical shake-up of structures. Insurgent Christianity in modern Africa would be a world-order experience with precedent in antislavery. Such issues belong with normative history, which as Walzer defines it would give primacy to the great political, social, and cultural shifts engulfing Africa today.

NOTES

Introduction

1. Alexandre Popovic, *The Revolt of African Slaves in Iraq in the Third/Ninth Century* (Princeton, N.J.: Markus Wiener Publishers, 1998).

2. Ibn Khaldún, *Al-Muqaddimah: An Introduction to History,* 3 vols., ed. and trans. Franz Rosenthal, 2d ed. (Princeton, N.J.: Princeton University Press, 1968), vol. 1, p. 304.

3. Bernard Lewis, *Race and Slavery in the Middle East: An Historical Inquiry* (New York: Oxford University Press, 1992), p. 53.

4. *Baba of Karo,* ed. Mary Smith (New Haven, Conn.: Yale University Press and London: Faber, 1954). The German, British, and French colonial authorities gave sanctuary to one local slave raider in Adamawa, Hamman Yaji, who said he enslaved over two thousand people between 1912 and 1920, apparently with colonial connivance. *The Diary of Hamman Yaji: Chronicle of a West African Muslim Ruler,* ed. James H. Vaughan and Anthony H. M. Kirk-Greene (Bloomington: Indiana University Press, 1995). Britain acted unwittingly to perpetuate slavery in northern Nigeria by requiring slaves to buy back their freedom, thus placing a heavy financial burden on slaves, who found freedom beyond their all too modest means. Britain finally abolished slavery in Muslim Nigeria in 1936. Paul E. Lovejoy and Jan S. Hogendorn, *Slow Death for Slavery: The Course of Abolition in Northern Nigeria, 1897–1936* (Cambridge: Cambridge University Press, 1993).

5. In the 1520s Afonso I complained bitterly to the king of Portugal and to the pope that his kingdom was being ravaged by Portuguese slave traders. Extracts in Basil Davidson, *The African Past: Chronicles from Antiquity to Modern Times* (Harmondsworth: Penguin Books, 1966), pp. 194–197.

6. See, for example, A. Guirre Beltran, "Tribal Origins of Slaves in Mexico," *Journal of Negro History,* 31, no. 2 (April 1946), 269–352, and Frederick P. Bowser, *The African Slave in Colonial Peru: 1524–1650* (Stanford, Calif.: Stanford University Press, 1974).

7. Cited in Jean Comby, *How to Understand the History of Christian Mission* (London: SCM Press, 1996), p. 60.

8. Richard F. Burton, *Wanderings in West Africa,* 2 vols. (London: Tinsley Brothers, 1863, repr. New York: Dover Publications, 1991), vol. 1, p. 266. In his "Memorial on the Slave Trade," Henry Brougham (1786–1868), radical politician and a lord chancellor, noted how slave traders found in the intricate riverain system on the West African coast snug anchorage and shelter, out of reach of the British naval patrol. He said supply had exceeded demand, and purchase prices had fallen from £20 or £25 to £5 or £6 per slave, while the selling price in the West Indies had risen sharply at the same time. Public Record Office, London, CO 267/43.

9. Orlando Patterson, *Slavery and Social Death* (Cambridge, Mass.: Harvard University Press, 1982).

10. For aspects of slavery and African state structures, see Paul E. Lovejoy, ed., *The Ideology of Slavery in Africa* (Beverly Hills, Calif.: Sage Publications, 1981).

11. *The African Repository and Colonial Journal* 3 (October 1828), 245.

12. John Barbot, *A Description of the Coasts of North and South Guinea, etc.* (London, 1732). Reprinted in Davidson, *The African Past,* p. 213.

13. Cited in Olaudah Equiano, *The Interesting Narrative and Other Writings,* ed. Vincent Carretta (London: Penguin Books, 1995), p. 244. Willem Bosman, *A New and Accurate Description of the Coast of Guinea, 1705,* 2d ed. (London: K. Knapton, 1721).

14. Lewis, *Race and Slavery in the Middle East,* p. 3.

15. Abolitionist sentiment, for example, deemed slavery to be a "masterpiece of iniquity, woven as it is of human wrongs, the oaths of the oppressor and the cries of the oppressed." What differentiated that cruelty from the chastisements of God, the abolitionists insisted, was that there was mercy and the possibility of a second chance with God but none with the slave dealer, as the story of the Egba Yoruba captive John Baptist Dasalu illustrated. In 1851 Dasalu fell captive to Gezo, the king of Dahomey, who sold him as a slave in Cuba from where he was eventually rescued through a series of remarkable events. He returned to Nigeria only to fall once more into the hands of the king of Dahomey, who had him and his fellow prisoners summarily executed. *Church Missionary Intelligencer,* 7 (1856), 241.

16. For Britain's role in abolition, see Roger Anstey, *The Atlantic Slave Trade and British Abolition: 1760–1810* (Atlantic Highlands, N.J.: Humanities Press and London: Macmillan, 1975). See also the classic study by Sir Reginald Coupland, *The British Anti-Slavery Movement* (London: Longmans, 1933, 2d ed. London: Frank Cass, 1964). In an important but little noticed article, Ralph A. Austen of Chicago examined the economic and political roots

of abolition in West Africa. Austen, "The Abolition of the Overseas Slave Trade: A Distorted Theme in West African History," *Journal of the Historical Society of Nigeria,* 5, no. 2 (June 1970).

17. For example, in 1771 Anthony Benezet published a work focused on the slave trade and conditions in Africa. Benezet, *Some Historical Account of Guinea . . . with an Inquiry into the Rise and Progress of the Slave Trade* (Philadelphia, 1771).

18. *Freedom's Journal,* the first black newspaper in America, edited by Joseph Brown Russwurm (d. 1851) and published in New York from 1827 to 1829, regularly printed articles on factual knowledge about Africa, including extended reviews of scholarly works on Africans and Africa.

19. Cited in Gordon S. Wood, *The Radicalism of the American Revolution* (New York: Vintage Books, 1993), p. 169.

20. Ibid., p. 186.

21. Cited in Bernard Bailyn, *The Ideological Origins of the American Revolution* (Cambridge, Mass.: Belknap Press of Harvard University Press, 1992), p. 230. On the issue of slavery in prerevolutionary ideology, see pp. 242ff.

22. *The African Repository and Colonial Journal,* 1, no. 1 (1826), 13ff.

23. Remarks of Mr. Custis of Arlington, on the occasion of nominating General Lafayette as a vice president of the society for life, *The African Repository and Colonial Journal,* 1, no. 1, (March 1825), 16.

24. E. W. Blyden, *The Three Needs of Liberia: A Lecture Delivered at Lower Buchanan, Grand Bassa County, Liberia, January 26, 1908* (London: C. M. Phillips, 1908), p. 2.

25. Lourenço da Silva de Mendouça, the Afro-Brazilian, led a delegation to the papal curia in the 1680s to protest the injustice of slavery, resulting in 1686 in the Vatican issuing a directive condemning slavery. But, concerning the effects on the ground, "the sequel was almost total anticlimax," as Spain and Portugal failed to intervene in their domains to enforce the rulings. Richard Gray, *Black Christians and White Missionaries* (New Haven, Conn.: Yale University Press, 1990), p. 24. Also Richard Gray, "The Papacy and Africa in the Seventeenth Century," in *Il Cristianesimo Nel Mondo Atlantico nel Secolo 17* (Vatican: Libreria Editrice Vaticana, 1997), pp. 283–305.

26. Turner's own explanation of *communitas* resorts to technical language; he speaks of "the units of space and time in which behavior and symbolism are momentarily enfranchised from the norms and values that govern the public lives of incumbents of structural positions." Victor Turner, *The Ritual Process: Structure and Anti-Structure* (Ithaca, N.Y.: Cornell University Press, 1982), p. 166.

27. The idea of territorial passage was formulated by Arnold van Gennep as a function of *communitas.* Turner expanded it. Van Gennep, *The Rites of*

Passage, trans. Monika B. Vizedom and Gabrielle L. Caffee (Chicago: University of Chicago Press, 1960), pp. 12, 192.

28. Michael Walzer, *The Revolution of the Saints: A Study in the Origins of Radical Politics* (Cambridge, Mass.: Harvard University Press, 1965), pp. 134–135.

29. Albert Bushnell Hart, *Slavery and Abolition: 1831–1841,* (1906, repr. New York: Haskell House, 1968), p. 210.

30. C. S. Lewis, *English Literature in the Sixteenth Century (Excluding Drama)* (London: Oxford University Press, 1954), p. 55.

31. For a review of the *Annales* school in the context of African history, see Steven Feierman, "African Histories and the Dissolution of World History," in Robert Bates, V. L. Mudimbe, and Jean O'Barr, eds., *Africa and the Disciplines* (Chicago: University of Chicago Press, 1993), pp. 167–210. See also Michael Adas, "Bringing Ideas and Agency Back In: Representation and the Comparative Approach to World History," in Philip Pomper, Richard H. Elphick, and Richard T. Vann, eds., *World History* (Oxford: Blackwell Publishers, 1998), pp. 81–104.

32. Walzer, *Revolution of the Saints,* p. 128.

33. Karl Marx, veteran of the progress tradition, may be called on as representative of this Western attitude toward non-Western cultures. Marx pilloried the societies of Asia, and non-Western societies in general, as reactionary because they transformed "a self-developing social state into never changing natural destiny, and thus brought about a brutalizing worship of nature, exhibiting its degradation in the fact that man, the sovereign of nature, fell down on his knees in adoration of Hanuman, the monkey, and Sabbal, the cow." Cited in Arthur Schlesinger, Jr., "The Missionary Enterprise and Theories of Imperialism," in John K. Fairbank, ed., *The Missionary Enterprise in China and America* (Cambridge, Mass.: Harvard University Press, 1974), p. 340.

1. The American Slave Corridor and the New African Potential

1. *The Life of Olaudah Equiano, or Gustavus Vassa, the African: 1789,* 2 vols. (London: Dawsons of Pall Mall, 1969), vol. 1, p. lx. The name Gustavus Vassa was adopted from that of a Swedish nobleman, who lived 1496–1560 and who led his Swedish countrymen to obtain their freedom from Denmark in the years 1521–1523.

2. *A Slaver's Log Book, or Twenty Years' Residence in Africa: The Original 1853 Manuscript by Captain Theophilus Conneau* (Englewood Cliffs, N.J.: Prentice-Hall, 1976), p. 60.

3. Christopher Fyfe, *A History of Sierra Leone* (London: Oxford University Press, 1962), p. 229.

4. Conneau, *Slaver's Log Book,* pp. 104–105.

5. Fyfe, *History,* p. 29.

6. David Brion Davis, *The Problem of Slavery in the Age of Revolution: 1770–1823* (Ithaca, N.Y.: Cornell University Press, 1975), p. 47.

7. *Life of Olaudah,* vol. 1, p. lvii.

8. Ibid., p. 2. See also G. I. Jones, "Olaudah Equiano of the Niger Ibo," in Philip D. Curtin, ed., *Africa Remembered: Narratives by West Africans from the Era of the Slave Trade* (Madison: University of Wisconsin Press, 1967), pp. 60–98.

9. *Life of Olaudah,* vol. 1, pp. 25–26.

10. Ibid., vol. 2, p. 35.

11. Ibid., vol. 1, pp. 218ff. Olaudah spoke with regret about how people in London he regarded as friends worked against him (see p. xlii).

12. Douglas Grant, *The Fortunate Slave: An Illustration of African Slavery in the Early Eighteenth Century* (London: Oxford University Press, 1968).

13. The eyewitness testimony is from Thomas Bluett, published in 1734. Reproduced as "The Capture and Travels of Ayuba Suleiman Ibrahima," in Philip D. Curtin, ed., *Africa Remembered: Narratives by West Africans from the Era of the Slave Trade* (Madison: University of Wisconsin Press, 1967), p. 46. Another Muslim, Prince 'Abd al-Rahmán, exercised a similar influence on the American public. *The African Repository and Colonial Journal,* 3 (October 1828).

14. Cited in Olaudah Equiano, *The Interesting Narrative and Other Writings,* ed. Vincent Caretta (London: Penguin Books, 1995), p. 273. Stephen J. Braidwood rejects racial motivation as the basis of opposition to Olaudah. Braidwood, *Black Poor and White Philanthropists: London's Blacks and the Foundation of the Sierra Leone Settlement, 1786–1791* (Liverpool: Liverpool University Press, 1994), pp. 153ff. Our judgment in this matter must depend finally on whether or not Olaudah's own account and related contemporary reports carry decisive weight.

15. Mary Beth Norton, "The Fate of Some Black Loyalists of the American Revolution," *Journal of Negro History,* 58, no. 4 (October 1973), 404. The Sierra Leone Company itself admitted that the London blacks had been reduced to the condition of St. Giles's blackbirds even "though their original circumstances were different." Extract in Carl B. Wadström, *Essay on Colonization, particularly applied to the Western Coast of Africa, with some Free Thoughts on Cultivation and Commerce; also Brief Descriptions of the Colonies already formed, or attempted, in Africa, including those of Sierra*

Leone and Bulama, 2 vols. (London: Darton and Harvey, 1794), vol. 2, p. 228.

16. Eric R. Wolf, *Europe and the People without History* (Berkeley: University of California Press, 1990), pp. 229–230.

17. *Life of Olaudah,* vol. 1, pp. 28–29.

18. Cited in James W. St. G. Walker, *The Black Loyalists: The Search for a Promised Land in Nova Scotia and Sierra Leone; 1783–1870* (London: Longman, 1976), p. 1.

19. Ibid.

20. Benjamin Quarles, *The Negro in the American Revolution* (New York: Norton, 1973), p. 28.

21. Walker, *Black Loyalists,* p. 2.

22. Cited in Quarles, *The Negro,* p. 165.

23. Herbert Aptheker, *American Negro Slave Revolts* (New York: Columbia University Press, 1943, repr. New York: International Publishers, 1978), p. 89.

24. Ibid., p. 87.

25. Ibid., p. 88.

26. Ibid., p. 89.

27. Marion Russell, "American Slave Discontent in the Records of the High Courts," *Journal of Negro History,* 31 (October 1946), 411–434. Cited also in John W. Blassingame, *The Slave Community* (New York: Oxford University Press, 1979), p. 361.

28. Russell, "American Slave Discontent," pp. 418–419.

29. Quarles, *The Negro,* p. 39.

30. Ibid.

31. Cited in Mary Stoughton Locke, *Anti-Slavery in America* (Boston: Ginn, 1901), p. 80. See also W. E. B. Du Bois, *The Suppression of the African Slave-Trade to the United States of America: 1638–1870* (1898, repr. New York: Russell and Russell, 1965), pp. 27–38.

32. Cited in Locke, *Anti-Slavery,* p. 73. Also Du Bois, *Suppression,* pp. 70–93.

33. Quarles, *The Negro,* pp. 41–42.

34. Thomas Jefferson, *Autobiography,* in *The Life and Selected Writings of Thomas Jefferson,* ed. Adrienne Koch and William Peden (New York: Random House, 1944, repr. 1993), p. 39.

35. Locke, *Anti-Slavery,* p. 76.

36. Cited in P. J. Staudenraus, *The African Colonization Movement: 1816–1865* (New York: Columbia University Press, 1961), p. 1.

37. Cited in Walker, *Black Loyalists,* p. 10; also in Robin Winks, *The Blacks in Canada: A History* (New Haven, Conn.: Yale University Press, 1972), pp. 31–32.

38. Cited in Winks, *Blacks in Canada*, p. 32.

39. Cited in Quarles, *The Negro*, p. 169.

40. Cited in ibid., p. 168.

41. In the South there were some 700,000 slaves by 1790, and 3.5 million in 1860. Sydney A. Ahlstrom, *A Religious History of the American People* (New Haven, Conn.: Yale University Press, 1972), p. 655.

42. Quarles, *The Negro*, pp. 62–63.

43. Winks, *Blacks in Canada*, p. 32.

44. Quarles, *The Negro*, p. 172.

45. Walker, *Black Loyalists*, p. 41.

46. Ibid., p. 54.

47. Winks, *Blacks in Canada*, p. 40.

48. Cited in Walker, *Black Loyalists*, p. 46.

49. Clarkson Papers, II, fol. 15, cited in Walker, *Black Loyalists*, p. 48.

50. Norton, "The Fate of Some Black Loyalists," p. 406.

51. In full it was called the Committee for the Relief of the Black Poor, founded in January 1786. Braidwood, *Black Poor and White Philanthropists*, pp. 63–127.

52. Wadström, *Essay*, vol. 2, pp. 227–228. Cited also in R. R. Kuczynski, *Demographic Survey of the British Colonial Empire*, 3 vols. (London: Oxford University Press for the Royal Institute of International Affairs, 1948–1953, repr. Fairfield, N.J.: Augustus M. Kelly, 1977), vol. 1, p. 40 n.

53. Cited in Forrest McDonald, *Novus Ordo Seclorum: The Intellectual Origins of the Constitution* (Lawrence: University Press of Kansas, 1985), p. 114.

54. Dr. Henry Smeathman, *Letters*, in Wadström, *Essay*, vol. 2, p. 200, emphasis in original.

55. Henry Smeathman, *Plan of a Settlement to be made near Sierra Leone, on the Grain Coast of Africa: Intended more particularly for the service and happy establishment of Blacks and People of Colour, to be shipped as freemen under the direction of the Committee for Relieving the Black Poor, and under the protection of the British Government* (London, 1786), pp. 16–17.

56. Anna Maria Falconbridge, *Narrative of Two Voyages to Sierra Leone, during the Years 1791–2–3, in a Series of Letters, &c.* (London, 1794, repr. London: Frank Cass, 1967), p. 66.

57. Letter dated Granville Town, 13 May 1791, in Falconbridge, *Narrative of Two Voyages to Sierra Leone*, p. 64. Cited also in Kuczynski, *Demographic Survey*, vol. 1, p. 51. The general wisdom was that Granville Sharp did not know about the white prostitutes. Yet it seems astounding he should be ignorant of so flagrant an abnormality. It is easier to assume he had knowledge, and qualms, about it.

58. Published in the *Public Advertiser,* 14 July 1787, reproduced in *Life of Olaudah,* vol. 1, p. xlii.

59. *Life of Olaudah,* vol. 1, pp. xli–xlii.

60. Ibid., p. xxxvii.

61. Olaudah, *Interesting Narrative,* p. 274.

62. See John Peterson, *Province of Freedom: A History of Sierra Leone, 1787–1870* (London: Faber and Faber, 1969).

63. Cited in Braidwood, *Black Poor and White Philanthropists,* p. 188.

64. Cited in Kuczynski, *Demographic Survey,* vol. 1, p. 45.

65. Ibid., p. 46.

66. See David Hancock, *Citizens of the World: London Merchants and the Integration of the British Atlantic Community, 1735–1785* (Cambridge: Cambridge University Press, 1995), pp. 1–2, 172–220; A. W. Lawrence, *Trade Castles and Forts of West Africa* (London: Jonathan Cape, 1963), pp. 77–78; and, for a detailed social history of the island, Edward Ball, *Slaves in the Family* (New York: Farrar, Straus and Giroux, 1998), pp. 419–445.

67. Braidwood, *Black Poor,* pp. 204–205.

68. In 1688 a group in Germantown, Pennsylvania, adopted a resolution against slavery, confirming official fears of Quakerism as a pro-abolition religion. See Albert J. Raboteau, *Slave Religion: The "Invisible Institution" in the Antebellum South* (New York: Oxford University Press, 1978), p. 111. See also Locke, *Anti-Slavery,* pp. 94, 96ff., 123, 142ff.

69. Anthony Benezet, *A Short Account of that Part of Africa Inhabited by Negroes* (1762), p. 78.

70. Cited in Quarles, *The Negro,* p. 35.

71. Benezet, *Account of Guinea,* 1788, cited in Olaudah, *Interesting Narrative,* pp. 272–273.

72. Locke, *Anti-Slavery,* p. 28. See also Thomas E. Drake, *Quakers and Slavery in America* (New Haven, Conn.: Yale University Press, 1950). The latter has an exhaustive listing of primary and secondary sources.

73. Benjamin Rush, *Address to the Inhabitants of the British Settlements, on the Slavery of the Negroes in America,* vol. 1, (1773), p. 9. Cited also in Locke, *Anti-Slavery,* p. 55.

74. John A. Woods, "The Correspondence of Benjamin Rush and Granville Sharpe, 1773–1809," *Journal of American Studies,* 1 (1967).

75. Cited in Quarles, *The Negro,* p. 42. The original document is housed in the New York Public Library.

76. David Brion Davis, *The Problem of Slavery in Western Culture* (New York: Oxford University Press, 1988), p. 434.

77. Sir Harry Johnston, *Liberia,* 2 vols. (London: Hutchinson and Co., 1906), vol. 1, p. 111.

78. Cited in Samuel Crowther and John Christopher Taylor, *The Gospel on the Banks of the Niger: Journals and Notices of the Native Missionaries Accompanying the Niger Expedition of 1857–1859* (London: CMS, 1859, repr. London: Dawsons of Pall Mall, 1968), p. 448.

79. Davis, *Slavery in Western Culture,* p. 214.

80. Captain F. W. Butt-Thompson, *Sierra Leone in History and Tradition* (London: H. F. and G. Witherby, 1926), pp. 93–94.

81. Gary B. Nash, "Thomas Peters: Millwright and Deliverer," in David G. Sweet and Gary B. Nash, eds., *Struggle and Survival in Colonial America* (Berkeley: University of California Press, 1981), pp. 69–85.

82. Walker, *Black Loyalists,* p. 32. Cited in Nash, "Thomas Peters," p. 78.

83. Walker, *Black Loyalists,* p. 53.

84. *Report of the Sierra Leone Company* (London, 1794), p. 5. Cited also in Kuczynski, *Demographic Survey,* vol. 1, pp. 54–55.

85. Fyfe, *History,* pp. 36–37.

86. Cited in Quarles, *The Negro,* pp. 182–183.

87. Fyfe, *History,* p. 41.

88. Cited in Christopher Hill, *Milton and the English Revolution* (Harmondsworth: Penguin, 1979), p. 253.

89. An article in *Freedom's Journal* (21 October 1828) assured its readers that "liberty must eventually be the portion of every descendant of Africa."

90. Locke, *Anti-Slavery,* p. 49.

91. Cited in Nathan Hatch, *The Democratization of American Christianity* (New Haven, Conn.: Yale University Press, 1989), p. 102.

92. Quarles, *The Negro,* p. 193.

93. Ibid.

94. Hatch, *American Christianity,* p. 103.

95. Cited in ibid.

96. Cited in ibid. The reference is to 1 Corinthians 1:27.

97. Quarles, *The Negro,* p. 193.

98. Davis, *Slavery in Western Culture,* p. 217.

99. Davis, *Slavery in the Age of Revolution,* p. 39.

100. Oliver O'Donovan, *The Desire of Nations: Rediscovering the Roots of Political Theology* (Cambridge: Cambridge University Press, 1996), p. 264.

101. For a general historical overview, see Hugh Thomas, *The Slave Trade* (New York: Simon and Schuster, 1997).

102. For a theological treatment of slavery as metaphor, see Dale B. Martin, *Slavery as Salvation: The Metaphor of Slavery in Pauline Christianity* (New Haven, Conn.: Yale University Press, 1990).

103. G. W. F. Hegel, *The Phenomenology of Mind,* trans. J. B. Baillie, 2d ed. (New York, 1964). Cited in Davis, *Slavery in the Age of Revolution,* p. 40 n. "It was

not so widely understood that Slavery might be injurious to the masters' morals also," echoes Sir Reginald Coupland, *The British Anti-Slavery Movement* (London: F. Cass, 1964), p. 8.

104. Ernst Troeltsch, *The Social Teaching of the Christian Churches,* trans. Olive Wyon, 2 vols. (London: Allen and Unwin, 1931, repr. Louisville: Westminster/John Knox Press, 1992), vol. 1, p. 132.

105. Davis, *Slavery in the Age of Revolution,* p. 41.

106. Ibid., p. 46.

107. Ibid., p. 42.

108. Davis, *Slavery in Western Culture,* p. 292.

109. See David Brion Davis, *Slavery and Human Progress* (New York: Oxford University Press, 1984).

110. William Wilberforce, *A Practical View of the Prevailing Religious System of Professed Christians in the Higher and Middle Classes in This Country Contrasted with Real Christianity* (1797, repr. London: SCM Press, 1958), pp. 57ff.

111. James Beverley and Barry Moody, eds., *The Life and Journal of the Rev. Mr. Henry Alline* (Hantsport, Nova Scotia: Lancelot Press for Acadia Divinity College, 1982), p. 217.

112. Walker, *Black Loyalists,* pp. 64–65. See also Stephen Marini, *Radical Sects in Revolutionary New England* (Cambridge, Mass.: Harvard University Press, 1982).

113. G. A. Rawlyk, *Ravished by the Spirit: Religious Revivals, Baptists, and Henry Alline* (Kingston: McGill-Queen's University Press, 1984), pp. 89–90.

114. Ibid., pp. 119f. Victor Turner, *The Ritual Process: Structure and Anti-structure* (Ithaca, N.Y.: Cornell University Press, 1969), pp. 94–140.

115. Cited in Walker, *Black Loyalists,* p. 66.

116. See C. Eric Lincoln and Lawrence H. Mamiya, *The Black Church in the African American Experience* (Durham, N.C.: Duke University Press, 1994), p. 3.

117. Rawlyk, *Ravished by the Spirit,* pp. 84–85.

118. Cited in Quarles, *The Negro,* p. 183.

119. *Report of the Sierra Leone Company* in Wadström, *Essay,* vol. 2, p. 78.

120. Ibid., p. 118.

121. Cited in Quarles, *The Negro,* p. 4.

2. "A Plantation of Religion" and the Enterprise Culture in Africa

1. The phrase "a plantation of religion" in the chapter title is drawn from the Salem divine John Higgenson, who was at pains to remind his contempo-

raries that New England was "originally a plantation of religion and not a plantation of trade." Joseph Gaer and Ben Siegel, *The Puritan Heritage: America's Roots in the Bible* (New York: Mentor Books, 1964), p. 24.

2. See Hugo Rahner, S.J., *Church and State in Early Christianity* (San Francisco: Ignatius Press, 1992), trans. Leo Donald Davis, S.J., from the German, *Kirche und Staat im Frühen Christentum* (Munich: Kösel Verlag, 1961), p. 191.

3. Christopher Dawson, *Religion and the Rise of Western Culture* (London: Sheed and Ward, 1950). See also Dawson's *The Making of Europe: An Introduction to the History of European Unity* (New York: Barnes and Noble Books, 1994).

4. For a discussion of the Puritan heritage in American history, see Perry Miller and Thomas H. Johnson, eds., *The Puritans: A Sourcebook of Their Writings*, Vol. 1, *The Theory of the State and of Society: This World and the Next*, rev. ed. (New York: Harper Torchbooks, 1963), Introduction, pp. 1–79.

5. R. H. Tawney has argued that there was a fundamental break between the medieval and modern ideas of economics and society, a break that consisted of "the contraction of the territory within which the spirit of religion was conceived to run." Tawney, *Religion and the Rise of Capitalism: A Historical Study* (Harmondsworth: Penguin Books, 1966), p. 272. In a different connection, Michael Walzer has argued that the independent, commoner social roots of the English Puritans, in contrast to their aristocratic Huguenot counterparts in France, enabled them to become a force for change. Freed from feudal attachments, the Puritans "anticipated in their own lives the politics of the revolution." Their independence and self-reliance pointed them "toward the overthrow of the traditional order." Walzer, *The Revolution of the Saints: A Study in the Origins of Radical Politics* (Cambridge, Mass.: Harvard University Press, 1965), pp. 114, 118.

6. The practice was widespread, as is reported in accounts of Ethiopia. See Julian Baldick, *Black God: The Afroasiatic Roots of the Jewish, Christian, and Muslim Religions* (London: I. B. Tauris, 1997), pp. 136–137.

7. J. Dupuis, *Journal of a Residence in Ashantee* (London, 1824), pp. 163–164. Cited also in Ivor Wilks, *Asante in the Nineteenth Century: The Structure and Evolution of a Political Order* (Cambridge: Cambridge University Press, 1975), pp. 679–680.

8. Eric R. Wolf, *Europe and the People without History* (Berkeley: University of California Press, 1990), p. 230.

9. Christopher Fyfe, *A History of Sierra Leone* (London: Oxford University Press, 1962), p. 30.

10. Carl B. Wadström, *Essay on Colonization, particularly applied to the West*

Coast of Africa, with some Free Thoughts on Cultivation and Commerce; also Brief Descriptions of the Colonies already formed, or attempted, in Africa, including those of Sierra Leone and Bulama, 2 vols. (London: Darton and Harvey, 1794), vol. 2, p. 11.

11. Fyfe, *History,* p. 38.

12. Ibid., p. 39.

13. *Report of the Sierra Leone Company,* in Wadström, *Essay,* vol. 2, p. 68.

14. Richard F. Burton, *Wanderings in West Africa,* 2 vols. (London: Tinsley Brothers, 1863, repr. New York: Dover Publications, 1991), vol. 1, p. 217. Burton also pilloried the recaptives in Cape Coast: see vol. 2, pp. 72–73.

15. Chief Justice Robert Hogan, letter of 25 May 1816, Public Record Office, London, CO 267/43.

16. Fyfe, *History,* p. 191. Paul Kahn has argued that the rule of law is deeply embedded in the American religious imagination, centering his argument on the famous Supreme Court case of *Marbury v. Madison* of 1803. Such an attitude to the law fits in well with the Judeo-Christian tradition of law as divine revelation. Kahn, *The Reign of Law: Marbury v. Madison and the Construction of America* (New Haven, Conn.: Yale University Press, 1997).

17. Fyfe, *History,* p. 218.

18. J. W. Loguen, *The Rev. J. W. Loguen, as a Slave and as a Freeman: A Narrative of Real Life* (Syracuse, N.Y.: J. G. K. Truair, Office of the Daily Journal, 1859), pp. vii–viii.

19. "An Account of the Life of Mr. David George, from Sierra Leone in Africa, Given by Himself in a Conversation with Brother Rippon of London, and Brother Pearce of Birmingham," in *The Annual Baptist Register for 1790, 1791, 1792, and Part of 1793,* ed. John Rippon p. 473.

20. For a discussion of George at Silver Bluff, see also Walter H. Brooks, "The Priority of the Silver Bluff Church and Its Promoters," *Journal of Negro History,* 7 (1922), 172–196.

21. George, "Account of the Life," pp. 475–476.

22. See also Albert J. Raboteau, *Slave Religion* (New York: Oxford University Press, 1978), p. 109.

23. George Liele, "An Account of Several Baptist Churches, Consisting Chiefly of Negro Slaves: Particularly of One at *Kingston,* in Jamaica, and Another at *Savannah* in Georgia," in *The Annual Baptist Register for 1790, 1791, 1792, and Part of 1793,* pp. 332–337, ed. John Rippon.

24. Ibid.

25. George, "Account of the Life," p. 480.

26. Cited in Anthony Kirk-Greene, "David George: The Nova Scotian Experience," *Sierra Leone Studies,* n.s., 14 (December 1960), 106.

27. Ibid., pp. 110–111.

28. Robin Winks, *The Blacks in Canada* (New Haven, Conn.: Yale University Press, 1972), p. 60.

29. Ibid., p. 67.

30. Ibid., p. 68.

31. George, "Account of the Life," p. 483.

32. R. R. Kuczynski, *Demographic Survey of the British Colonial Empire*, 3 vols. (London: Oxford University Press for the Royal Institute of International Affairs, 1948–1953, repr. Fairfield, N.J.: Augustus M. Kelley, 1977), vol. 1, p. 67.

33. Kirk-Greene, "David George," p. 115.

34. Cited in Kuczynski, *Demographic Survey*, vol. 1, p. 69. However, about a year later there was a dramatic improvement, at any rate enough to lead the company's attending physician, Dr. Winterbottom, to assure the directors in October 1793 that the settlers "appear now to be so well accustomed to the climate that there is little reason to apprehend any great mortality among them."

35. Cited in ibid., p. 73, n. 4.

36. Maroons were descendants of slaves who fled to the mountains of Jamaica after the armies of Oliver Cromwell took the island and drove off the Spaniards in 1655. See Richard Price, ed., *Maroon Societies: Rebel Slave Communities in the Americas*, 3d ed. (Baltimore: Johns Hopkins University Press, 1996).

37. Kuczynski, *Demographic Survey*, vol. 1, p. 73.

38. John Newton, *Thoughts upon the African Slave Trade* (London, 1788). Excerpted as "A Reformed Slave Trader's Regrets," in David Northrup, ed., *The Atlantic Slave Trade* (Lexington, Mass.: D.C. Heath, 1994), pp. 80–89. For a theological study of Newton, see D. Bruce Hindmarsh, *John Newton and the English Evangelical Tradition* (Oxford: Clarendon Press, 1996). Newton was not an antislavery activist: he merely regretted his personal role in the cruelties of the trade.

39. For a discussion of Puritan preaching, see Perry Miller and Thomas H. Johnson, eds., *The Puritans: A Sourcebook of Their Writings*, vol. 1 (New York: Harper Torchbooks, 1963), pp. 64–79.

40. Walzer, *Revolution of Saints*, p. 117.

41. Paul Seaver, *The Puritan Lectureships: The Politics of Religious Dissent, 1560–1662* (Stanford, Calif.: Stanford University Press, 1970), p. 144.

42. *The Life of Olaudah Equiano, or Gustavus Vassa, the African: 1789*, 2 vols. (London: Dawsons of Pall Mall, 1969), vol. 1, pp. 91–92.

43. Raboteau, *Slave Religion*, p. 181.

44. Herbert Aptheker, *American Negro Slave Revolts* (New York: Columbia University Press, 1943, repr. New York: International Publishers, 1978), p. 83.

45. Raboteau, *Slave Religion,* p. 215.

46. Cited in ibid., pp. 215, 218.

47. Ibid., p. 129.

48. Cited in ibid., p. 133.

49. See Eugene D. Genovese, *Roll, Jordan, Roll: The World the Slaves Made* (New York: Vintage Books, 1972), p. 256.

50. *The Souls of Black Folk* (London: Longmans, 1903, repr. New York: Signet Classics, 1969), p. 211.

51. Cited in Andrew F. Walls, "A Christian Experiment: The Early Sierra Leone Colony," in G. J. Cuming, ed., *The Mission of the Church and the Propagation of the Faith, Studies in Church History,* vol. 6 (Cambridge: Cambridge University Press, 1970), p. 119.

52. Cited in Raboteau, *Slave Religion,* p. 236.

53. See Fyfe, *History,* pp. 201–202.

54. *Extracts of the Journal of George Lane,* 17 February 1822, no. 43, Methodist Missionary Society Archives, School of Oriental and African Studies, London; hereafter cited as MMS Archives.

55. Walls, "A Christian Experiment," p. 118.

56. John Marrant, *A Narrative of the Lord's Wonderful Dealings with John Marrant, a Black,* 4th ed. (London: Gilbert and Plummer, 1785), pp. 23–24.

57. Ibid., pp. 38–39.

58. Ibid., p. 40.

59. Olaudah Equiano lists John Wesley as a subscriber to the cause of abolition. *Life of Olaudah,* vol. 1, prefix.

60. Whitefield had laid elaborate plans for Bethesda as "the Princeton" of the South but failed in his efforts to get the necessary backing for it from all the parties concerned. There is no indication in his plans that he saw Bethesda as in any way allied with the cause of abolition. In fact he used the offer of slaves working for Bethesda College as a recommendation for its viability. See Harry S. Stout, *The Divine Dramatist: George Whitefield and the Rise of Modern Evangelicalism* (Grand Rapids, Mich.: Wm. B. Eerdmans, 1991), pp. 257ff.

61. Edwin Welch, *Spiritual Pilgrim: A Reassessment of the Life of the Countess of Huntingdon* (Cardiff: University of Wales Press, 1995), p. 131. For the poem in question, see Stout, *Divine Dramatist,* p. 284.

62. See *Journal of Negro History,* 57 (1972), 212.

63. Welch, *Spiritual Pilgrim,* pp. 146–147.

64. Ibid., p. 147.

65. *The Sierra Leone Mission Supported by the Churches of the Countess of Huntingdon's Connexion and the Free Church of England,* report by Rev. Joseph

Bainton, Hon. Secretary, and Mr. T. Manly, Tunbridge Wells, Hon. Treasurer, no date, p. 7.

66. Cited in Fyfe, *History,* p. 260.

67. Lamont D. Thomas, *Rise to Be a People: A Biography of Paul Cuffe* (Urbana: University of Illinois Press, 1986), p. 37.

68. Henry Noble Sherwood, "Paul Cuffe," *Journal of Negro History,* 8 (April 1923), 160.

69. Massachusetts Archives, Yale University Library, vol. 186, 134–136. Cited also in Sherwood, "Paul Cuffe," p. 162.

70. Cited in Seaver, *Puritan Lectureships,* p. 136.

71. The petitions of both James Wise and Samuel Brown can be found in the MMS Archives, box 279.

72. Letter of James Wise to Rev. John Beecham, 17 May 1833.

73. The authorities in Freetown proscribed the petition. Robert Purdie, the colony's secretary, published a public notice on 20 December 1814, saying it had been illegal and forbidden under English law since 1664 to make use of the petition, with sanctions reserved for offenders. Robert Purdie, "Notice," Freetown, 20 December 1814, Public Record Office, London, CO 267/40.

74. Macaulay's letter can be found in Rosalind Cobb Wiggins, ed., *Captain Paul Cuffe's Logs and Letters, 1808–1817: A Black Quaker's "Voice from within the Veil"* (Washington, D.C.: Howard University Press, 1996), pp. 84–85.

75. Ibid., p. 108.

76. Sherwood, "Paul Cuffe," pp. 174–181.

77. Letter of Charles MacCarthy, 31 May 1816, Public Record Office, London, CO 267/42.

78. Sherwood, "Paul Cuffe," p. 204. Also Wiggins, *Cuffe's Logs,* pp. 441–442.

79. Thomas Clarkson, "Society for the Purpose of Encouraging the Black Settlers at Sierra Leone, and the Natives of Africa Generally, in the Cultivation of their soil, and by the sale of their produce," 28 January 1814, Public Record Office, London, CO 267/41.

80. Sherwood, "Paul Cuffe," p. 184.

81. Ibid., p. 189. Also Wiggins, *Cuffe's Logs,* pp. 116–117.

82. Sherwood, "Paul Cuffe," p. 190.

83. Ibid., p. 192. This is a reference to Micah 6:8.

84. Sherwood, "Paul Cuffe," p. 192. Wiggins, *Cuffe's Logs,* p. 234.

85. Sherwood, "Paul Cuffe," p. 192.

86. Wiggins, *Cuffe's Logs,* p. 128.

87. Sherwood, "Paul Cuffe," pp. 195–196. Wiggins, *Cuffe's Logs,* pp. 252–253, 434–435.

88. Wiggins, *Cuffe's Logs,* p. 434.

89. William Allen, *William Allen,* vol. 1 (Philadelphia: Henry Longstreth, 1847), p. 134.

90. Ibid., p. 138. Also Wiggins, *Cuffe's Logs,* p. 180.

91. Wiggins, *Cuffe's Logs,* p. 342.

92. Sherwood, "Paul Cuffe," p. 213.

93. *Second Annual Report of the American Colonization Society,* p. 153. Cited in Sherwood, "Paul Cuffe," p. 218.

94. *First Annual Report of the American Colonization Society,* p. 5. Cited in Sherwood, "Paul Cuffe," p. 220.

95. George Washington was one of the largest slave owners in eighteenth-century colonial America, and at his death he owned 317 slaves. Walter H. Mazyck, *George Washington and the Negro* (Washington, D.C.: Associated Publishers, 1932). The descendants of these slaves now gather annually at Mount Vernon.

96. Fyfe, *History,* pp. 55–56.

97. Anna Maria Falconbridge, *Narrative 1794* (London, 1967), p. 201.

98. Fyfe, *History,* p. 202.

99. *Report of the Court of Directors of the Sierra Leone Company to the General Court, Held at London, on the 19th of October, 1791,* in Wadström, *Essay,* vol. 2, pp. 66–67.

100. Andrew F. Walls, "The Nova Scotian Settlers and Their Religion," *Sierra Leone Bulletin of Religion,* 1 (June 1959) 21–22.

101. Milton alluded to this once when he exulted: "Let them chant while they will of prerogatives, we shall tell them of Scripture; of custom, we of Scripture; of acts and statutes, still of Scripture." Cited in Walzer, *Revolution of the Saints,* p. 130.

102. Liele, "Account of Several Baptist Churches," p. 335.

103. Christopher Fyfe, "The Countess of Huntingdon's Connexion in Nineteenth Century Sierra Leone," *Sierra Leone Bulletin of Religion,* 4, no. 2 (December 1962), 56–57.

104. *Register of Missionaries (Clerical, Lay, and Women) and Native Clergy: From 1804 to 1904* (London: CMS, n.d.), p. 6.

105. Fyfe, *History,* p. 129.

106. A Baptist chapel had been built in Kissy, where Christianity had been introduced by a Nova Scotian. MacCarthy bought the chapel to discourage further Baptist work there, for Baptists were suspect as antinomians. He accordingly intervened actively in all the village settlements in Freetown. Fyfe, *History,* pp. 130, 131. Johnson warned converts against dwelling on the doctrine of election. CMS Archives, University of Birmingham, CA1/E7, 23c.

107. Christopher Fyfe, "The Baptist Churches in Sierra Leone," *Sierra Leone Bulletin of Religion*, 5, no. 2 (December 1963) 56–57.

108. John W. Blassingame, *The Slave Community: Plantation Life in the Antebellum South*, rev. ed. (New York: Oxford University Press, 1979), p. 145.

109. Liele, "Account of Several Baptist Churches," p. 336.

110. Blassingame, *Slave Community*, p. 146.

111. Fyfe, *History*, p. 69.

112. Raboteau, *Slave Religion*, pp. 238–239.

113. Christopher Fyfe, "The West African Methodists in the Nineteenth Century," *Sierra Leone Bulletin of Religion*, 3, no. 1 (June 1961), 23–24.

114. Cited in Raboteau, *Slave Religion*, p. 199.

115. Albert Bushnell Hart, *Slavery and Abolition: 1831–1841* (1906, repr. New York: Haskell House, 1968), pp. 211–212.

116. Liele, "Account of Several Baptist Churches," p. 336. The reference to being entangled in the affairs of the world concerns Liele's conscription in Jamaica as a trumpeter to the Kingston militia and "in carrying all the cannon that could be found lying about this part of the country."

117. However, although Freemasonry in Freetown came to play an important social and political role, it was typically seen as a pillar of civil society, not as a challenge to it. Abner Cohen, "The Politics of Ritual Secrecy," *Man*, 6 (September 1971), 427–448. Reprinted in Edward A. Tiryakian, ed., *On the Margins of the Visible: Sociology, the Esoteric, and the Occult* (New York: John Wiley and Sons, 1974), pp. 111–151.

118. Gary B. Nash, "Thomas Peters: Millwright and Deliverer," in David G. Sweet and Gary B. Nash, eds., *Struggle and Survival in Colonial America* (Berkeley: University of California Press, 1981), p. 82; A. W. Lawrence, *Trade Castles and Forts of West Africa* (London: Jonathan Cape, 1963), p. 30.

119. Falconbridge, *Narrative, 1794*, p. 148.

120. Letter of Samuel Brown, 27 February 1819. no. 43, MMS Archives.

121. Letter of John Baker and J. Gillison, 24 June 1819. no. 50, MMS Archives.

3. Abolition and the Cause of Recaptive Africans

1. *Report of the Sierra Leone Company* (London, 1794), p. 7. Cited also in R. R. Kuczynski, *Demographic Survey of the British Colonial Empire*, 3 vols., (London: Oxford University Press for the Royal Institute of International Affairs, 1948–1953, repr. Fairfield, N.J.: Augustus M. Kelley, 1977), vol. 1, p. 56.

2. Kuczynski, *Demographic Survey*, vol. 1, p. 157 and n. 2.

3. It was reported that the last slave ship sailed up the Savannah River in the

United States was in 1858. Francis Butler Simkins, *Pitchfork Ben Tillman* (Baton Rouge: Louisiana State University Press, 1944). In 1860 a slave ship, the *Wildfire,* was brought to Key West, Florida, with a cargo of black slaves. *New York Times,* "Arts and Ideas," 13 December 1997.

4. MacCarthy's memorandum can be found in the Public Record Office, London, CO 267/42.

5. Letter of William Davies, 10 August 1815, MMS Archives, box 279.

6. Cited in Andrew F. Walls, "A Colonial Concordat: Two Views of Christianity and Civilization," in Derek Baker, ed., *Church, Society, and Politics,* vol. 12 of *Studies in Church History* (Oxford: Blackwell, 1975), p. 296, n. 10.

7. Walls, "A Colonial Concordat," p. 299.

8. Ibid., p. 296.

9. Christopher Fyfe, *A History of Sierra Leone* (London: Oxford University Press, 1962), pp. 130, 131.

10. Letter of Robert Hogan, 25 May 1816, Public Record Office, London, CO 267/43.

11. Cited in Walls, "A Colonial Concordat," p. 301.

12. Cited in ibid.

13. A. P. Kup, "Freetown in 1794," *Sierra Leone Studies,* n.s., 11 (1958), 163.

14. *Report of the Sierra Leone Company* (March 1798), 47–48, cited in Anthony Kirk-Greene, "David George: The Nova Scotian Experience," Sierra Leone Studies, n.s., 14 (December 1960), 117–118.

15. Letter of William Davies, Extracts, 13 June 1817, MMS Archives, box 279.

16. Letter of Samuel Brown, 14 February 1817, MMS Archives, box 28.

17. Petition cited in Andrew F. Walls, "The Nova Scotian Settlers," *Sierra Leone Bulletin of Religion,* June 1959, 27. Also Grant Gordon, ed., *From Slavery to Freedom: The Life of David George* (Hantsport, Nova Scotia: Lancelot Press for Acadia Divinity College, 1992), pp. 139–141.

18. Cited in George Shepperson and T. Rice, *Independent African: John Chilembwe and the Origins, Setting, and Significance of the Nyasaland Native Rising of 1915* (Edinburgh: Edinburgh University Press, 1958), p. 163.

19. Fyfe, *History,* pp. 201–202.

20. Walls, "The Nova Scotian Settlers," p. 30.

21. Fyfe, *History,* pp. 293–294.

22. Samuel Crowther and John Christopher Taylor, *The Gospel on the Banks of the Niger: Journals and Notices of the Native Missionaries Accompanying the Niger Expedition of 1857–1859* (London: CMS, 1859, repr. London: Dawsons of Pall Mall, 1968), p. 88.

23. Fyfe, *History,* pp. 227–228.

24. Earl Grey, *The Colonial Policy of Lord John Russell's Administration,* 2 vols.

(London: Richard Bentley, 1853, repr. New York: Augustus M. Kelley, 1970), vol. 2, pp. 281–282.

25. Mark Onesosan Ogharaerumi, "The Translation of the Bible into Yoruba, Igbo, and Itsekiri Languages of Nigeria, with Special Reference to the Contributions of Mother Tongue Speakers" (Ph.D. diss., University of Aberdeen, Scotland, 1986), pp. 15–16.

26. The account is given in Charles Marke, *Origin of Wesleyan Methodism in Sierra Leone and History of Its Missions* (London: Charles H. Kelly, 1913), pp. 58–59.

27. Christopher Fyfe, "The Life and Times of John Ezzidio," *Sierra Leone Studies*, n.s., 4 (June 1955), 220.

28. Edmund Burke, *Reflections on the French Revolution,* cited in Fyfe, "John Ezzidio," p. 218.

29. Marke lacked formal education and was not, unlike his colleagues, trained in England. Yet he read widely and became a fluent English speaker and writer. His *Wesleyan Methodism,* a 240-page book, is written in flawless, fluid prose.

30. Marke, *Wesleyan Methodism,* p. 59.

31. Cited in Barbara Prickett, *Island Base* [a history of the Methodist mission in the Gambia] (Bo, Sierra Leone: private printing, n.d. [1971?]), p. 110.

32. Fyfe, "John Ezzidio," p. 221.

33. Ibid., p. 223.

34. Ibid., p. 216.

35. Richard F. Burton, *Wanderings in West Africa,* 2 vols. (London: Tinsley Brothers, 1863, repr. New York: Dover Publications, 1991), vol. 2, p. 48.

36. Andrew F. Walls, "A Christian Experiment: The Early Sierra Leone Colony," in G. J. Cunning, ed., *The Mission of the Church and the Propagation of the Faith* (Cambridge: Cambridge University Press, 1970), p. 128. Basil Davidson takes a different and unsympathetic view of the social role of recaptives as local mediators of Western culture and civilization: Davidson, *The Black Man's Burden: Africa and the Curse of the Nation-State* (London: James Currey Publishers, 1992), pp. 21–51, 102–103.

4. The Niger Expedition, Missionary Imperatives, and African Ferment

1. Johnson's *History* was commenced in the 1880s and published in London in 1921 and subsequently.

2. Samuel Johnson, *The History of the Yorubas* (London: Routledge and Kegan Paul, 1921, repr. 1969), p. 192.

3. On this see Babatunde Agiri, "Slavery in Yoruba Society in the Nineteenth Century," in Paul E. Lovejoy, ed., *The Ideology of Slavery in Africa* (Beverly Hills, Calif.: Sage Publications, 1981), pp. 123–148.

4. Johnson, *History*, p. 296.

5. T. B. Freeman, *Journal of Various Visits to the Kingdom of Ashanti, Aku, and Dahomey* (London, 1844). Reproduced in *The African Repository and Colonial Journal*, 20, no. 4 (April 1844), 99, 101.

6. See Paul Ellingworth, "Mr. Freeman's Case," *Journal of Religion in Africa*, 27, no. 1 (1997).

7. Cited in J. F. A. Ajayi, *Christian Missions in Nigeria, 1841–1891: The Making of a New Élite* (Evanston, Ill.: Northwestern University Press, 1969), pp. 27–28.

8. Samuel Crowther, extracts from journal, cited in Ajayi, *Christian Missions*, p. 27.

9. Ajayi, *Christian Missions*, p. 28.

10. See T. F. Buxton, *The Slave Trade and Its Remedy* (London, 1840).

11. Cited in Ajayi, *Christian Missions*, p. 34.

12. T. J. Bowen, *Adventures and Missionary Labors in Several Countries in the Interior of Africa* (New York, 1857, 2d ed. London: Frank Cass, 1968), pp. 339–340.

13. Ibid., pp. 342f.

14. Cited in Ajayi, *Christian Missions*, p. 144.

15. Bowen, *Adventures*, p. 322. Bowen founded missions in Yoruba country at Ijaye, where he baptized his first convert in 1854, at Ogbomosho in 1855, at Abeokuta in 1856, and soon thereafter at Oyo.

16. Cited in Ajayi, *Christian Missions*, p. 17.

17. Cited in J. D. Y. Peel, "For Who Hath Despised the Day of Small Things? Missionary Narratives and Historical Anthropology," *Comparative Study of Society and History*, 37, no. 3 (July 1995), 603.

18. Ibid., p. 31.

19. Cited in ibid., p. 30.

20. Ibid., p. 42.

21. Quinine, also known as the "bark," after the cinchona tree from which it is extracted, was used earlier as a prophylactic. Members of the 1854 expedition up the Niger led by Dr. Baikie were given daily quinine rations. Robert Campbell, the companion of Martin Delany, said he used quinine as a prophylactic in 1859 and found it effective against bilious fever, but he continued to believe that the fever came from "marsh miasmata," Campbell, *A Pilgrimage to My Motherland: An Account of a Journey among the Egbas and Yorubas of Central Africa, 1859–60*, in M. R. Delany and Robert

Campbell, *Search for a Place: Black Separatism and Africa* (Ann Arbor: University of Michigan Press, 1969), pp. 245–246. But only after 1897 did such remedies receive more than anecdotal attention.

22. Kenneth Dike says there were 162 whites of whom 54 died. *The Origins of the Niger Mission: 1841–1891* (Ibadan: Ibadan University Press for the CMS Niger Mission, 1962), p. 6.

23. Cited in Jesse Page, *Samuel Crowther* (London and New York, n.d.), p. 57. The reference is to Acts 14:17. That idea of natural religion as sign of divine favor is developed by Paul in Romans 1:19–21, where no one is excluded from divine favor or exempt from divine judgment.

24. Rev. James Frederick Schön and Samuel Crowther, *Journals,* 2d ed. (London: Frank Cass, 1970), pp. 50–53.

25. Page, *Samuel Crowther,* London ed., p. 127; New York ed., p. 107.

26. Sir Edward E. Evans-Pritchard, *Magic, Witchcraft, and Oracles among the Azande* (Oxford: Clarendon Press, 1936).

27. Jesse Page, *Samuel Crowther,* London ed., p. 126; New York ed., p. 106.

28. Ibid., London ed., pp. 126–127; New York ed., pp. 106–107.

29. Ibid., London ed., pp. 181–182.

30. Schön and Crowther, *Journals,* p. 177.

31. Samuel Crowther, 30 September 1851, citing Isaiah 62:1, in a personal inscription in *The Church Missionary Intelligencer,* 1850. Isa. 62:2 goes on to speak about God's righteousness being extended to the Gentiles and rulers, a thought that would have been very much in Crowther's own mind.

32. E. A. Ayandele, *The Missionary Impact on Modern Nigeria, 1842–1914: A Political and Social Analysis* (London: Longman Group, 1966), p. 206.

33. Henry Venn instructed the missionaries in Nigeria that, although they could baptize slaveholders and wives of polygamists, baptism must be refused to polygamous men. Cited in Ajayi, *Christian Missions,* p. 107. This ruling, however, did not come close to settling the matter. If a man divorced all his wives but one in order to receive baptism, he would confront Venn with the awkward theological problem of remedying the offense of polygamy with the sin of divorce. Most missionaries avoided the issue.

34. Modupe Oduyoye, "The Planting of Christianity in Yorubaland: 1842–1888," in Ogbu Kalu, ed., *Christianity in West Africa: The Nigerian Story* (Ibadan: Daystar Press, 1978), pp. 251–252.

35. Peel, "For Who Hath Despised," p. 597.

36. Geoffrey Moorhouse, *The Missionaries* (London: Eyre Methuen, 1973), p. 102.

37. Ibid.

38. Ibid.

39. Schön and Crowther, *Journals*, pp. 62–63.

40. Edward Wilmot Blyden echoed Crowther on this matter: *The Three Needs of Liberia: A Lecture Delivered at Lower Buchanan, Grand Bassa County, Liberia, January 26, 1908* (London: C. M. Phillips, 1908), pp. 5–6, 33–34.

41. Speaking in Lagos, Blyden remarked on this conflict: *The Return of the Exiles and the West African Church: A Lecture Delivered at the Breadfruit School House, Lagos, West Africa, January 2, 1891* (London: W. B. Whittingham, 1891), pp. 14–15.

42. Cited in Ajayi, *Christian Missions*, p. 224.

43. Ibid.

44. Cited in ibid., p. 250.

45. Peter R. McKenzie, *Inter-religious Encounters in West Africa: Samuel Ajayi Crowther's Attitude to African Traditional Religion and Islam* (Leicester: University of Leicester, 1976), p. 27. This is the most detailed account on the subject.

46. Cited in Ajayi, *Christian Missions*, p. 97.

47. On the debate among Presbyterians on slavery see James H. Smylie, "The Bible, Race, and the Changing South," *Journal of Presbyterian History*, 59 (Summer 1981).

48. Cited in Ajayi, *Christian Missions*, p. 104.

49. Letter to Venn, cited in ibid., p. 105.

50. This distinction between domestic slavery and the slave trade has an eminent chain of transmission, one of whose distinguished links was Cardinal Lavigerie, founder of the White Fathers. See Richard F. Clarke, ed., *Cardinal Lavigerie and the African Slave Trade* (London: Longmans, Green, 1889), p. 313.

51. Cited in Ajayi, *Christian Missions*, p. 181.

52. Cited in ibid., p. 182.

53. Townsend was compiler of the first Yoruba hymn book and of a Yoruba primer, and editor and publisher of the Yoruba fortnightly publication *Iwe Irohin*. See *Register of Missionaries (Clerical, Lay, and Female) and Native Clergy from 1804 to 1904* (London: CMS, n.d.), pp. 41–42.

54. Cited in Ajayi, *Christian Missions*, p. 183.

55. Cited in ibid., p. 184. Crowther's journal entries show him in impressive form when it came to matters of language and translation. Page, *Samuel Crowther*, London ed., p. 108; New York ed., p. 91.

56. Cited in Floyd J. Miller, *The Search for a Black Nationality: Black Emigration and Colonization, 1787–1863* (Urbana: University of Illinois Press, 1975), p. 87.

57. Cited in ibid., p. 203.

58. M. R. Delany and Robert Campbell, *Search for a Place: Black Separatism and*

Africa, incorporating *Official Report of the Niger Valley Exploring Party,* by M. R. Delany, and *A Pilgrimage to My Motherland: An Account of a Journey among the Egbas and Yorubas of Central Africa, in 1859–60,* by Robert Campbell (Ann Arbor: University of Michigan Press, 1969), pp. 112–113.

59. Cited in Miller, *Search for a Black Nationality,* p. 205.

60. Delany and Campbell, *Search for a Place,* pp. 104–105.

61. Ajayi, *Christian Missions,* p. 191.

62. Delany and Campbell, *Search for a Place,* p. 77.

63. Ajayi, *Christian Missions,* pp. 191–192.

64. Richard F. Burton, *Abeokuta and the Cameroons Mountains: An Exploration,* 2 vols. (London: Tinsley Brothers, 1863), vol. 1, p. 269.

65. Ibid., p. 270 n.

66. Ibid., p. 268.

67. Delany revised his views after he saw what missions were accomplishing in Africa. Delany and Campbell, *Search for a Place,* p. 102.

68. Ajayi, *Christian Missions,* p. 195.

69. Ibid., p. 255.

70. Cited in ibid., p. 253 n.

71. James Bertin Webster, *The African Churches among the Yoruba: 1888–1922* (Oxford: Clarendon Press, 1964), pp. 56, 61.

72. Cited in ibid., p. 68.

73. Andrew F. Walls, "The Legacy of Samuel Ajayi Crowther," *International Bulletin of Missionary Research,* January 1992, pp. 19–20.

74. C. B. Wadström, *An Essay on Colonization, particularly applied to the Western Coast of Africa, with some Free Thoughts on Cultivation and Commerce; also Brief Descriptions of the Colonies already formed, or attempted, in Africa, including those of Sierra Leone and Bulama,* 2 vols. (London: Darton and Harvey, 1794), vol. 1, pp. 23–24.

75. Ajayi, *Christian Missions,* pp. 51–52.

76. Walter Miller, the pioneer CMS official in north Nigeria, where he arrived in tow with the new British colonial rulers, observed that whereas the administrators aligned themselves with the chiefs and rulers, missionaries had the trust of the ordinary people, suggesting a divergent effect of colonialism and mission on local societies. Walter Miller, *Success in Nigeria? Assets and Possibilities* (London: Lutterworth Press, 1948), p. 77.

77. Basil Davidson offers a different assessment, seeing the recaptives as doubly alienated from Africa by their enslavement and by their rescue at the hands of Britain. Davidson, *The Black Man's Burden: Africa and the Curse of the Nation-State* (London: James Currey, 1992), pp. 21–51. Burton also was highly critical of the recaptives, "the semi-civilised African returning to the 'home of his fathers.'" Burton, *Wanderings in West Africa,* 2 vols. (London,

1863, repr. New York: Dover Publications, 1991), vol. 1, p. 210. In their different ways, Davidson and Burton raise the question of the relevance of recaptive values to Africa's political and moral transformation. Related to this question is Mahmood Mamdani's critical assessment of the effects of colonial rule on local elites and peasants. Mamdani, *Citizen and Subject: Contemporary Africa and the Legacy of Late Colonialism* (Princeton, N.J. Princeton University Press, 1996). See my Conclusion for further reflections on the subject.

5. American Colonization and the Founding of Liberia

1. See Hugh Hawkins, ed., *The Abolitionists: Immediatism and the Question of Means* (Boston: D.C. Heath, 1964), pp. 31–32.
2. Cited in P. J. Staudenraus, *The African Colonization Movement: 1816–1865* (New York: Columbia University Press, 1961), p. 1.
3. Thomas Jefferson, *Autobiography,* in *The Life and Selected Writings of Thomas Jefferson,* ed. Adrienne Koch and William Peden (New York: Random House, 1944, repr. 1993), p. 49.
4. Cited in Staudenraus, *African Colonization,* pp. 3–4.
5. St. George, Tucker, *A Dissertation on Slavery: With a Proposal for the Gradual Abolition of It, in the State of Virginia* (Philadelphia: Printed for Mathew Carey, 1796).
6. Staudenraus, *African Colonization.*
7. Early Lee Fox, *The American Colonization Society, 1817–1840* (Baltimore: Johns Hopkins University Press, 1919), p. 41.
8. Staudenraus, *African Colonization,* pp. 6–7.
9. Ibid.
10. See Andrew F. Walls, *The Missionary Movement in Christian History: Studies in the Transmission of Faith* (Maryknoll, N.Y.: Orbis Books, 1996), pp. 246–247.
11. Samuel Hopkins, *The System of Doctrines, Contained in Divine Revelation, Explained and Defended . . . ,* 2d ed. (Boston, 1811), vol. 1, pp. 466ff.; Oliver Wendell Elsbree, "Samuel Hopkins and His Doctrine of Benevolence," *New England Quarterly,* 8 (1935), 540–545.
12. William Wilberforce, *A Practical View of the Prevailing Religious System of Professed Christians in the Higher and Middle Classes in This Country Contrasted with Real Christianity* (1797, repr. London: SCM Press, 1958), p. 66.
13. This was Thomas Foster preaching at the Devon assizes in 1630. Michael Walzer, *The Revolution of the Saints: A Study in the Origins of Radical Politics* (Cambridge, Mass.: Harvard University Press, 1965), p. 174.
14. Cited in Staudenraus, *African Colonization,* p. 18.

15. Cited in ibid., pp. 19–20.

16. Cited in ibid., p. 20.

17. Ibid.

18. For a study of this messianic theme in American history see Ernest Tuveson, *Redeemer Nation: The Idea of America's Millennial Role* (Chicago: University of Chicago Press, 1968).

19. The concept is discussed in Frederick Merk, *Manifest Destiny and Mission in American History: A Reinterpretation* (Cambridge, Mass.: Harvard University Press, 1963), p. 261.

20. Cited in Staudenraus, *African Colonization*, pp. 21–22.

21. Clay said "prejudices more powerful than laws, deny them the privileges of freemen." Fox, *American Colonization Society*, p. 33.

22. *Speech of the Hon. Henry Clay before the American Colonization Society in the Hall of the House of Representatives, January 20, 1827* (Washington, D.C., 1827), p. 6. Clay expanded on this theme in *The African Repository and Colonial Journal*, 14, no. 1, (January 1838), 17–19.

23. Staudenraus, *African Colonization*, p. 37.

24. Cited in ibid., p. 38.

25. Ibid., p. 44.

26. Cited in ibid., p. 46.

27. Cited in ibid., p. 47.

28. Ibid., p. 49.

29. Cited in ibid., p. 52.

30. Cited in ibid., pp. 52–53.

31. Cited in ibid., p. 61.

32. Ibid., p. 64.

33. O. B. Frothingham, "Colonization," *Anti-Slavery Tracts*, 3 (n.d.), 1.

34. The constitution, called the "Plan of Civil Government for the Colony of Liberia," contained fifteen articles with a detailed outline of authority and administration. Reproduced in *Freedom's Journal*, 28 March 1829.

35. William Goodell, *Slavery and Anti-Slavery: A History of the Great Struggle in Both Hemispheres, with a View of the Slavery Question in the United States* (New York: William Harned, 1852), p. 352.

36. Benjamin Anderson, the African American explorer, gives an account of his forays into the kingdom of King Boatswain in his book *Narrative of a Journey to Musardu: Capital of the Western Mandingoes* (1870, repr. London: Frank Cass, 1971), with a helpful introduction by Humphrey J. Fisher.

37. Sir Harry Johnston, *Liberia: With an Appendix on the Flora of Liberia*, 2 vols. (London: Hutchinson, 1906), vol. 1, p. 141.

38. Fox, *American Colonization Society*, p. 73.

39. Cited in Leroy Fitts, *Lott Carey: First Black Missionary to Africa* (Valley Forge, Penn.: Judson Press, 1978), p. 34.

40. Cited in ibid., pp. 46–47.

41. Samuel Wilkeson, *A Concise History of the Commencement, Progress, and Present Condition of the American Colonies in Liberia* (Washington, D.C.: Madisonian Office, 1839), pp. 37–38.

42. Fitts, *Lott Carey*, p. 63.

43. See Svend E. Holsoe, "A Study of Relations between Settlers and Indigenous Peoples in Western Liberia, 1821–1847," *African Historical Studies*, 4, no. 2 (1971), 331–362.

44. E. W. Blyden, *The Three Needs of Liberia: A Lecture Delivered at Lower Buchanan, Grand Bassa County, Liberia, January 26, 1908* (London: C. M. Phillips, 1908), pp. 1–2.

45. See J. D. Hargreaves, "African Colonization in the Nineteenth Century: Liberia and Sierra Leone," *Sierra Leone Studies*, n.s., 16 (June 1962), 189–203.

46. Goodell, *Slavery and Anti-Slavery*, p. 563. See also [Thomas R. Hazard,] *A Constitutional Manual for the National American Party: In Which Is Examined the Question of Negro Slavery in Connection with the Constitution of the United States, by a Northern Man, with American Principles* (Providence, 1856).

47. Cited in Fox, *American Colonization Society*, p. 24.

48. Cited in ibid., p. 28.

49. Cited in ibid., p. 29.

50. Cited in ibid.

51. *The African Repository and Colonial Journal*, 1 (1826), 14.

52. Alexis de Tocqueville, *Democracy in America*, trans. George Lawrence, ed. J. P. Mayer (New York: Harper and Row, 1966, repr. Harper Perennial Library, 1988), pp. 354ff.

53. For the connection with the rise of African nationalism, see George Shepperson, "Notes on Negro American Influences on the Emergence of African Nationalism," *Journal of African History*, 1 (1960).

54. C. H. Huberich, *The Political and Legislative History of Liberia*, 2 vols. (New York: Central Book, 1947), vol. 1, p. 41.

55. His work was noted in *The African Repository and Colonial Journal*, 16, no. 1 (January 1840).

56. De Tocqueville, *Democracy*, 359–360.

57. Goodell, *Slavery and Anti-Slavery*, p. 351.

58. Ibid.

59. Reproduced in Frothingham, "Colonization," p. 7. Octavius Brooks Froth-

ingham (1822–1895), a Unitarian and independent clergyman and a cousin of Henry Adams, was an antislavery activist.

60. Louis Filler, *The Crusade against Slavery* (New York: Harper and Brothers, 1960), pp. 91, 192.

61. Buchanan's tenure as governor was described in *The African Repository and Colonial Journal,* 16, no. 12 (15 June 1840), 177–188; 16, no. 18 (15 September 1840), 276–282.

62. Goodell, *Slavery and Anti-Slavery,* p. 351.

63. C. Abayomi Cassell, *Liberia: History of the First African Republic* (New York: Fountainhead Press, 1970), p. 49.

64. Cited in Floyd J. Miller, *The Search for a Black Nationality: Black Emigration and Colonization, 1787–1863* (Urbana: University of Illinois Press, 1975), p. 87.

65. J. R. Oldfield, *Alexander Crummell (1819–1898) and the Creation of an African-American Church in Liberia* (Lewiston, N.Y.: Edwin Mellen Press, 1990), p. 12.

66. Cited in ibid., p. 27.

67. Ibid., pp. 108–109.

68. Ibid., pp. 50, 54.

69. W. E. B. Du Bois, *The Souls of Black Folk* (New York: Signet Classics, 1982), pp. 233–244.

70. London, *Times,* 8 October 1887.

71. Cited in Hollis R. Lynch, *Edward Wilmot Blyden: Pan-Negro Patriot, 1832–1912* (New York: Oxford University Press, 1970), p. 75.

72. L. Sanneh, *Piety and Power: Muslims and Christians in West Africa* (Maryknoll, N.Y.: Orbis Books, 1996), pp. 67–84.

73. In Lynch, *Blyden,* p. 76.

74. Ibid., p. 241.

75. Cited in ibid., pp. 14–15.

76. Blyden, *Needs of Liberia,* pp. 33–34.

77. E. W. Blyden, *The Return of the Exiles and the West African Church: A Lecture Delivered at the Breadfruit School House, Lagos, West Africa, January 2, 1891* (London: W. B. Whittingham, 1891), pp. 27–28.

78. Cassell, *Liberia,* p. 344.

79. Blyden, *Needs of Liberia,* p. 2.

80. E. W. Blyden, *The Aims and Methods of a Liberal Education for Africans: Inaugural Address, January 5, 1881* (Cambridge, Mass.: John Wilson and Son, 1882), p. 18.

81. Bell I. Wiley, ed., *Slaves No More: Letters from Liberia, 1833–1869* (Lexington: University Press of Kentucky, 1980), pp. 16f.

82. The declaration is reproduced in Johnston, *Liberia*, pp. 199–218, 202. The sentiment is echoed in *Freedom's Journal*, 25 January 1828.
83. Cited in Fitts, *Lott Carey*, p. 46.

Conclusion

1. David Brion Davis, *Problem of Slavery in the Age of Revolution: 1770–1823* (Ithaca, N.Y.: Cornell University Press, 1975), p. 46. Roger Anstey writes that evangelicalism gave Divine Providence a historical dimension through a heightened consciousness of personal sin and personal redemption. Anstey, *The Atlantic Slave Trade and British Abolition: 1760–1810* (Atlantic Heights, N.J.: Humanities Press, 1975), p. 164.
2. E. W. Blyden, *The Return of the Exiles and the West African Church,* (London: W. B. Whittingham, 1891), p. 6.
3. *The African Repository and Colonial Journal,* 3 (October 1828), 246.
4. See the poem on 'Abd al-Rahmán in *Freedom's Journal,* 24 October 1828.
5. Michael Walzer, *The Revolution of the Saints: A Study in the Origins of Radical Politics* (Cambridge, Mass.: Harvard University Press, 1965), p. 128.
6. *The African Repository and Colonial Journal,* 2 (February 1827), 387.
7. James Mackay, "The Liberian Emigrant's Song," *The African Repository and Colonial Journal,* 20 (September 1844).
8. Cited in J. F. A. Ajayi, *Christian Missions in Nigeria, 1841–1891: The Making of a New Élite* (Evanston, Ill.: Northwestern University Press, 1969), pp. 27–28.
9. M. R. Delany and Robert Campbell, *Search for a Place: Black Separatism in Africa* (Ann Arbor: University of Michigan Press, 1969), p. 107.
10. Joseph Gaer and Ben Siegel, *The Puritan Heritage: America's Roots in the Bible* (New York: Mentor Books, 1964), p. 24.
11. It can be argued that the critical alliance between Puritan doctrine and the new politics of Elizabethan England has its counterpart in a corresponding alliance between evangelical doctrine and the social activism of antislavery. Walzer's description of Puritan political radicalism echoes many of the features of what has been presented in this book of antislavery and antistructure. See Walzer, *Revolution of the Saints,* pp. 124–125.
12. In a special issue of its journal, the American Anti-Slavery Society took up antislavery as a human rights issue. *The Anti-Slavery Examiner,* 6 (1838), "The Bible against Slavery: An Inquiry into the Patriarchal and Mosaic Systems on the Subject of Human Rights," 4th ed. This remains one of the strongest contemporary intellectual statements that we possess on the human rights character of antislavery.

13. *Five Slave Narratives: A Compendium,* 2d ed. (London: Charles Gilpin, 1849, repr. New York: Arno Press and the New York Times, 1968), p. xii.

14. William Goodell, *Slavery and Anti-Slavery: A History of the Great Struggle in Both Hemispheres with a View of the Slavery Question in the United States* (New York: William Harned, 1852), p. 563.

15. Gaer and Siegel, *The Puritan Heritage.*

16. Gordon S. Wood, *The Creation of the American Republic, 1776–1787* (1969, repr. New York: Norton, 1993), pp. 344–389.

17. Charles Beard, *An Economic Interpretation of the Constitution of the United States* (New York: Free Press, 1965, orig. pub. Macmillan, 1935).

18. Merrill Jensen, *The New Nation: A History of the United States during the Confederation, 1781–1789* (New York: Vintage Books, 1950).

19. See, for example, John Dewey's reflection on the theme in his *Freedom and Culture* (Buffalo, N.Y.: Prometheus Books, 1989).

20. See Sir Reginald Coupland, *The American Revolution and the British Empire* (London: Longmans, Green, 1930).

SOURCES

I consulted various archives and libraries in connection with the writing of this book. These included

The Library of Congress, Jefferson Building, for the papers of the American Colonization Society;

The British Library in the British Museum, Russell Square, London;

The Methodist Missionary Society Archives, housed at the School of Oriental and African Studies, University of London;

The Church Missionary Society Archives, deposited in the University of Birmingham, Main Library, Edgbaston, Birmingham, England;

The Public Record Office, Kew Gardens, London;

The archives of the Day Missions Library in the Divinity Library at Yale University. The Divinity Library also holds original editions of slave narratives, testimonies, and accounts;

The Sterling Memorial Library, the main University library at Yale;

The Beinecke Rare Book Library at Yale, which holds the *African Repository,* the official publication of the African Colonization Society.

On a sabbatical leave in Cambridge, England, I consulted the private papers of Lady Selina, the countess of Huntingdon. I am grateful to Edwin Welch, the curator of Lady Selina's papers, for permission at short notice to use the archives. When I lived in Sierra Leone I consulted widely the national archives then housed in Fourah Bay College, Freetown. I have also been able to make use of some materials I obtained many years ago when I was doing independent research in the New York public archives in Albany, New York, on the subject of the antislavery movement in Britain. I subsequently visited Hull in the north of England, the home of William Wilberforce. Early in my life in the United States I was introduced by Marie Gadsen, then of Atlanta University, to an African American community in rural Georgia whose roots were in the antebellum South. At Hampton Institute (now Hampton University)

Charles Flax introduced me to the richness of Negro spirituals and other aspects of African American religious culture. In the Bahamas I visited the Baptist Church in Nassau, home to many of the African Americans who went there after the end of the American Revolutionary War. In the company of a senior CMS official I visited Abeokuta, Nigeria. Similarly, I was fortunate to be able to visit Liberia before the civil war, when I traveled from Monrovia to several national centers, including Gbarnga, the site of Cuttingdon College, a historic educational institution. In Ghana I visited Cape Coast, a cradle of recaptive African life.

INDEX